BIGFOOT

Kenneth Wylie

BIG

FOOT

A Personal Inquiry
into a Phenomenon

ᘔ ᘔ ᘔ ᘔ ᘔ ᘔ ᘔ ᘔ ᘔ ᘔ ᘔ ᘔ ᘔ ᘔ

The Viking Press ᘔ New York

First published in 1980 by The Viking Press
625 Madison Avenue, New York, N. Y. 10022
Published simultaneously in Canada by
Penguin Books Canada Limited

LIBRARY OF CONGRESS CATALOGING IN PUBLICATION DATA
Wylie, Kenneth
Bigfoot.
Bibliography: p.
Includes index.
  1. Sasquatch.   I. Title.
QL89.2.S2W94   001.9'44   80-14576
ISBN 0-670-16509-3

Acknowledgment is made to Doubleday & Company, Inc., for permission
to reprint lines from the poem "In a Dark Time," Copyright © 1960 by
Beatrice Roethke, Administratrix of the Estate of Theodore Roethke, in
The Collected Poems of Theodore Roethke.

All photos courtesy of René Dahinden, Copyright © 1967, 1969, 1971,
1977, by René Dahinden.

Maps by Paul J. Pugliese, GCI

To Ethel Brewer Wylie

Preface

The origins of my interest in the Bigfoot mystery are somewhat obscure, even to myself. Like most people, I had heard scores of tall tales about the hairy woodland giant, stories I dismissed as fairy tales but found fascinating nevertheless.

Some years ago, after I gave up an academic career in New York City to devote all my time to free-lance writing, my earlier, casual interest was piqued by a series of seemingly unrelated incidents, especially by repeated references in books and documents I was reading while researching a projected book about human–animal relations and by a flurry of local reports in Michigan, not far from my rural home in the northwest corner of the state. During the summer of 1978, prompted by my editor at Viking, I began to look into the subject more thoroughly. By the end of that summer I had become convinced that there was indeed more to this strange phenomenon than mere sensational foolishness. I began to realize that belief in the existence of a hairy manlike monster—a huge and elusive beast, often seen but never found, that leaves prodigious footprints in widely scattered regions—had emerged as a genuine phenomenon, more than a passing fad. For me, the commonly heard phrase "Something is out there," a sentiment I did not share, was echoed by "Something strange is going on out there," something worth serious investigation. Was there really any evidence for such an eldritch beast, apparently seen by so many earnest witnesses, or was all the publicity and hoopla pure bunk? Why did so many intelligent people, including some highly educated and widely experienced naturalists, believe in such an improbability? And why among the general public did so many want to believe?

Through a period of more than a year of intensive research and analysis, combined with extensive travel, my skepticism remained firmly rooted in my sense of rationality. However, I gradually became aware that the more I learned about the Bigfoot phenomenon, the more my initial doubt became tinged with a kind of hope, wistful but genuine nonetheless. This disturbed me at the same time that it stimulated my curiosity. I suppose I had almost become a "Bigfoot buff" myself, one of those whose fascination for the subject is not easily shaken by the laughter and scorn of others.

This book is the result of my investigation, my own attempt to seek the truth about the Bigfoot phenomenon.

I believe that I am well prepared by experience, upbringing, education, and inclination to research and write a book of this sort. I have been a professional historian for most of my adult life. Oral traditions and ethnology are special fields of interest, and I have lived for extended periods among non-Western peoples. My lifelong pleasure in the outdoors has sustained a passion for natural history and wildlife study, and deepening ecological concern. I hardly claim personal knowledge of the full range of wilderness regions where Bigfoot, or Sasquatch, has been sighted, but I have investigated some of the most celebrated areas. I do not pretend to be an expert in every one of the aspects of this mystery (no one person could claim this), but I have looked into nearly every angle on the subject. This book reflects the deliberate range of my search. I have not been satisfied with interviews only with leading biologists at our premier museums. I have also talked with scores of laymen and with the best known among North America's self-appointed Bigfoot experts.

Even though the opinions and conclusions in this book are entirely my own, I owe a great deal to many people. The list of those who have helped is too long to include everyone, but there are a few whose continued support requires acknowledgment. My deepest appreciation goes to Toby Eady and Barbara Burn, without whom this book would never have been started. My good friend Richard Van Gelder has been vastly helpful from first to last. Harold Marcus, and Coty, too, provided gracious and necessary hospitality during my extensive library research. My old friend Roger Landrum has provided bedrock support and trenchant criticism. Richard W. Thorington, Jr., of the Smithsonian Institution, was most helpful. Rollin Baker gave brief, hilarious, and memorable comment. Marjorie Halpin, William Scharf, and John Eisenberg offered crisp and useful counsel. Among the Bigfoot aficionados René Dahinden, Barbara Wasson, and John Green deserve my special thanks for their willingness to cooperate in spite of my open statements of skepticism, and for their patience. Bob Gimlin and Wayne King gave me time for important interviews. The family of Zane Gray (no relation to the late naturalist-novelist Zane Grey) proved the meaning of traditional hospitality. David Grath provided some sparks that proved to be significant, and Brian Price added important suggestions. Closer to home, Marty and Jenny really made it all possible.

Kenneth Wylie

Contents

Preface   VII

1. Shadow in the Shade, Echo in the Woods   I

2. Relic Humanoids or Unknown Apes?   25

3. Giants in the Earth   59

4. A Biological Connection?   92

5. Conundrums and Controversies   120

6. Scientists and Bigfoot Buffs   144

7. More Buffs and Some Boffola:
   An Abominable Snow Job?   172

8. Common Sense About Evidence   196

9. Beasts, Blood, and Things That Go Bump
   in the Night   224

Appendix A   237

Appendix B   241

Bibliography   253

Index   259

Illustrations follow page 58.

BIGFOOT

1. Shadow in the Shade, Echo in the Woods

In a dark time, the eye begins to see,
I meet my shadow in the deepening shade;
I hear my echo in the echoing wood—
A lord of nature weeping to a tree,
I live between the heron and the wren,
Beasts of the hill and serpents of the den.
                    THEODORE ROETHKE

It is a dark summer night and the winding road is marked on each side by the looming forest of mixed hardwood and evergreen. The road crosses occasional watercourses where dense stands of white cedar and tamarack push close to the shoulders, overarching the rushing waters out of which trout rise to feed in silence. A light breeze coming off the enormous lake moans in the treetops far above, but it is quiet on the floor of the woods, where the understory is alternately dense and sparse, filled with tag alder, red-osier dogwood, and willow, or littered with bracken through the more open spaces, where poplars grow between the spaced, shimmering birches, rising to the hills of thick maple and beech. An occasional white pine stands sentinel above the line of deciduous trees, remnant of the vast virgin forest that a century ago spread the breadth of the peninsula and beyond, around the huge lakes in both directions, into Ontario and east to Maine, west into Wisconsin and beyond.

A lone car winds down the road north of Charlevoix, not a

mile or two from the pounding surf of Lake Michigan. Suddenly a large, monsterlike figure emerges rapidly from the brush at the roadside, plunging into the full glare of the headlights as it pushes the foliage aside with huge arms. Abruptly the creature halts its headlong rush, its arms hanging down. The driver slows quickly to avoid a crash—a common circumstance in a land full of deer and other wildlife. She is familiar with the road and the region. Her companion screams, startled, expecting a collision with the unfamiliar creature. She, too, is accustomed to the wild animals of the Michigan northland. Her husband is a hunter and an outdoorsman, and she shares his knowledge and interest. She knows the woods well. Recovering her composure, she realizes that this strange thing is no deer; nor is it a bear. She has seen both many times. For one thing, it stands upright on two legs, like a man, its head turned toward the car in an alert and curious stare. But it is much too large to be a normal human, and too massive of build. Its body is dark, its face flat, without a snout—like that of a man, or perhaps an ape, but it is not the face of a man.

The two women glide by in awed disbelief. Quickly they turn the car around for another look. But the creature has disappeared into the darkness. The surrounding region is mostly low and woody swamp, a lonely place. There are no buildings nearby, and the night is dark, so the two women go on their way. Aware of potential scorn at what they have seen, neither is willing to tell her story publicly. Not for several years.

Some years pass. It is the late summer of 1976, just before dawn. The night has been dank and foggy. The place is about fifty miles to the east of Lake Michigan, near the center of Michigan's upper palm. Vast stands of jack pine sprawl across low sandy ridges, interspersed with scattered oaks and thickets of fast-growing aspen. This is breeding country for the rare Kirtland's warbler. It is also one of those mostly uninhabited regions where the National Guard makes summer bivouac; thousands of young men annually march for a few weeks through the woods, maneuvering, practicing with—but rarely firing—rifles, automatic weapons, howitzers, and handling

tanks and other heavy equipment. Much of the area near Grayling is set aside as a military reserve for this purpose. Encounters with animals are not uncommon; city boys from downstate,
and from Ohio and Indiana, pause in their routines to watch
deer bound away into the forest, an osprey rise above a small
lake, a great blue heron wade at the edge of a marsh.

John Howe is awakened by a prolonged and repeated beep-
ing sound, from a horn of some kind. He sticks his head out the
window and shouts for quiet, but the noise continues for some
time. His house is not far from Kyle Lake, part of which is
within the military reservation, where there has been considerable activity lately involving large vehicles. Finally, three badly
frightened young Guardsmen from Ohio show up at Howe's
house. They have spent most of the night in an armored personnel carrier. Scared and shaken, the young men tell Howe
that they have been attacked in the night by an unknown animal of great size and strength. The three frightened men are
not quite certain what they have seen, but they are sure that the
thing wasn't a familiar animal—a bear, for example. They agree
that the creature attacked them, attempting to gain entry to the
personnel carrier by banging on its sides, prying at the hatch,
and rocking the large vehicle repeatedly on its large springs.
During the attack the creature broke off the radio antenna and
a rearview mirror; thus, the terrified youths could not radio the
nearby military camp for help. Eventually they moved the vehicle, and the monster disappeared.

Howe dutifully phones the sheriff's office. While waiting, he
has the opportunity to question the Guardsmen more closely.
He is not the kind of man to accept tall tales easily, but Howe is
convinced that the Guardsmen have been legitimately frightened, whatever the cause. Eventually, Deputy Steven Walter,
of the Crawford County Sheriff's Department, arrives. The
young men are interviewed, and a police report is written up.
An investigation into the incident reveals no tracks or further
evidence.

It is the following spring, and rain has not fallen on the
parched forests for many weeks. The family of Zane Gray, a re-

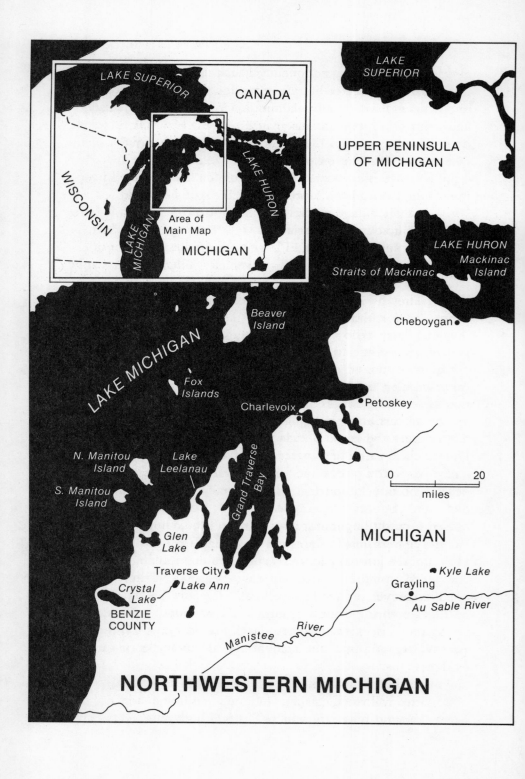

LAKE SUPERIOR

CANADA

LAKE SUPERIOR

WISCONSIN

LAKE MICHIGAN

LAKE HURON

Area of
Main Map

MICHIGAN

UPPER PENINSULA
OF MICHIGAN

LAKE HURON
Mackinac
Island

Straits of Mackinac

Cheboygan ●

Beaver
Island

LAKE MICHIGAN

Fox
Islands

Charlevoix

Petoskey ●

N. Manitou
Island

Lake
Leelanau

Grand Traverse Bay

S. Manitou
Island

MICHIGAN

Glen
Lake

0   20
miles

Traverse City ●

Kyle Lake ●

Crystal
Lake

Lake Ann

Grayling ●

BENZIE
COUNTY

Au Sable River

Manistee   River

NORTHWESTERN MICHIGAN

tired Michigan state trooper and respected businessman who has since been elected sheriff of Benzie County, are temporarily living in a remote woodland cabin owned by a relative while construction proceeds on their new house a few miles away.

The Lake Ann region, like most of Benzie County, is largely wilderness. Much of it lies within the huge Fife Lake State Forest in northwestern lower Michigan—not to be confused with the Upper Peninsula beyond the Straits of Mackinac, or the "UP," as Michiganders call it. Through most of the year it is magnificent country, especially lovely in spring. On the slopes above the valley where the Platte River winds its brief but enchanting way down to Lake Michigan, wild cherry and serviceberry bloom under the canopy of greater trees. Along the feeder streams choked in the low places with deep stands of white cedar, red-osier dogwood competes with sprawling sandbar and pussy willows for the little light that filters down from above. Across the higher flats and sandy stretches, where dirt farms once spotted the remnants of the ancient pine and hardwood forests, now man-leveled, sumac and hawthorn are interspersed in early flower among jack pines and old spruces, and dense clusters of poplar saplings carpet the descending slopes to larger creeks where junipers and yews give way in their deeper green to the pastel of tamarack and cedar in the bottomlands.

This is a land of deer and of deer hunters, of grouse, woodcock, wood duck, and teal. Of rabbit and raccoon, and of the occasional bobcat or bear. But it is not normally a hard land. When drought lingers for any time, the understory of this rich landscape remains fairly open. An animal of any size going through will normally leave signs, tracks that remain for days in soft sand or mud, scats that harden and only slowly pulverize as the flies gather, broken branches that heal slowly until the westerlies again bring the great cumulonimbus clouds over the cold lake from Wisconsin. These hot, dry days in May are not much appreciated, though they are good for tourists, builders, and workers. Just to the north, in picture-book Leelanau County, the huge cherry orchards are suffering. Dust from the unpaved roads already coats the foliage for many feet on either side.

It is around midnight and the Gray family are asleep. Suddenly their pet beagle, tied outside, begins to bark frantically. The racket continues for some time and then subsides. Those within the little cabin settle again into sleep. Then at about two A.M., Gray's wife and daughter—with the latter's new baby— are awakened by a horrible scream so drawn out and loud that it alerts all the household except for Zane himself, who is a bit hard of hearing. Inside, their friendly Labrador is crouched and silent, obviously frightened. Outside, the indescribable cater- wauling continues. The cabin is completely surrounded by woods and lies a good distance from any inhabited structure, so that the sound is disconcerting indeed. By the time Gray is awakened by the others the screaming has died away. Mrs. Gray does not believe that such a sound, sustained for such an extended time and at such a pitch, could be made by a human being. However, the noise does not resume, so everyone re- turns to bed.

The next afternoon, the 23rd of May, the youngest of the Gray sons, Mike, age 17, decides to look around with some of his friends. They find what appear to be large footprints about five hundred feet from the road, on a sandy knoll. The tracks are just visible, because the ground is exceptionally dry and no new growth has yet come through the carpet of old autumn leaves. The imprints can be felt clearly, but they are not clear to the eye. They make an apparent outline similar to that of a huge human foot, complete with toes. None is clear enough to photograph.

A few days pass. It is the 28th of May. One of Zane's older sons, Dave, has begun excavation for a new house for himself and his young wife, perhaps a quarter mile from the woodland site where Zane has commenced construction on his own house. Three sides of Dave's cement-block basement have been laid on a brushy slope that descends to a deeply wooded creek bed beyond. The excavation is still open to the north, facing the hill that falls away with increasing angle to the swampy for- est below. Fresh sand from the excavation is spread out in a flat terrace in front of the new foundation, in a swath perhaps two or three hundred feet wide and half as many deep.

Dave has been working most of the day with his father. Now in the early afternoon he drives over to unload some lumber at his own site. Dave is carrying the lumber around to the open north side of his foundation when he spots huge manlike footprints clearly marked in the fresh and unspoiled sand. Dave is a strapping fellow, and, as his father says, "not afraid of anything," but he feels the goose pimples rise on his back. To him it seems that whatever made the tracks had casually walked up the slope to the new construction from the woods below, taken a good look into the excavation, and then veered away down the hill into the scrubby woods to the northeast.

Brought to the site by his son, Zane is understandably stimulated by this strange sequence of events, and is further intrigued by the configuration of the footprints—only the familiar bootprints of his sons mar the otherwise unmarked sand in the freshly excavated terrace. He carefully makes a plaster-of-paris casting of the best of the eighteen-inch footprints. Zane also films the tracks in color with an eight-millimeter camera.

By the end of the month the news of this discovery has spread widely through the region and the story begins to appear in newspapers throughout the state and elsewhere.

Meanwhile, a Mrs. Browning, who lives some distance down a country road not far from the Gray property, informs Zane that she had noticed a very powerful, unpleasant smell wafting into her house from the woods on the same night of May 28. For most of the next day she had thought little of it, but with the news of Gray's discovery of huge tracks, Mrs. Browning unhesitatingly tells Zane about the odor. She also reveals the fascinating details of her experience—reported at the beginning of this chapter—on the road north of Charlevoix several years earlier. She explains that she has kept that incident to herself to avoid the disbelief that would surely result from public disclosure. Mrs. Browning knows Gray as a man of unquestionable honesty. She no longer sees a reason to keep her previous sighting of a strange monster to herself.

During the next few days Gray and his sons conduct a thorough search of the woods. More footprints are found about a mile away, on another country road. The tracks wind out of the woods and onto the sandy edge of the road and then back across a field where new pines are planted in furrows. But it is difficult to locate the imprints in the drought-hardened ground. As Zane puts it, "I thought I had enough ability to follow tracks anywhere, but at that particular time, it had been so dry so late in the year, I couldn't follow the tracks back into that field, and I lost them."

Nevertheless, Zane soon finds a large, flattened dropping on an abandoned railroad bed that runs in an east–west line beyond the creek to the north of the Grays' new houses. This deposit of fecal matter appears to be too large to have come from any known wild animal in the area.

"I was raised on a farm nearby," Zane says, "and this dropping was shaped something like a pile of cow manure, about one and a half inches deep and about seven across, shaped like a cow pie. It hadn't been there long—I'd say less than a week—but with no rain on it all that time, it was fairly dry. The consistency of it wasn't like any cow's. It was more like a horse's manure. Of course, horse manure is always like little dumplings, even when it's piled up, and this was flat, but the consistency was like a horse's, all chewed up, not like a cow's. As you know, cows chew their cud and their droppings show it. Also, this dropping had dark hair sticking out of it, not as fine as a horse's hair from the body but not as long or as coarse as the hair from the mane or tail."

Zane also points out that no other prints from such sharp-hoofed animals as horses, cows, and deer could be found on the old grade. He thoughtfully adds that a human, or another animal with a soft bare foot, might easily walk through the grade without leaving a noticeable track.

Gray is careful to stick to specifics. He relates exactly what he and his family have seen, heard, and found. He avoids speculation about what all of these things might mean. He is thoroughly aware of the widespread publicity and its impact. When questioned about the implications, he is forthright, but unwilling to make guesses. Nevertheless, he adds, with a quizzical expression on his handsome face, "That manure surprised me!"

Two thousand miles almost due west across the vast expanse of North America the coastal range drops quickly to the Pacific breakers of Oregon's iron-bound coast. Extending in northward and southward branches, with the great rampart of the Cascades rearing only a few miles inland across a verdant valley, these western mountains are largely wild and uninhabited. Lush and varied in their vegetation, they are covered in dense forest and often impenetrable bush. The rain-drenched slopes, especially those facing west, produce tall hemlock, Douglas fir, huge pines, and red cedars. The sharp gorges are studded with aspen and thick clusters of rhododendron, sorrel, bitter cherry, laurel, and vine maple; the broken swales are spotted with huckleberry, dogwood, and buckthorn; the bogs and swamps are filled with sedges, sphagnum, and cattails and are surrounded on their fringes by thick willows and alders.

These mountains are one of the earth's last natural refuges from the ravages of man and provide a home for various rare animals and plants, which are vanishing almost as quickly as the machines of industrial man can slash into them and lay them waste.

The towering National Forest around Mt. Hood is a typical relic wilderness despite Portland's urban sprawl only forty-five miles away. Beneath the brilliant white volcanic cone of Mt. Hood, vast tracts of forest roll away in all directions. Segments of this huge virgin forest are periodically logged by private firms that acquire leases from the Department of Agriculture. These operations are carried out on a large scale, with massive modern equipment.

Such an operation is under way on the heavily wooded slopes of Fir Mountain, about twenty miles south of the Columbia River gorge. It is a sunny summer day in 1974. A local logging crew is hard at work when a crane operator follows the motion of his rig across the tangled landscape of manmade debris. His eyes catch a standing figure along the edge of yet-uncut forest. Confused, he looks to check the position of his two companions, but they are hard at work behind him and his crane. He moves the crane boom to get the advantage of its shade and studies the strange figure. It is an erect, hairy creature, massive, perhaps six to six and a half feet tall, of uniform color—black, or nearly so. It seems to be watching him. Then the creature turns and moves back into the trees. Its movements are coordinated, graceful, purposeful.

A day later the three men are back at work in the same place. Taking a break from the hot sun, they move into the forest shade on the edge of the clear-cut zone. The leading man spots a huge form in the bushes, which rises and moves away. The conifers are dense but the underbrush is fairly clear, and the great, manlike figure can be seen as it moves up the steep slope. It is covered in thick black hair; its shoulders and body are huge, its legs thick and muscular. It walks wholly upright, with a rapid, silent stride. The lumberjack runs after the creature, bravely determined to get a better look, but the strange being disappears quickly into the scrub beyond. All three loggers have seen the creature this time, one of them for a second time. Questioned soon afterward, the men agree that the figure was no bear, nor any other known wild animal. Nor do they think it was human.

Several hundred miles to the south the rugged Siskiyou Mountains rise in isolated glory above California's Klamath River, which rushes to the Pacific some miles to the west, in a section of Redwood National Park. These high Siskiyous are part of the huge Six Rivers National Forest, one of the most varied ecosystems in North America and a refuge for several endangered wild animals, including the wolverine and cougar. One of the larger tributaries of the Klamath is a deep-cleft mountain stream called Bluff Creek, along which a notorious series of huge, humanoid footprints have been found. Bluff Creek is also the scene of a famous filming of a Sasquatch, which is the commonly accepted name for the legendary North American Bigfoot, as distinguished from the Himalayan yeti. This film is considered authentic by many investigators.

It is early afternoon, October 20, 1967, and Roger Patterson and Bob Gimlin are riding their tough little horses up the rugged bottom of Bluff Creek, more than thirty miles from the nearest paved road. They are in file, Patterson leading, Gimlin behind, handling the packhorse. Their rifles are in scabbards. Patterson's rented sixteen-millimeter movie camera is in his saddlebag. He is a self-promoting, self-taught Bigfoot hunter who has already written a book on the subject.* He has searched long and hard for the legendary creature, and this time, just in case, he has cameras with him, ready to take both still and moving pictures. Gimlin is a sometime construction worker, a toughened, wiry man, smallish, like Patterson, and an expert horseman. Gimlin is far more skeptical about the object of their search than Patterson is. He has come along partly out of curiosity and a sense of adventure and partly because he has a break between jobs. Now both men have been in the Siskiyou wilderness for at least two weeks. The glorious autumn colors are at their peak, and the men have filmed panoramic scenes here and there, but so far nothing has been found, not a single track.

The horsemen are rounding a tight bend in the arroyo of the creek when suddenly they encounter a large, hairy creature, standing erect, on the far side of the stream, about eighty to a hundred feet away. Apparently the strange being has been caught in the open by surprise as the horsemen emerged around a bend in the creek bottom where a fallen tree has created a barrier and the water rushes through with considerable noise. The horses rear and buck, and Patterson's mount falls sideways to the right, but the nimble rodeo rider slides free expertly and pulls the movie camera from the saddlebag. The creature has already begun to walk deliberately and rapidly away to the right, but it seems to be in no hurry. Patterson rushes on foot across the little stream, stumbling in the soft sand, camera in hand, trying to catch this strange thing on film. The camera is filming, in the meantime, and catching nothing but sky, earth, and trees. Finally Patterson gets his footing and steadies the camera. The creature continues to swing along in an unhurried stride. Patterson shouts back to his partner, "Cover me."

---

*Many of the more important books and articles mentioned in the text are listed in the bibliography.

Patterson remembers previous reports of three kinds of tracks along Bluff Creek, apparently made by three different monsters. He is concerned that other creatures might be around.

Gimlin in the meantime has calmed his horse, and now he rides across the creek and also dismounts, sliding his 30/06 rifle free, bringing it to the ready. The strange figure pauses, wheels its upper body around, and takes a long look back at Gimlin, who holds his fire.

As they tell the story, the two cowboys had long before agreed never to shoot at such a creature unless absolutely necessary. They maintain that they have been impressed by the arguments of certain other Bigfoot hunters that to kill such a wild and unknown creature, perhaps related in some way to humans, would be indefensible.

Meanwhile, the creature has moved behind the partial obstruction of some trees, but it quickly emerges again into full view, its back plainly visible as it moves away.

Then Patterson curses in frustration. "Jesus. I'm out of film."

Earlier he had used most of the film on nearby scenery. Now there is nothing he can do. His horse has run off, and the extra rolls are in the saddlebag. The creature continues to move rapidly—but still not running—around one bend in the creek, then another, until it finally disappears at a distance of two or perhaps three hundred yards.

There is a brief discussion about what to do next. Gimlin reluctantly accepts Patterson's reasoning that to continue pursuit without film would prove nothing, so they go to retrieve the stray horse. They can always track the creature later. For the remainder of the afternoon they photograph and make casts of the many clear tracks in the sandy silt of the creek bottom. They also measure the tracks and study them for depth, trying to make a reasonable estimate of the weight of the creature. Gimlin at one point stands on a stump near the tracks and jumps into the earth. His high-heeled cowboy boots make an indentation in the earth no deeper than the tracks. They follow the tracks for perhaps a mile up the rough creek bed until they disappear up a steep rocky cliff.

Still excited, Patterson and Gimlin then drive out to nearby Willow Creek, where they tell their story to a man at a variety store. Later that night they drive to a larger town and mail the exposed film to Yakima, Washington, their home base, whence it is taken to Seattle to be developed.

The creature they have seen and filmed is a female, apparently, with large, pendulous breasts clearly visible. It appears to be at least six and a half feet tall, perhaps taller, and of enormous bulk. The body is covered in very dark hair. Only the palms of the hands and the soles of the feet seem to be hairless, and perhaps part of the face. The legs are short in relation to the torso, and the arms are long. The overall proportions are similar to those of a heavyset human being, but the neck seems nonexistent, the large head emerging directly from long, sloping shoulders. The head is peaked, with a ridge on the cranium that rises toward the back. The impressions of the feet in the silt measure about fourteen inches in length and five and a half inches wide, sunk, on average, about half an inch into the ground. The feet are plantigrade—using both sole and heel—as in a human being, with five toes that decrease progressively in size, although the difference between the largest (inside) toe and the smallest (outside) is less than in humans.

Both men have a distinct impression that the creature moves with the powerful grace of a wild animal, or of an athlete. Every motion is assured and economical, the arms swinging in balanced opposition to the thrust of the muscular legs. Gimlin recalls a powerful, musky odor that lingers in the air for a time after the creature has disappeared.

Patterson and Gimlin are determined to remain in the Bluff Creek region to act as guides for other Bigfoot hunters, whom they have alerted by phone. A group from Canada is expected in a day or so, and there are many tracks to study, and perhaps other signs. Unfortunately, it begins to rain hard early on the morning of October 21, and at dawn it is clear that they are in for a long, hard storm. They scramble about trying to cover some of the better footprints with pieces of cardboard, acquired the previous night in Willow Creek. But soon it is clear that if they wish to save the truck and the horses, and to assure their own safety, they will have to get out. Eventually they escape the treacherous floods and mud slides of Bluff Creek and make their way, exhausted, to Yakima. Soon after, they discover that the film has come out all right.

Within months this film becomes the center of a controversy, and the arguments regarding its authenticity have yet to be resolved.

Several hundred miles to the north the great coastal evergreen belt continues into British Columbia's rugged and mountainous littoral and well into the interior. Here the coniferous rain forest is equally dense, although the understory of deciduous growth is not as lush and varied as in California and Oregon. A woodsman exploring the region near Mica Mountain encounters what he at first takes for a grizzly bear. But he is an experienced hunter, and he quickly realizes that the creature is very different—well over six feet tall, broad, and hairy, the coat dark brown and silver-tipped. Heavy breasts are visible from the front. The massive frame is straight, and the long arms reach nearly to the knees. The feet are wider than a human's; but, more intriguing, the strange being walks erect, placing its heel down first. The head is sloped upward to the back, the lips protruding beneath a flat nose, the ears humanlike. The eyes seem small and dark. The neck is so thick and short as to be almost nonexistent. The strange apparition retreats quickly, watching the surprised man over its shoulder as it goes.

Many years earlier, in 1924, a lumberman named Albert Ostman has, by his account, a weird and traumatic adventure in the British Columbia wilderness. While camping in the region of Toba inlet, opposite Vancouver Island, he is carried away in the night, while still ensconced in his sleeping bag, by an eight-foot-tall, hairy giant. After miles of harrowing travel, slung over the creature's back like a sack of flour, Ostman is dumped unceremoniously on the ground.

Morning reveals a deep gorge, and around him move four hairy humanoid giants, including the huge male that carried him off, a female about seven feet tall, a younger male of about the same size, and a young, immature female. By his account Ostman remains among these creatures for at least six days, so he gets an extraordinary chance to observe the giants at close range. Unmolested but closely watched, he is apparently free to move among them and observes that they are humanlike except for their coats of hair and their great size. They seem to possess no tools, although their hands and other extremities are similar to those of man. They seem to spend little time foraging or hunting, at least during the period of Ostman's captivity, although the adult male wanders off from time to time. The younger male hovers about him a great deal, curious and playful, and Ostman notices that the big toe on the foot is longer than the other toes and well separated from them; the feet are padded underneath, like a dog's. The female has wide hips and visible breasts. All the beasts are covered with hair except on the soles of the feet and the palms of the hands, and on the nose and eyelids. Ostman guesses that the large male weighs more than 700 pounds, the female about 550, the younger male at least 300. The younger creatures seem to be the offspring of the mature giants.

Eventually Ostman escapes and somehow makes his way back to civilization. Ostman rarely travels again in the British Columbia wilderness—never alone—and he never returns to the site of his abduction. Indeed, he keeps the whole extraordinary story to himself for more than thirty years, for fear of scorn, until 1957, when stories about the hairy giants of British Columbia are beginning to attract considerable publicity.

The above are among hundreds of similar incidents reported with increasing frequency during the last few decades, especially from the Pacific Northwest and northern California, and to a somewhat lesser extent from Alberta, Idaho, and Montana. Although most of these accounts were once confined almost entirely to these regions, reports of a similar nature have been coming in from all over North America in the last ten or fifteen years. In the United States these sightings have been most heavily concentrated in Florida and Texas, and somewhat less heavily in the Midwest, especially in Illinois, Arkansas, Missou-

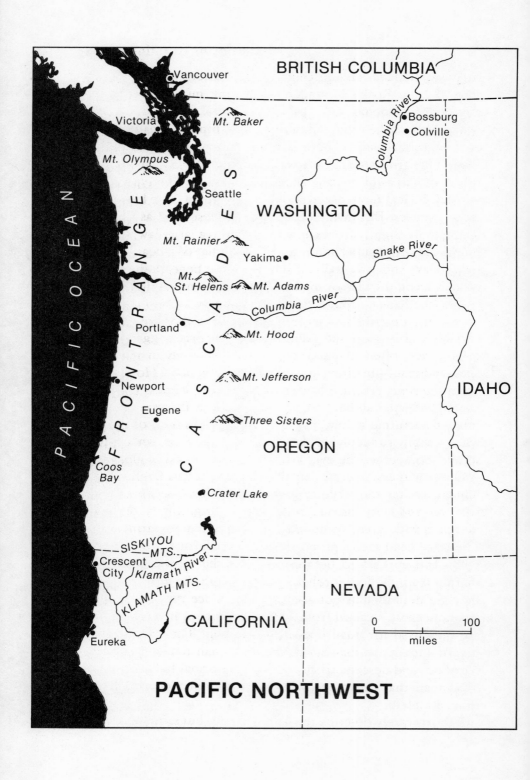

ri, Iowa, Indiana, and Michigan. The Eastern states, Appalachia, and the Rocky Mountain states rank much lower in the number of incidents.

The bulk of the reports describe huge, bipedal creatures covered with dark hair. There is rarely much anatomical detail, though the arms are almost always described as long and powerful, the torso as heavy, the shoulders as huge. The typical eyewitness, such as those noted above, rarely gets a close look at the facial features. But invariably the face is described as flat, projecting only slightly from a low forehead to a large jaw, vaguely humanoid, or apelike, and not at all like that of a bear, with its long, heavy snout. Usually, if skin is visible beneath the mantle of hair, or on the face or the hands, it is remembered as dark in color. The hands, though rarely seen clearly and up close, are universally described as large but similar to those of man, invariably hairless on the palms. Many reports suggest small, bright eyes, often of dark color, set closely—as in monkeys, apes, and man—on either side of a flat or pug nose. However, if the mysterious creature is seen at night, the witness often describes reflected amber, red, or green, as in the case of many smaller nocturnal animals, such as cats, porcupines, or skunks, when caught suddenly in the glare of light from an artificial source. Sometimes the eyes are actually described as glowing.

Often witnesses recall that the creature seems frighteningly human, yet far too large to be human, at least seven or eight feet tall and very broad, built like a weightlifter, the head merging with great, rounded shoulders, the forearms huge. The large head seems proportionately small for the bulk of the body, and appears to be crested, with the crown sloping up sharply from the low forehead. And though the arms are long, they are described as not at all apelike, since they do not project noticeably forward from a canting torso, as in a gorilla, nor are they used for quadrupedal locomotion. The impression is that of a great ape that can stride like a man rather than shamble about and descend to all fours in its normal fashion, or of a huge man that can move with the speed and economy of a trained athlete.

Reports rarely describe the feet in detail, but samples of footprints abound, numbering in the thousands. Usually these measure between fourteen and eighteen inches in length, some more than twenty inches, and about five to eight inches in width. Based on what is known about other large mammals, such huge feet might support a creature easily more than eight or even nine feet tall and weighing anywhere between five hundred and fifteen hundred pounds.

Only in the Southeast does this pattern vary noticeably. In Florida, Louisiana, and parts of Texas, reports have most often described a smaller creature of around five feet in height that emits an awful stench. Locally, this mysterious creature is known as the "skunk ape." Like the giants of the mountainous Northwest, the skunk ape is beginning to acquire a literature all its own.

Actually, these stories—these descriptions, footprints, weird noises in the night, and so on—seem to fit a pattern of protean but pervasive lore, both oral and written, that goes back to the early nineteenth century among European immigrants and, if Indian legends are included, centuries earlier. And such lore is not confined to the Northwestern coast or even to North America; it is ubiquitous, international, intercontinental.

Halfway around the world the greatest mountains on earth rear skyward in a vast wall between the lowlands of the Indian subcontinent and the uplands of Tibet and central Asia. The first published reports of huge two-legged creatures in the Himalayas date back to the nineteenth century when British travelers took note of stories told by Sherpa guides and other native peoples, especially in Nepal. Before the end of the nineteenth century undefinable tracks were widely reported, but it was not until well into this century that tales of actual sightings filtered out.

The Himalayas are not only the highest mountains in the world; they are also unusual in their flora and fauna, as they make a kind of transitional barrier between the subtropical zones that creep up to their southern slopes and the cold, arid plateau that extends beyond their northern slopes all the way to the Gobi Desert and the plains of Takla Makan. (Or, in zoogeographic terms, the rampart of the Himalayas marks a separation between the immense Palearctic region, essentially all of Eurasia north of the tropics, and the smaller but more varied Oriental region, essentially tropical Asia and its adjacent islands.) The lush forests of the Himalayan valleys are themselves remarkable. Because of the rapid changes in altitude, there are exceptionally rich successions of vegetation that include botanic habitats that range from tropical to arctic. Monsoons produce cloud forests in the middle zones, and great forests of oak, fir, alder, magnolia, rhododendron, and other larger growths shelter an incredible diversity of smaller plants. Within these deep valleys and ridges are sheltered several plant and animal species that have long since become rare or extinct in the more populous zones on either side of the rampart.

Perhaps this is one reason that tales of manlike beasts in the Himalayas have long had currency, even among scientists. In 1925 a respected British photographer and Fellow of the Royal Geographic Society, N. A. Tombazi, reported the sighting of such a creature in the Zemu Glacier region. He reported that it walked upright and occasionally stopped to uproot dwarf rhododendrons before it disappeared into some thick scrub. Still there was no great hullabaloo. Such incidents were known from forty years before, although they were not widely reported. Even Tombazi's report that the creature left clear, bipedal footprints in the snow did not arouse much controversy or interest. Presumably the scientific world assumed the creature to be either a yet-unknown species of mountain ape or a large monkey of some sort, despite the bipedal footprints. After all, in 1925 the gorilla had not yet been classified according to its two "races" or subspecies; this did not come until 1929.

Subsequent years brought many explorers, mountaineers, and biologists, as well as that most adventurous and peripatetic of now-extinct British breeds, the big-game hunter. By the end of the 1940s the Himalayas were fairly well explored—although some regions remained quite unknown even into the 1970s—and the list of alleged sightings, footprints, odors, and other signs of a large, hairy, apparently two-legged creature had grown considerably. The awareness that something quite unusual might exist in the Himalayan wilderness gradually began to spread beyond the borders of the British raj. Speculative articles and reports of strange incidents began to appear in scientific and popular journals. One of the most interesting of these reads very much like the tale told by Ostman in the Pacific Northwest.

A lone traveler in the Himalayas, snow-blind and almost dead from exposure, is rescued by a hairy being about eight or nine feet tall and carried miles to its cave, fed, nursed to recovery, and released. After his return to civilization the gentleman, one Captain d'Auvergne, wrote an article about his adventure for an Indian research journal in which he suggested that the creature was human, a survivor from prehistoric times, a descendant of a local race that had taken to the inner mountains to avoid persecution and had hence degenerated, somehow acquiring gigantic proportions and the habits of a beast.

Most people paid little attention to this fascinating and growing body of information until the famous and successful assault on Mt. Everest that began with a careful reconnaissance by mountaineer-explorer Eric Shipton in 1951. During that expedition Shipton and his companion, Michael Ward, discovered and photographed a remarkable series of large footprints while crossing the Menlung Glacier near the Tibet-Nepal border. The Sherpa porters had at once responded, "Yeti, sir, yeti." The tracks appeared to be extremely fresh, apparently made only a few hours earlier, impressed into a thin layer of crystalline snow carpeting the firm glacial ice. Shipton's celebrated photograph of one of these prints is exceptionally sharp, revealing a large foot about twelve and a half inches long and seven and a half inches wide. The heel is nearly as broad as the front of the foot, quite unlike that of a man, but clearly not similar to that of any known bear. In the Himalayas only bears approximate or exceed human size among mammals with plantigrade feet. Furthermore, the hallux, or large inner toe, is very large, although shorter than the long second toe and separated from and opposable to the other four, suggesting a creature more primitive than modern man. Apes have nearly opposable big toes. However, unlike the toes of apes, the four remaining toes appear in the photograph to be short and stubby.

Of equal importance in Shipton's opinion was the observation that the tracks indicated two creatures moving together, in a bipedal mode of locomotion. Shipton reported that he found a place where one of the animals had jumped across a crevasse about three feet wide, and he had clearly noted the takeoff point of one foot and the clear imprint of toes where the other foot landed.

Shipton's photograph soon became world famous, and it has since emerged as the primary piece of indirect evidence that an unknown animal of apparent apelike or humanoid nature exists in the Himalayas. Because of Shipton's association with the successful ascent of Everest by Edmund Hillary and his Sherpa companion, Tenzing Norgay, in 1953, his find brought an aura of respectability to the mysterious phenomenon. Newspapermen, students of the unusual, and other curious people began for the first time to compile a record of previous incidents. Within a year of the famous Everest climb, the mass-circulation British newspaper the *Daily Mail* had financed an expedition to search for the legendary creature. Mass publications printed detailed descriptions of the beast, gleaned from Sherpa lore and other native tales. The yeti's body is most often described as between five and five and a half feet tall, somewhat stocky or apelike in shape but with a human quality imparted by its two-legged gait. Its hair is usually described as reddish brown, of coarse texture, sometimes with white patches on the chest. The hair on the shoulders is longest. The face is flat and hairless, similar to that of an ape. The jaw is large and heavy, the teeth are large but apparently not fanged, and the mouth is wide. The head is said to have a ridged crown rising to a conical shape. The free-swinging arms are long, reaching nearly to the knees, and are apparently used regularly when climbing steep or rocky slopes. There is no tail.

The world was captivated at once. What a marvelous mystery, and in such a legendary and remote place. The international press had a field day. Within a few months an earlier misinterpretation of the word *me-teh* (roughly meaning "man-sized wild thing" in the Sherpa dialect) had again been mis-translated into the English "abominable snowman." Now the name matched the lore. What could be more fascinating, more romantic, than the idea of a huge mammal, not yet neatly clas-sified into the cubbyholes of contemporary zoology, not yet dissected, still an apparition, possibly akin to man, hovering on the edge of human knowledge (like a ghost on the fringes of consciousness)? Indeed, the longer the duration of the mystery, the more romantic, the more intriguing.

Curiosity about such a titillating mystery could hardly be contained by a single continent. Rudimentary research by jour-nalists quickly revealed similar legends among peoples in other parts of the world, including certain mountainous parts of the Soviet Union. Somewhat unexpected was the information that a body of lore about gigantic hairy monsters existed along the mountainous Northwest coast of North America.

It took a while before American newspapers and other publi-cations could come up with a term as appropriate as "abomina-ble snowman," but the Everest expedition and its hatch of books and memoirs had tilled the soil. In late August 1958 a road-construction crew at work about twenty miles north of Klamath, California, encountered huge footprints that seemed to appear only at night in the fresh dirt of the new roadbed. The tracks seemed to come down to the road from the steep hillsides, across the road, and toward a nearby creek. Some ap-peared to follow the road, skirting the massive earth-moving equipment before disappearing again into the woods. The prints were about sixteen inches long and seven inches wide at the ball of the foot, narrowing to about five at the heel. The stride seemed to be about four feet on average. The foot was akin to that of a flat-footed human, without a visible arch. The similarity among all the footprints indicated a single specimen.

Apparently some weeks passed, with the tracks repeatedly appearing overnight only to be obliterated during the next day's construction. For some reason news of this extraordinary find did not get out until a publicity-wise bulldozer operator made arrangements to have plaster casts prepared by a local taxidermist. A newspaper in nearby Eureka responded with a story, complete with a photo of the construction worker holding his casting of the sixteen-inch footprint. The story was on the Associated Press wires within days, and it quickly appeared throughout North America, photo and all. Somewhere along the way the caption BIGFOOT was added.

It would hardly be fair to say that the press invented our North American hairy monster. Alleged sightings and footprints clearly antedate the above events, probably by more than a century, if we are to credit the record compiled by various Bigfoot researchers. Nevertheless, the written record is sparse and uncertain—and open to interpretation—prior to about 1958. The oral or folkloric tradition is equally uncertain. On the other hand, the record of sightings, footprints, and other so-called evidence compiled in the twenty-odd years since is varied and vast. There have been thousands of reports, published and unpublished, that more or less fit into the category of the Bigfoot phenomenon. So, in this sense, the phenomenon itself is of recent vintage; perhaps related in its mass-media aspects to other unexplained phenomena that have cropped up during the postwar era, the beginning of the atomic age.

This hardly means that all of the evidence regarding the existence of Bigfoot is meaningless or unworthy of investigation. It does mean that the entire matter falls into a huge category of doubt. Frauds, con men, and gullible suckers are naturally attracted to the Bigfoot sphere like moths to a flame. Bigfoot stories continue to have a strangely insubstantial quality, akin to the reports of UFOs or the alleged mysterious disappearances in the "Bermuda Triangle." So it is easy for most self-respecting people simply to ignore the whole matter or dismiss it as fabulous junk.

The phenomenon will not so easily go away, however. *Something* is going on, something that cannot be explained away by scornful dismissal or even by elegantly preconceived rationalizations. Even if these incidents, these footprints, are the product of whimsy, phantasmagoria, the fruits of overripe imagination, or perhaps modern manifestations of ancient myths and subconscious memory, the phenomenon as a whole demands a serious and unbiased investigation. It is not enough to say that such a pervasive and frequent phenomenon is either faked or implicitly absurd simply because it seems to contradict the mainstream of current scientific or academic fashion. Anyone with historical perspective knows that the halls of orthodoxy at any given time are strewn with the bones of once "universal" truths, littered with the discarded fragments of outmoded explanations. It is only the present that is assured its theories are coherent, its explanations immutable.

Thus, good detective work is necessary in order to sift and balance the odds and ends of evidence, to test the clues and separate what might be real from what is obviously fake. Then one must concentrate on what seems most consistent, most plausible, most sensible. And, in the true spirit of scientific inquiry, one must be willing to risk the label of "deviate" and go where the evidence leads, even if people consider the subject to be the realm of crackpots and cranks.

It would be foolish, nevertheless, to accept any theory at face value—no matter how coherent it might seem—unless it has been subjected to the rules of evidence as we understand them and tested by the most basic scientific methods. For example, within the confines of our present knowledge, flights of fancy about unknown or half-understood "dimensions" or "separate realities" will accomplish little. Such speculations properly belong in the realm of parapsychology, where the rules of evidence apparently do not apply. Simply because the Bigfoot mystery has been labeled as "paranormal" does not justify removing it from the sphere of rigorous scientific inquiry, as if all the painstaking accumulation of scientific knowledge since the Renaissance—indeed since Aristotle—is of no import. The Bigfoot phenomenon deserves to be treated seriously on its merits and should not forthwith be relegated to the realm of pseudoscience.

2. Relic Humanoids or Unknown Apes?

Orthodox primatology has not recognized, and apparently, has no clues for analyzing the evidence of the continued existence on earth of higher primate forms distinct from both the Pongidae and *Homo Sapiens.*

DMITRI BAYANOV AND IGOR BOURTSEV
in *Current Anthropology,* December 1974

I am convinced that the Sasquatch exists, but whether it is all that it is cracked up to be is another matter altogether. There must be *something* in north-west America that needs explaining, and that something leaves man-like footprints.

DR. JOHN NAPIER in *Bigfoot: The Yeti and Sasquatch in Myth & Reality*

The Literature

Most people cannot afford just to galivant off hunting for Big-foot at the drop of a hat, the way deer hunters from Detroit invade the north woods of Michigan every November. It would be convenient if they could. By now the mystery would probably be solved. We might have our creature, dead or alive, and the amateurs would have long since given way to the pros.

But the amateurs prevail. Our Bigfoot is marvelously elusive. No one seems to be able to agree exactly which is the best place to look. One expert says emphatically that the unknown monsters live only in the Pacific Northwest. Another strongly disagrees, pointing out that the sightings and other data from Michigan, Florida, and Texas are every bit as good as the stuff from Washington and Oregon. Anyway, most people can only read about the creature. But for the curious and unsuspecting reader trying to get a handle on the subject, perhaps wanting to do a bit of investigating on his own, the printed matter on Bigfoot is contradictory, confusing, and downright misleading. So it is important early on to set up some standards, some basis for comparison.

Most of the Bigfoot literature is very useful—even the worst of it—because it so neatly reflects the array of viewpoints, the warring factions, that have clustered around the phenomenon since the late 1950s. Books and articles on Bigfoot, which did not exist a few years ago, now proliferate. In their profusion and confusion they are a mirror of the elusive phenomenon itself.

The majority of the books and articles fit into a category that I call the "true believers," akin to the works of Erich von Däniken *(Chariots of the Gods)* or the stories printed in such sensationalist tabloids as *The National Enquirer.* These are written with the premise that the creature must exist and that any and all skepticism is either part of a conspiracy among scientists and academic types to suppress the truth—apparently because it would somehow upset the apple cart—or the result of blind unwillingness to "face the facts."

Premier among such are the works of John Green, one of the first people to publish anything on Bigfoot and long considered a leading authority on the subject. Green, a journalist from British Columbia, apparently began from a position of open skepticism, back in the early 1950s. But like many Bigfoot buffs he soon became convinced that the bulk of the data—the sightings, footprints, and so on—taken together, proved the existence of the creature. And, once that premise had been formed, Green decided the next step was to find out what the strange apparition was all about. He has since collected an impressive array of information from all over North America and published it as evidence. In so doing Green has greatly helped to popularize the widespread belief that the mysterious Sasquatch not only exists throughout North America but that it can be tentatively classed as to type and described in terms of its anatomical structure and behavior. Recently Green has gone so far as to suggest that there is no mystery at all. He states, for example, that Bigfoot is gentle, friendly, harmless to humans, timid yet curious. He reassures readers that they need not worry if they encounter one of the hairy giants; it will assuredly do no harm.

Green is an experienced journalist, capable of leading the unprepared reader down an alluring garden path of fascinating stories. In his early books Green introduced his Sasquatch in classic anecdotal fashion. Thus the cumulative effect of case after case, incident after incident, can be convincing to the inexperienced reader. Data heaped up in support of speculative theories that lack a shred of hard evidence to support them can take on the mantle of "proof" even when there is none. For example, Green devotes an entire chapter in his most recent book, *Sasquatch: The Apes Among Us,* to a description of the giant's physical attributes, its alleged size, and so on, and he states categorically that it is "solitary" by nature—all this without a single piece of hard evidence or verifiable observation.

In this recent book Green has made an attempt to analyze systematically more than fifteen hundred sightings and other reports, and his handling of select examples from the massive bulk of data compiled over a period of more than twenty years is unquestionably useful. Green has arranged this material neatly, according to state and province, thus providing future investigators with a convenient primary source. No doubt *Sasquatch: The Apes Among Us* will become a major reference, a guide to the public manifestations of Bigfoot.

Unfortunately, Green's analysis of the data that he so carefully presents is arbitrary, apparently based on his personal choice as to what is good or bad evidence.* For example, the most systematic tabulation of data gleaned from eyewitness reports does not add up to a body of scientific proof. It merely adds up to more "soft" evidence, ultimately conjectural in nature, since it is wholly unverifiable. In the final analysis, discriminating read-

---

*See the summary of my interview with Green in Chapter 6.

ers will recognize Green's prolific contribution to Bigfoot literature for what in essence it is, mostly polemic that falls into the "preaching to the converted" category, demanding a suspension of disbelief similar to that required to enjoy an episode of *Battlestar Galactica.*

Most of the other popular books on Bigfoot make John Green look like a rigorous scholar by comparison. Pulp paperbacks such as *Bigfoot,* by B. Ann Slate and Alan Berry, and *Creatures of the Outer Edge,* by Loren Coleman and Jerome Clark, not only subscribe to the premise that Bigfoot exists but also seem to suggest that it may have supernatural qualities. Berry and Slate seem to believe that it can disappear into thin air, or move about with or without making its huge tracks, according to whim.

Some of this material fits better into specialized publications dealing with the "paranormal," such as *Flying Saucer Review* or *UFO Report.* Perhaps this is where the phenomenon actually belongs. Clark and Coleman have led the way with "far-out," supranormal explanations for Bigfoot, explanations that do not require strict adherence to known scientific rules. That is, these authors do not question the validity of reports or the "fact" of Bigfoot at all; they have little interest in biological or earthly theories. Coleman and Clark attempt to make the case that sightings of Bigfoot and of UFOs are related, even parallel, phenomena. They suggest, with considerable persuasive force, that the apparently futile struggles by Bigfoot buffs to "prove" that such apparitions are "real" are doomed to failure precisely because these strange giant forms are not of this world. Exactly what they are is left largely unexplained.

Fitting rather loosely into the category of true believers is the rather turgid work of certain self-styled "hominologists" based in the Soviet Union. Several of their highly technical briefs have recently been published in various scientific journals, including the prestigious *Current Anthropology.* Basically, these hominologists believe that Sasquatch, as well as its alleged Asiatic cousin, is some kind of relic humanoid, a survivor from another age, a member of a primate group they call "troglodytes." There is, for some, an undeniable appeal in such speculations.

There is also a lot of sensationalist magazine literature on Bigfoot. Popular magazines such as *Saga, Pursuit* (published by the Society for the Investigation of the Unexplained), *True, Fate,* and *Argosy* have returned again and again to the Bigfoot theme, especially in the past dozen years or so. *Argosy* alone published several articles on Bigfoot during the early seventies, not all of these arguing in favor of the hypothesis. This is not to say that any Bigfoot article published in a mass-circulation magazine is automatically useless but only to suggest that we be aware of the potential exploitation by the press of a titillating subject.

Probably the most popular book on Bigfoot in recent years has been *The Search for Bigfoot: Monster, Myth, or Man?,* by Peter Byrne, an Irish-born former big-game hunter who has successfully promoted himself as the only full-time professional Bigfoot investigator in this country. In addition to searching for the elusive monster in North America, Byrne has organized expeditions to the Himalayas, one of his old stomping grounds, to seek the yeti. Apparently Byrne does nothing on a small scale, and until very recently he was head of a privately financed "Bigfoot Information Center" based in Oregon. This closed down during the summer of 1979, for unexplained reasons. During his years in Oregon, Byrne apparently attracted a sizable coterie of supporters, some of them obviously well-to-do, who were willing to finance his research into the Bigfoot phenomenon. There seems to have been considerable faith among Byrne's supporters that his investigations might one day yield exciting results, and in his writings Byrne certainly encouraged this hope. This is not to suggest that these hopes were entirely misplaced, for Byrne seems to have energy and the born adventurer's sense of the right moment. Also, his search during the last dozen years or so has certainly been organized and systematic.

Unfortunately, Byrne's book is disappointing and not very convincing. Byrne is careful to pay lip service to minimum standards of scientific objectivity, and he professes a scientific method in his research. But, taken as a whole, *The Search for Bigfoot* is little more than a loosely organized collection of familiar Bigfoot lore, wrapped around some high-sounding appeals to the conservation ethic. Byrne maintains that his "system" of classifying sightings and footprint reports has effectively narrowed the general pattern of such reports to geographical regions called "Area I," centered in the coastal ranges and the Cascades of the Pacific Northwest, and Area II, parts of Idaho and southern and southwestern British Columbia. Byrne flatly states that there are no *credible* reports from outside these two areas. Data from the Midwest, the Southeast, and Texas must therefore be discounted. Since it makes good sense to limit the potential range of any putative Sasquatch to the mountainous Northwest, where such a beast could presumably find shelter in remote areas, Byrne's statement appears to be both scientifically objective and logical. However, the unspoken implication is less evident: namely that Byrne has somehow effectively separated the credible from the incredible. Thus the reader is led to the assumption that if evidence outside these regions is not credible, then evidence of a predictable pattern found within Areas I and II must therefore be credible. Like Green's apparently coherent speculations about Sasquatch's physical appearance and habits, there is no hard evidence to back up such subjective conclusions about Bigfoot's habitat. In the end such assumptions rest on speculation based on selective use of evidence that cannot be substantiated. So, Byrne's otherwise more cautious approach to the mystery is in the end scarcely more reliable than Green's. Furthermore, *The Search for Bigfoot* is far less useful for reference and much less interesting than Green's work.

Byrne has also published a monthly called *Bigfoot News,* which began in 1974 and ended its run in the summer of 1979. A superficial reading of back issues of this intriguing sheet conveys the impression that an awful lot of important information is being collected about Bigfoot and that a great deal of painstaking, systematic analysis is proceeding. There seems to be no doubt that Byrne and his associates have been more careful in the sifting of information than most, and Byrne has set up a "rating system" that appears to be useful.* But a close reading of *Bigfoot News,* from issue to issue, is disappointing, especially

---

*See Chapter 7.

when compared with the compilations of John Green. There is a great deal of pseudoscientific talk, but little of substance, just additional reports that are in essence no different from earlier reports. Indeed, a good part of *Bigfoot News* is given over to simplistic explanations designed to "inform" schoolchildren who are interested in Bigfoot.

Much more fascinating and instructive among these popular books is *Sasquatch,* by René Dahinden and Don Hunter. The book, although written by Hunter, a journalist, is really Dahinden's story. René Dahinden is another Bigfoot hunter whose record of involvement goes back to the mid-fifties, when he became one of John Green's first associates. But Dahinden did not remain long under Green's wing. He is the classic loner, a feisty one-man sparkplug of passion, irascible, litigious, dedicated, almost a phenomenon in himself. From the beginning of his search—which for Dahinden has always been an overwhelmingly *personal* matter—he has exhibited great tenacity. However, through many years of gradual and difficult self-education, Dahinden has seen his early hopes greatly eroded. Concerned by the frauds, hoaxes, and other dubious activities with which many of his former Bigfoot colleagues have been associated, Dahinden has become a tough, though inconsistent, critic.

The Dahinden book, which is as much about Dahinden as it is about Bigfoot, is unusually revealing. It is a must for any serious student of the subject primarily because Dahinden's candid recapitulation of his adventures in search of Sasquatch is, like a Ross MacDonald thriller, an exercise in progressive disillusionment that finally leads to an unraveling of the threads of deception. A case in point is Dahinden's hilarious description of the Pacific Northwest (or "Slick") Expedition of 1959–1960, which was supposed to gather the best people in the field and collect real evidence. The spectacle of grown men running around in the woods trying to "lure" a presumed male giant by means of used sanitary napkins purloined in the night from service-station bathrooms and tacked to trees around the expedition's camp proved to be too much even for Dahinden. At the time his faith was perhaps stronger than his sense of criticism, but his personal sense of integrity was offended.

This so-called expedition, financed by the late Tom Slick, a Texas millionaire who backed several similar hunts in the Americas and in the Himalayas, attracted a motley bunch of two-bit hustlers and confidence men. Quickly the sincere searchers, including John Green, were shoved into the background. From the first the expedition was doomed to failure. Wholly disorganized and without leadership, focus, or plan, it degenerated into a foolish wild-goose chase. This was only one of many experiences over the years that clearly infuriated Dahinden.

The Dahinden-Hunter book is interesting for other reasons, too. Despite his early disillusionment, Dahinden remained impressed by the controversial Patterson-Gimlin film noted earlier. He knew both men well, and came to trust Gimlin especially, though his faith in Patterson was somewhat shaky. Bolstered by his frequent study of the film over many years, Dahinden is convinced that it, along with a handful of footprints and other data, is evidence enough to continue his search. His travels to the Soviet Union and Europe in the early 1970s to consult with the Russian hominologists and other experts are neatly summarized in the book, along with useful, if rather uncritical, outlines of the hominologists' many elaborations and theories.

Sadly, the Dahinden-Hunter book is short on consistent analysis. Like Dahinden himself, the book is ultimately paradoxical, raising more doubts than it allays. Dahinden's hard-won realization that the great majority of alleged Bigfoot reports, including footprints, are dubious at best seems finally incongruous with his persistent faith that this quest will one day succeed.

The most recent study as of this writing is *Sasquatch Apparitions,* by Barbara Wasson, a privately printed paperback published early in 1979. This little book is a serious attempt to investigate the primary elements of the Bigfoot phenomenon: the nature of the evidence itself, the most notorious incidents—including some of those already noted herein—the geographical regions and ecological zones, and, most important, the investigators themselves. A practicing psychologist, Wasson is apparently the first Bigfoot investigator to attempt an objective analysis of the people who have been most intimately involved in the Bigfoot business since it started. To a limited extent she succeeds, revealing potential motives, life patterns, conflicts, and character traits among the many Bigfoot searchers, which, taken as a whole, cannot be very reassuring to anyone who studies the subject. The majority of the central figures in the Bigfoot drama appear to be rather confused, sometimes pathetic people whose lives might be quite empty without their Bigfoot involvement. Several appear to be manipulative borderline cases, accomplished liars, or ne'er-do-wells. A few seem to be highly motivated, able, and bright, sincerely interested in doing all they can to resolve the mystery, come what may.

Unfortunately, Wasson is herself peripherally involved in one of the cliques that have so deeply segmented the Bigfoot cognoscenti. When discussing certain individuals—René Dahinden, for example—she is by turns penetrating and vague. Perhaps this is because of Wasson's friendship with Dahinden and her personal involvement in the internecine struggles that he has done so much to instigate. In any case she pulls back from the hard conclusions that her own evidence would seem to suggest.

Sasquatch Apparitions is, nevertheless, an important contribution to a growing body of Bigfoot literature that is otherwise mostly self-serving, repetitive, and misleading. Wasson shows why so much of the Bigfoot evidence is unreliable and why some of it is disturbingly provocative, but in the end she seems unable to sustain her objectivity. Like Dahinden, she so badly wants her apparition to prove real that she makes a statement founded more on hope than on reason.

By far the most important book in this mixed bag is John Napier's *Bigfoot: The Yeti and Sasquatch in Myth and Reality.* Dr. Napier is one of the world's leading primatologists, and also one of the world's few experts in primate locomotion. His qualifications are unquestionable, and his book ought to be the last word on the subject. I fear, however, it is not.

Napier's book is indeed detailed, brilliant, crammed with significant zoological, anthropological, and literary material. He is devastatingly critical of some of the more notorious Bigfoot stories so often reprinted uncritically. For example, Napier effectively demolishes an often-repeated story told by an escaped Siberian prisoner of war named Slavomir Rawicz in his adventure book *The Long Walk.*

According to Rawicz, after he and several friends escaped from a Siberian prison camp, apparently in 1941, they made their agonizing way across thousands of miles of desert and mountain to freedom in India. Rawicz further alleged that while traversing the Himalayas, in February 1942, he and his companions encountered two creatures at least eight feet tall and covered with rusty-brown hair. His elaborate description of these creatures is so convincing at first reading, so full of apparently pertinent detail, that it has been widely reprinted in half a dozen Bigfoot books. Unfortunately, as Napier points out, Rawicz's book has been criticized by many Himalayan experts, who suspect it is largely a work of fiction. The text is full of geographical errors and inconsistencies, apparent fabrications and discrepancies. At one point in his narrative Rawicz says that an overland march from the Tsangpo River (an upper tributary of the Brahmaputra) to the Himalayas took two months, a trip that should have taken five days at the most. Also, Rawicz and his compatriots would have had to cross the major highway between Umruchi and Lanchow, then busy with wartime traffic, in order to move south into the Tibetan massif. They would necessarily have arrived at this road after months of isolation and deprivation. Why, then, did Rawicz not mention the road, and why didn't he and his companions attempt to get help from a passing vehicle?

Napier further argues that the greatest weakness in the celebrated Rawicz tale is that it perpetuates the popular misconception that Tibet and Nepal are total wildernesses where fugitives can wander for months without human contact. In reality, once the escapees crossed the Tibet-Nepal or the Bhutan frontier— apparently Rawicz's book doesn't say which—they could hardly have avoided any number of widely scattered villages where shelter and food could have been obtained. Even if Rawicz and company were for some reason avoiding the network of village trails, they would have been forced to wallow through the bottoms of rock-cliffed gorges filled with lush, often impenetrable tropical vegetation, but not a word about any such topography appears in Rawicz's story.

Finally, as if this were not enough, Napier points out inconsistencies in Rawicz's account of the two hairy monsters. The creatures seem to combine several of the precise anatomical characteristics of the gorilla, for example a strange two-legged gait that is simultaneously "shuffling" and "waddling." Napier argues convincingly that such a gait, combined with the heavy upper torso Rawicz describes, would not be functional for a yeti living at high altitudes in the Himalayas.

Napier's book is very useful as a guide to such pseudoscientific foolishness. He brings a combination of scientific erudition and personal wit to the whole yeti question, which he strives to reveal as a fantasy based on mythology. He is almost convincing. Surely no self-respecting writer on this subject could henceforth dare to quote the Rawicz account as "evidence" of the yeti's existence or as supporting evidence for the North American variety.

Napier's powerful aversion to the possible existence of the yeti does not apply equally to the Sasquatch. Despite the fact that apes do exist in southeastern Asia and once existed in inner Asia, and despite the fact that apes have never been known to exist anywhere in the Americas, Napier argues that the evidence for the Sasquatch is much stronger. In so doing he seems to have deviated from the rigor of his discipline; at least, that is what many of his scientific colleagues think.

Napier has based his pro-Sasquatch stance almost entirely on the abundant footprint evidence in North America; there is a relative scarcity of such evidence in Asia. He does not believe that all these footprints, many of them seeming to fit a biological pattern, can be ignored; he believes they could have been made by a real but unidentified creature. So in the end Napier launches his own tentative guess, though he admits it is still not based on hard evidence, that there is an unknown bipedal primate of some kind wandering about the Pacific Northwest wilderness. And like many who have studied this question, Napier is not ready to dismiss all the sightings, myths, and legends as mere fantasy.

It is all too easy to make fun of a position such as the one Napier has courageously taken, especially when one is ignorant of the mass of data on which it is based. My critical comments about the worst of the above books should not be confused with my comments about Napier's book, as Napier has few peers in his knowledge of his subject. Unlike so many of his openly scornful scientific brethren, Napier has *investigated* the phenomenon. Reading Napier, one gets the impression that he moved from an initial stance of almost outright disbelief to an open-minded stance, finally leaning hard in the direction of belief because this is where his open-minded search has taken him. His position, whether ultimately proved right or wrong, is an intellectually honest one.

It is also an index of Napier's reliability as an unbiased student of this phenomenon that he curries no favors with one side or the other. He is distrusted by the true believers because of his doubts about the authenticity of the Patterson-Gimlin film (see Appendix A for a summary of Napier's arguments), and he is dismissed by the disbelievers because he dares to make a tentative case for the existence of Bigfoot. This doesn't mean that his book is without flaws, some of which are noted later.

The biggest and most outwardly impressive study is *Abominable Snowmen: Legend Come to Life*, by the late monster-buff-extraordinaire Ivan T. Sanderson. Published in 1961, the book is now out of print. Its bulk and its vast leaps back and forth in time and space would probably discourage all but the most dedicated buffs, but it is worth a careful reading. Sanderson was a zoologist who had an encyclopedic knowledge of the weird and unusual. His knowledge of animals—well known a few years ago because of his frequent television appearances—seems to have been exceeded only by his fertile imagination. Scientists invariably count imagination as an asset, but Sanderson's seems to have gotten away from him. Long before he wrote this big book, he had separated himself from most of his fellow zoologists because of his willingness to believe in the reality of all kinds of unproved popular legends. For example, he wrote in an otherwise brilliant book on elephants that mammoths still roamed North America after Columbus's arrival and perhaps survived here into the early seventeenth century. He was capable of making such conjecture read almost like fact. But, of course, he could produce no proof.

Thus Sanderson's work fits into the true-believer category. Sanderson not only believed in the corporal reality of Bigfoot but also postulated several species of hairy giants widely distributed throughout the globe, some of them products of quite separate evolutionary lines.

One of Sanderson's longtime partners in the pursuit of such phenomena was Bernard Heuvelmans, a Belgian zoologist who wrote a popular book, published in 1959, called *On the Track of Unknown Animals.* In this book Heuvelmans included a chapter entitled "The Not-So-Abominable Snowman," which presents a neat, almost eloquent précis of the best evidence then available regarding the legendary Asiatic creature. Some interesting work has been done since, but it is significant that nothing really new has been brought forth in the last twenty years. Regarding the evidence gathered in North America, Heuvelmans basically agreed with his colleague Sanderson. In 1969 he published a fascinating but almost certainly erroneous article that purported to classify the infamous "Minnesota Iceman" as a genuine biological specimen representing the "unknown" North American hominid. The alleged creature, frozen in a block of ice, was, alas, soon thereafter shown to be almost certainly a model made in Hollywood.

Anthropologists have shied away from the Bigfoot business almost entirely. Perhaps they are even more worried about guilt by association than are the zoologists. However, at least one anthropologist has seriously researched the matter. He is Grover Krantz, of Washington State University. Krantz is satisfied, as a result of his painstaking study of many footprints and of at least two handprints, that the mysterious animal exists in nature. Krantz has published little, considering the plethora of information that has poured forth in recent years—or perhaps because he recognizes that most of this information is of poor quality. But he has edited an interesting collection, *The Scientist Looks at the Sasquatch,* and this includes his three major articles on the structure of the Sasquatch hand and foot.

Krantz's work is interesting for several reasons. For one, he suggests that the Sasquatch has a hand with a nonopposable thumb; that is, its thumb apparently cannot touch all the other fingers at their tips, as the human's can, for efficient grasping and manipulation. This does not jibe with much of the "observed" activity of the alleged Sasquatch—including the Ostman tale about being slung over a huge monster's shoulder and the many reports of objects being thrown and moved about with great dexterity and strength—and it raises questions about the food-gathering practices of the supposedly omnivorous cold-adapted animal, whose foraging would have to vastly exceed that of a grizzly bear, for example.

Also, one wonders about a hominid, almost universally agreed to be bipedal, that would place its hands flat to the ground to produce prints like those studied by Krantz. These alleged handprints come perilously close to suggesting quadrupedal locomotion or at least a mode of combined bipedal *and* quadrupedal locomotion. Although this would seem appropriate in an animal with a high center of gravity—like the gorilla or orangutan—it hardly goes well with the "observed" evidence (including the Patterson-Gimlin film) suggesting the great creature's powerful two-legged stride. Generally Krantz has based his theory on very shaky data. Despite the fact that he brings an anthropologist's training to the question, Krantz suffers from the same problem that all Sasquatch experts do: there is no hard evidence, no physical evidence, to work with.

I should add in fairness that Krantz's anthology does include some interesting pieces by anthropologists and other scholars who do not believe in the existence of Sasquatch but who are willing to keep an open mind. Some of the comments about the unwillingness of the scientific world to take a close and sustained look at the phenomenon are pertinent. For this reason *The Scientist Looks at the Sasquatch* is worthwhile. Also, the article by Wayne Suttles, "On the Cultural Track of the Sasquatch," is a must. In it Suttles brilliantly sums up the

Amerindian lore of the Northwest coast, though I fear his conclusions will not be very satisfying to most of those who want
to believe.

Bigfoot and the Media

Even as I write, a program by the Smithsonian Institution,
entitled "Monsters, Mysteries and Myths," is flickering on television, and my children are watching attentively. "Dramatiza-
tions" have also been put together to simulate alleged sightings
of Bigfoot, the Loch Ness monster, and the abominable snowman. This particular television piece is not a bad job. But it bol-
sters an important point.

I have already noted that a strong case can be made that
our media have, in effect, created the Bigfoot phenomenon.
Even a child can see how readily the subject lends itself to
sensationalism.

It is no accident that John Green, premier Bigfoot investigator, was a newspaperman. To trace the history of the Bigfoot
phenomenon in newspapers, and to a somewhat lesser extent in
books and magazines, is to parallel the public career of Mr.
Green, which is not to say that he or any other publicist for Bigfoot is not sincere in his efforts but merely to suggest an obvious and significant relationship.

Green's first presentation of the Sasquatch, by means of an
unconnected series of anecdotes—a time-honored journalistic
device—was followed in later years by material taken from
newspapers and magazines dating into the previous century.
For the most part, Green wisely avoided using more reliable
historical documents. Then, after a body of devotees had gradually emerged, Green expanded his reportage to include carefully selected accounts from the Amerindian myths and legends
and other sources. From the beginning Green was fully conscious, and said as much, that he was challenging orthodox science in his presentation of this material, and this is one factor
that has attracted widespread interest. Green has admitted that
the core of his fascination for the subject derives from the fact

that the scientific establishment scorns or ignores the Bigfoot phenomenon.

Thus, at least in the print media, no one has matched Green's influence over the years, and it is probable no one will. His early pieces contained a strong element of whimsy—this was apparently before he became a believer—and the "believe it or not" tone in his writing has been strong ever since. He presents a direct challenge to the reader that is undeniably attractive. Even when Green decided finally to tabulate the heaps of data from thousands of eyewitness reports in his attempt to create a composite portrait of the Sasquatch, his technique remained essentially journalistic, openly that of an amateur scientist. The implicit goal is not to convince skeptics among scientists, who can hardly be impressed by anything short of physical evidence, but to convince or at least arouse the interest of laymen. To this end, a kind of breathless quality of presentation in Green's writing has remained intact throughout the years.

Green was, of course, quickly joined by others, as noted earlier. Probably the most effective practitioner in terms of the visual media has been Peter Byrne, who became a minor TV personality partly because of his effectiveness before the camera. With the help of some of his colleagues who had close connections to the film industry, such as Alan Landsburg, Byrne probably did more to popularize Bigfoot in North America than all the other Bigfoot hunters put together. Byrne is the only Bigfoot expert, for example, to be featured in the Smithsonian program mentioned earlier.

Of course, the impact of the famous Patterson-Gimlin film has been enormous. It has been seen by millions in its several commercial manifestations. The divisive impact of this film within the fraternity of Bigfoot buffs, despite increasing claims that it is valid, is an indication of its significance. This is largely because the "P-G film" is the only one to date that is not laughably absurd in its depiction of a supposed Bigfoot. Unless or until some other film comes along that is obviously "better," the P-G film will probably remain at the center of the controversy, a kind of eye in the hurricane that blows the winds of Sasquatchery hither and yon, against the battered shores of reason.

And this brings us to the central role of the media in helping to create, if not actually in creating, a modern corpus of legend, perhaps even a new mythology of our age. Since the work of Frazer, Tylor, Freud, and Jung, we have known that most tales, whether in the category of simple folklore or more elaborate mythology, tend to depict social realities on the simplest level and then to employ extraordinary solutions to everyday problems. This is so whether the solutions are actual or symbolic. Mythology has always introduced fabulous elements so as to broaden the range of adventure and prowess through which resolution of a problem is achieved, and thus to inspire awe. In this sense the simplest folklore and the most elaborate ancient myths overlap with current stories of unexplained phenomena, whether they are about Bigfoot or UFOs. Obviously this is true whether or not the UFOs or Sasquatch really exist.

The anthropologist Claude Lévi-Strauss achieved what many believe to be a breakthrough in our understanding of the functions and meaning of myths when he connected three previously unrelated developments. The first of these is the realization that the myths of "primitive" peoples are highly relevant to understanding the society in question. One could add that this principle applies to any society, no matter how "advanced." The second is Sigmund Freud's "discovery" of the unconscious and its intimate relation to myth, a discovery much advanced by Jung. And the third is Lévi-Strauss's own idea that myth is a primal method of interaction and communication among people, at least equal in significance to kinship exchanges through marriage and the resulting family ties, and to all-important economic exchange. Lévi-Strauss even went so far as to suggest that myth forms a "fourth or auditory" mode of communication, along with music, rhythmical sounds, and language itself. He implies that without it we are less than human.

To argue that the rather spare anecdotes about Bigfoot reported by Green and others are not worthy of a place in the corpus of mythology, legend, and folklore is to misinterpret the role of the modern media as they confront, and exploit, a phenomenon like Bigfoot. In a society like ours the media are capable of reducing a classic tale to nothing but a foolish and titillating image, one that flickers and dies on the television screen and then fades from our consciousness. But the same media are also capable of fomenting mystery, of exploiting the most antirational or prescientific thought. There isn't much difference, really, between the hype that a televised "ghost story" is based on a "true story" and the half-serious, almost comic presentation of Bigfoot a few years ago in *The Six Million Dollar Man,* in which the creature had supernormal powers and "outer-space" or otherworldly connections. A thesis could be written on the media manifestations of Bigfoot just in the last dozen years. The "Wookie" named Chewbacca in the epic film *Star Wars* is a recent example. Bigfoot has even been exploited in advertisements to sell trucks and other products.

I have no doubt that sincere investigators such as Dahinden and Green would object to such use of the image they have promoted so successfully over the years. Green has made it clear that his preferred view is of a monster that is really nothing more than an unknown animal, in no way exceptional among the many other animals on earth, except perhaps in its elusive nature and the fact that its existence is largely denied by the academic community. But this does not alter the fact that the mass media have largely taken over, certainly in popular consciousness, with new images and with embellishments to add to the old. The result is a more typically satisfying beast of full-fledged mythic quality, possessing the ambiguous and potentially threatening qualities of what Jerome Clark and Loren Coleman have called the "manimals." Thus Bigfoot turns up in many movies, television shows, novels, and magazine articles that deal with the paranormal or the occult; in these the creature is often shown as coming from another world and having supernatural strength, like the legendary giants of old. The popular movie of a few years back, *The Legend of Boggy Creek,* is an example. This was based on widespread reports of a hairy monster roaming the woods of the Louisiana-Arkansas border in the mid-1950s. So, too, does the creature in Slate and Berry's *Bigfoot* possess potential supernatural qualities. Thanks to the modern media, the Bigfoot image has been restored to its place in the mythic pantheon, for better or for worse.

In the meantime, Green, Byrne, and other aficionados persist in arguing for the concept of a relic ape or subhuman of some kind, a substantially predictable living fossil that for some reason did not become extinct when it should have. But even this view has a mythic quality, because of the lack of hard evidence to support it and because the monster is located in a remote and legendary time—that is, in prehistory. The mythology of Bigfoot will almost certainly grow in our time, and it will do so with the aid of our mass media.

Further details on the mythology of forest giants and hairy humanoids will be discussed in Chapter 3. But it is worth pointing out here that if indeed we have a modern myth in this Bigfoot phenomenon, one created in our own time and emerging as we watch, perhaps compounded of half-remembered elements from our past as well as out of present need, there is every reason to pay it full attention.

The Theories

Theories about Bigfoot vary widely. Probably the most popular theory is what I call the "relic-humanoid hypothesis." This is based on the idea that earlier forms of mankind, or of large primates related to man but stemming from a divergent line of evolution, have survived as relics into the present. The Soviet hominologists have postulated the survival of Neanderthaloid types in remote regions, final remnants of once-flourishing populations of subhumans that dominated much of Eurasia more than 100,000 years ago. The gist of this theory is that Neanderthal man—in his ancient and in his alleged modern form—represents a line of evolution separate and distinct from that of mankind, that he was intelligent and adaptable but without speech, elaborate tools, and "culture" as we know it. This is the strange being variously called *kaptar* and *alma* in various regions of inner Asia; and, so the argument goes, it is quite real and not the stuff of legend or myth.

The late Boris F. Porshnev, a philosopher and historian who was an active amateur in the study of mankind's origins, seems first to have suggested this hypothesis. Eventually he resurrected the outmoded term *Troglodytidae*—a term originally used by Linnaeus to describe man's supposed cave-dwelling ancestors—to classify his "new" family so that it could be distinguished from that of man, *Hominidae.*

More recently some of Porshnev's followers, particularly Igor Bourtsev and Dmitri Bayanov, have further elaborated this theory, delving into the mythological record for what they interpret as literary evidence for the existence of such creatures. They say that unlike humans, these troglodytes are nocturnal rather than diurnal and mostly solitary in behavior rather than social. They have also pushed Porshnev's tentative idea that the North American Sasquatch may represent an "archaic" divergent form of the troglodyte family; its much greater size and other characteristics are apparently the result of either geographic isolation or environmental conditioning.

A variation on this theory holds that some kind of large apeman, probably in the line of Louis Leakey's famous fossil discovery *Australopithecus robustus,* or "large southern ape"—also called *Paranthropus,* or "marginal ape"—has continued into the present. Omnivorous, cunning, having certain qualities of both man and ape, these creatures lurk in wildernesses where humans rarely go; they are few in number and endangered, but probably not dangerous. This is the argument advanced by Gordon Strasenburgh, an American Bigfoot expert. After all, it is argued, *Paranthropus* seems to have been primarily vegetarian, not much of a hunter, probably scavenging what little meat it ate, although it certainly caught small animals and insects. Like the baboon and the bears, such a creature might have adapted to the changing environment of the earth through the geological ages and become furtive because of man's implacable hostility (perhaps stemming from his remote kinship); but, like its more successful and dangerous human cousin, the apeman was ubiquitous, able to spread in small but significant numbers across the once-connected continents during a period of glaciation.

This theory further assumes that such a creature, although

tropical in origin, would have become "cold-adapted" to survival in high mountains and inhospitable northern climes through the evolution of a luxuriant coat of hair, a more broadly omnivorous diet suitable to the colder climate, and a presumably "preadapted" intelligence, hardly on the order of man's but nevertheless of a high order. The argument goes that man, after all, also adapted from an originally tropic environment to populate all the zones of the earth through periods of great climatic severity.

Strasenburgh's theory probably attracts more adherents in North America than abroad. The towering Sasquatch is hard to fit into a theory that presumes Neanderthal connections. *Paranthropus*, on the other hand, although approximating the size of a modern human, was robust, and might have given rise over a much longer span of time to a modern hairy giant because of its alleged adaptation to northern climes—following what is known as Bergmann's rule, which states that warm-blooded animals of the same genus or species (bears, for example) often increase in body size in cold regions in order to reduce heat loss.

Another widespread theory can be called the "Gigantopithecus hypothesis." This is based on the fossilized remains—actually only a few teeth and parts of huge jaws—first found in Chinese apothecary shops before World War II by the celebrated anthropologist G. H. von Königswald and described in his book *Meeting Prehistoric Man*. Briefly, this theory assumes the continuation of a creature descended from the line of a gigantic ape that roamed uplands in south-central and southeastern Asia millions of years ago. Although no other parts of any fossil skeleton from this creature have yet been found, analysis of the teeth and jaw fragments from *Gigantopithecus* (Giant ape) indicates an animal that stood perhaps eight or nine feet tall, weighed six hundred pounds or more, and was apparently largely graminivorous, or grass-eating. Differences in the size of the fragments and the teeth indicate that the male of the species was much larger than the female.

Without skeletal remains the exact shape and size of this ancient giant is a matter of conjecture. Nevertheless, an elaborate theory about the origins of Bigfoot, and of the abominable snowman especially, has been based on these tantalizing clues. According to this theory, Sasquatch and the yeti are huge apes, adapted, unlike gorillas or orangutans, to cold environments, to alpine or near-alpine conditions, or to temperate forest habitats. Presumably such apes would be anatomically more akin to the gorilla than to modern man, but partially bipedal, if not wholly.

An interesting variation on this hypothesis stems from the speculations of a respected contemporary of von Königswald, Dr. Franz Weidenreich, who argued in his book *Apes, Giants and Men* that the so-called *Gigantopithecus* fossils indicate a giant humanoid rather than an ape, and that this creature is linked in its evolutionary history to later and smaller humanoids such as the *Pithecanthropus* types (Peking man and Java man, also called *Homo erectus*). Weidenreich, entirely innocent of the later use to which his theory would be put by the Bigfoot fraternity, suggested that the scientific name for the huge creature ought to be changed to *Gigantanthropus,* in order to emphasize its humanlike qualities. Now, of course, a number of Bigfoot writers have made use of Weidenreich's speculations and proposed that Sasquatch, as well as the yeti, is related to man, however distantly, and that this close relationship accounts for the two-legged rather than quadrupedal gait, the apparently humanlike structure of the feet and hands, and its apparent intelligence and adaptability.

This theory, although it also suggests a relationship to man, differs from the relic-humanoid hypothesis primarily in that it suggests the creatures in question are rare but successful products of a line within hominid evolution that diverged from that of man long before the Neanderthal types had evolved; perhaps it is related to man in the distant way that a chimp is related to a gibbon.

The theory most acceptable to scientists in general, if any theory is acceptable at all, is the view that assumes the yeti, at least, to be a surviving form of ape, perhaps diverging from the ancestral orangutan, whose rather large fossilized bones have been found on the Asian mainland—though the orang is now confined to Asiatic islands. This seems to fit better with sightings in the Himalayas that indicate a creature approximately of human height but of greater weight, with arms that reach to the knees, a heavy upper torso, and relatively short legs. Furthermore, the yeti is often described as having reddish-brown hair and a head that slopes sharply back from the brow, coming to a pointed crown. Both are characteristics of living orangs. Sherpas, when asked to pick out what seems most like the yeti from an assortment of photographs of apes, monkeys, and other large primates, have picked the orangutan at once.

Since it is known that both the ancestral orangutan and at least one species of huge terrestrial primate did roam mainland Asia in prehistoric times, it is certainly not impossible that a few might survive today in the Himalayan wilderness or in other isolated regions of Asia. The irregular topography of the Himalayan region might conceal an intelligent primate long after other apes have been classified. The ability of certain large mammals to elude documentation by science is religiously exaggerated by Bigfoot buffs, but the possibility remains. As many experts have noted, the inner regions of the Himalaya are inadequately represented in two-dimensional maps, and few people venture into these congested gullies, canyons, and gorges. Most trails, as Napier noted, follow the high contours of the ridges, plunging to cross the streams at convenient and less dangerous places and rising again to the high ground. The huge area of the lower slopes within the uninhabited gorges is virtually unexplored.

Of course, for those who remain skeptical that Bigfoot or the yeti represents any kind of apelike or humanlike creature, there are many explanations that hold them to be bears or other large mammals well known to science, or even actual human beings gone wild. There is no doubt that many sightings and some footprints can be thus explained, as cases of mistaken identity. Bears do rear on their hind legs, though they cannot properly walk without descending to all fours. They also have plantigrade feet, and their hind feet leave prints similar enough to those of man that amateurs might easily make errors of identification. For centuries people have erroneously considered the bear to be mankind's closest kin in the world of animals. The whole question of "bear legends," which have wide currency among the earth's peoples, has yet to be seriously studied. Today's urbanized folk have mostly forgotten how important the bear was in the lore of our European ancestors, as well as in that of Amerindians and most Asiatic peoples. Richard Adams's best-selling novel *Shardik* is merely a modern version, fantastic as it is, of an ancient theme.

The feral, or "wild-child," theme is also an ancient one. Generally it goes like this: An infant is abandoned or somehow lost to the wilderness. It is found and nursed by a species of wild animal, usually a predator, such as the wolf. The young human thrives despite lack of contact with its own kind and learns the elusive skills of the wild beasts. Eventually, like Kipling's Mowgli or Burroughs's Tarzan, the feral child emerges as an awesome combination of human intelligence and superhuman strength and physical skill. Commonly, and quite unlike Tarzan and Mowgli, the feral human becomes a hairy creature that hovers curiously at the edge of human contact, seen only in fleeting glimpses, afraid of direct contact with its own kind but drawn to it by bonds of consanguinity. This wild-child theme, which is in some ways akin to the medieval idea of the "wild man" discussed in the next chapter, has many variations from culture to culture, but it actually has little to do with reality. Reports of "wolf children" in India and elsewhere are spurious, as apocryphal as the Roman legend of Romulus and Remus. It is known that infant humans, if separated from regular contact with their own kind, do not develop simple motor skills, cannot even learn to walk upright.

Some hold that creatures identified as Sasquatch were actually overlarge humans gone wild. There are hermits, of course, whose alienation is complete enough to sustain a solitary existence in places where humans rarely go. A number of Japanese soldiers holed up in the jungles of Pacific islands for more than thirty years, often surviving entirely alone. A large and cunning hermit living entirely off the land in the Pacific Northwest *might* be mistaken for Bigfoot, but there are problems with this idea. Aside from differences in range and size, there are incongruities having to do with detailed physical descriptions, as well as the evidence of the footprints themselves.

Of course, there are some farfetched explanations that cannot be included in any of the above categories simply because they pay no attention to known scientific rules. Most of these, as I indicated above, fall into the realm of the paranormal. Some writers assume Bigfoot to be some kind of image projected by flying-saucer crews, or perhaps even the crew members themselves. And some put the sightings, footprints, etc., into the world of the occult. I'll not try to examine the details of these far-out beliefs with the same seriousness of purpose that the "rational" explanations demand. But the fact that many people attribute Bigfoot to "otherworldly" realms or dimensions is significant in itself.

Finally, there are some whose theories do not really fit into any of the above categories. Sanderson is the best example, as he created what must be considered an extraordinary and all-encompassing theory, marked as much by its imaginative qualities as by its sweeping assumptions. Sanderson did not believe that there might be only one or even two species, such as Bigfoot and the yeti. Rather, he suggested that there were several unknown primate species—as many as four or five. In *Abominable Snowmen: Legend Come to Life,* Sanderson argued that one of these is closely related to modern man, a degenerate subhuman of some kind confined to inner Asia. A second species is presumably a gigantic ape, probably descended from *Gigantopithecus,* not related to man except in the most distant way and found both in Asia and in the West. He presumed Sasquatch to be of this type, or at least a subspecies of it. A third species, found in south-central Eurasia, Sanderson identified as a "subhominid" not quite up to the level of a "subhuman" or a relic humanoid, but not an ape, either. The fourth type, according to Sanderson, is a so-called "proto-pygmy," a smallish creature of subtropical or tropical adaptation and confined to the rain forests of southern Asia, Africa, South America, and perhaps the forested swamps of the southeastern United States, where sightings of the "skunk ape" have occurred in recent years.

It is fairly clear that Sanderson combined most of the ingredients of the several theories into one, even before most of these theories had been postulated. Of course, as Napier says in his *Bigfoot: The Yeti and Sasquatch in Myth and Reality,* it boggles the mind "that there should be a whole *Systema Naturae* of unknown, living monsters, as is suggested by Sanderson's classification." What Sanderson has to say requires close attention, however. Of all those who properly fit the true-believer category, Sanderson had the most impressive credentials. He was an intrepid traveler all his life, and a scientific gadfly with extensive experience in primate studies. Some of his popular works, including his elephant book, *The Dynasty of Abu,* remain minor classics despite their frequent flights of fancy. Toward the end of his life, Sanderson seems to have been genuinely obsessed by the mystery of the Bigfoot, yeti, and other creatures. Before he died, he was taken willingly to the bosom of the most dedicated Bigfoot believers, to whom he lent an aura of marginal respectability. In the end of the 1950s and throughout the '60s Sanderson's writings did a great deal to popularize his obsession. The recent increase in popular interest in the phenomenon can be largely attributed to Sanderson. His widely read magazine articles and his book clearly had a lot to do with popular concepts—most of them still current—as to what Bigfoot is like. For example, Sanderson was the first to provide the general public with a psuedoscientific explanation of the creature in the Patterson-Gimlin film. This was in an article in *Argosy* magazine early in 1968, complete with several color photographs and testimonials by various interested scientists, including Dr. John Napier. Napier's tentative, even ambivalent conclusions about the film (see Appendix A) were included in fine print near the end of the magazine article, neatly separated from the sensationalist opening segment with its larger print and arresting illustrations.

There is no doubt that the Bigfoot phenomenon lends itself

well to fancy. There appears to be a vast audience ready to believe the worst about organized science and at the same time willing to believe in the most farfetched theories, whether in the realm of mysticism, parapsychology, or psychic phenomena. Many Bigfoot writers have exploited this popular attitude, implying that the scientific authorities really know more than they let on, and sometimes even suggesting that scientists deliberately suppress evidence for obscure reasons. Such sensationalism tends to discredit any and all association with the Bigfoot search in the eyes of serious scholars. Many scientists simply dismiss the phenomenon as one of several "fringe" areas to be avoided. It scares them, and any direct association is considered a sure road to academic ruin.

Indeed, it is true that the considered views of serious students of the subject, like Dr. Napier's, tend to be drowned out by the strident pronouncements of the cranks. Napier's reputation has no doubt suffered among his zoologist colleagues because he dared write an open-minded book about Bigfoot. But Napier is not alone among authoritative writers who caution against hasty disdain or dismissal. In his recent best-selling book *The Snow Leopard,* Peter Matthiessen lucidly describes his own feelings regarding the legendary yeti, and he reports that his companion during their harrowing Himalayan trek, the celebrated ethologist George Schaller, is convinced that "an animal unknown to science" occurs in the Himalayan uplands, though Schaller discounts ninety-five percent of the material on the yeti as nonsense.

Perhaps this is a good rule of thumb. For it is the other five percent of the material that is so consistently disturbing because it cannot easily be explained away. As Matthiessen notes, "The case *against* the existence of the yeti—entirely speculative and necessarily based on assumptions of foolishness or mendacity in many observers of good reputation—is even less 'scientific' than the evidence that it exists."

Twenty years ago the novelist John Masters—author of *Coromandel; The Night Runners of Bengal; Far, Far the Mountain Peak;* and many other popular novels of British India—wrote a sardonic article for *Harper's* urging readers to keep their minds open because the subject deserves level-headed study. Masters was convinced from his many years of experience in and around the Himalayas that something yet unclassified by science was out there, accounting for the strange footprints, the widespread legends among the Sherpas and other native peoples, and the recurrent sightings by pilgrims, travelers, naturalists, and mountaineers.

Surely the same should apply to North America. Rigorous separation of the obviously faked, the fanciful, and the apocryphal from the small but seemingly consistent body of more reliable data is required. This is a task of some difficulty since, as we shall see, the majority of the reports do not stand up well to close investigation. But there *is* that disturbing five percent.

The Evidence

Many assume that the most convincing evidence for the existence of any unknown thing would be eyewitness accounts. Sightings, although they are often dramatic and important, are actually among the least reliable types of evidence. The truth is that without photographic documentation, or the existence of physical data to back it up, what any person claims to see is simply impossible to "validate," to use a favorite word of the true believers among Bigfoot hunters. "Seeing is believing" is one of those old saws that has no force among scientists, scholars, or cops, all of whom need additional *hard* data to make their case.

Obviously, when more than one person sees something, the evidence is more compelling, particularly if the persons involved are not known to one another or connected in any other way. But even when two or more people agree that they have witnessed something, the evidence remains shaky; in fact, the "evidence" in such cases is nothing more than memory, actually recorded only in the fallible minds of the viewers. Without documentation—that is, without the capacity to duplicate, replicate, or substantiate the alleged sighting—one does not of course have hard evidence. For this reason all the accounts

summarized earlier, including the incident in which three loggers claimed to see a Bigfoot, are properly classified as unsubstantiated, and therefore they really prove nothing. The fact
that a thousand separate people claim to have seen ghosts does
not, after all, prove that ghosts exist.

Of course, there are ways to check up on eyewitness accounts. Other evidence is sometimes available to support what
a person claims, such as footprints or a spoor of droppings or
other matter.

Still, it is wise to remember that fish stories are just that,
without at least a good photograph with a clear background for
size comparison, or without the fish itself. If a hunter claims to
have bagged a record deer but cannot produce the carcass or
the head and its rack of horns, he is believed only when he
tracks down its remains. Since before the time of the Code of
Hammurabi, more than three thousand years ago, an eyewitness to a crime dared not make public accusation without supporting evidence—proof of a theft, for example, by producing
the purloined goods in someone else's possession, or the body
of the putative victim in the case of murder, and so on.

Bigfoot sightings, or incidents that are loosely classified as
such, by now number well over a thousand. I doubt that even
John Green has collated all of these. The great majority are unverifiable, to put it bluntly. Most fall into certain obvious
groupings, according to such factors as geography, patterns of
consistency, immediate physical surroundings, time of year,
time of day, and the reputation of the witness. Peter Byrne's
system of rating eyewitness accounts on a scale of one to ten
creates only the impression of verifiability. In fact, there are a
very few accounts that are supported by physical evidence, and
the greatest number of these seem to be supported by footprints. Indeed, it appears that the only accepted eyewitness account backed by photographic evidence is the celebrated
incident at Bluff Creek, October 20, 1968, the source of the
Patterson-Gimlin film.

Footprints are in a sense "verifiable" by means of castings
and photographs, but any rational investigator of the thousands

of alleged Sasquatch footprints will quickly discover that the vast majority of them are fake. Why this is so is a subject worth serious study; it is enough to state here that the opportunity for perpetrating elaborate pranks and hoaxes designed to fool the gullible public is far greater than most Bigfoot buffs are prepared to admit.

Also, many of the so-called Bigfoot tracks are simply cases of mistaken identity. Bigfoot buffs like to tell us that any experienced hunter or woodsman can immediately identify the tracks of a bear or the composite tracks of other mammals and easily separate them from those of man and his relatives (past or present). In fact, tracks of all kinds vary enormously according to weather, terrain, the gait of the animal, and so on. It is possible for an animal no bigger than a fox to produce what appear to be huge bipedal footprints in the snow.

Nevertheless, there remain a quantity of huge, manlike footprints that appear to be genuine, that cannot easily be explained away by one of the above-mentioned possibilities. These are most heavily concentrated in the Pacific Northwest, within an area roughly bounded by the Pacific Ocean on the west, by the foothills of the Klamath Mountains of California on the south, by the northern part of the Great Basin on the east, and by the limits of the Pacific montane rain forest on the north.

Bigfoot hunter Byrne and others claim that within this vast region the majority of giant footprints fit into a clear and consistent pattern: usually between fourteen and eighteen inches long and about four to eight inches wide, often with a broad heel that is proportionally wider than that of a human. Many of these footprints seem to indicate five toes of similar size, arranged in an upward slant from the outside of the foot, as in humans, but in man the big toe is appreciably larger, whereas in the apes it is greatly separated from the other toes. There are other differences between these "typical" Bigfoot prints and those of mankind. Dr. Napier has noted an apparent ridge of sand or soil pushed up between the ball of the foot and the toe-line, with another less marked ridge dividing the ball of the foot into two parts. Also, in at least some of the prints carefully studied by Napier, the foot shank itself is shaped somewhat like a lopsided hourglass.

Napier has further distinguished himself from most of the investigators by calling attention to the disturbing fact (which he fails ultimately to explain) that some of the best footprints do not fit this pattern at all. These seem to be far more humanlike, except for their size, of course, with the big toe considerably larger than the others, the shank of the foot tapering more or less gradually to the narrower heel, and with a curved ridge behind the toes. Napier correctly points out that such variation is much greater than one would expect to occur within a single species.

Equally disturbing is the fact, mostly ignored by apologists for Bigfoot, that there are many prints that do not fit into either of these patterns. These have been found all over North America, including the Pacific Northwest. Some appear to be nearly rectangular, with the toes almost straight across the top. Some are wedge-shaped and have only three toes. Some are shaped more like the celebrated abominable-snowman print in Shipton's photograph. Of course, serious Bigfoot hunters dismiss these variant footprints as fakes, arguing that they have to be fraudulent because they do not conform to the preconceived pattern of consistency. And since these "inconsistent" prints have been reported from all over the continent, as well as throughout the Northwest, they would seem to bolster the view that the only "good" footprints are confined to the Northwest, and thus the Sasquatch's range is presumed to be limited to that region. The trouble is that acceptable footprints that conform to the preconceived standards *also* have been found all over North America, as John Green repeatedly tells us. Thus, he maintains, the range of the Sasquatch must include the breadth of the continent.

Such arbitrary selectivity may seem to solve one problem, but it poses another. Many of the "unacceptable" footprints have been found in circumstances that are quite convincing, especially some of the recent finds in Iowa and the Dakotas, as reported in *The Minnesota Archaeologist.* If these are fake, the argument that it would require a broad conspiracy to fake so many of the good footprints would be undermined. If pranksters and hoaxers can fake unacceptable tracks that fit a consistent pattern, they can certainly fake acceptable ones. In the end, the standards for comparison are arbitrary simply because no physical specimen of Sasquatch has ever been found.

Another factor that is rarely considered is who finds the footprints. Many of the most famous prints have been discovered by well-known Bigfoot hunters. For example, Ivan Marx and Bob Titmus are responsible respectively for the celebrated "cripple" footprints from Bossburg, Washington, near Colville, and for the most commonly cited examples of the Bluff Creek tracks. Some of the most important footprints that Napier selected for his analysis were found by known Bigfoot buffs, including Roger Patterson, Ivan Marx, René Dahinden, and Bob Titmus. Surely the most reliable footprint evidence must come from people with unquestioned credibility and character, and people who have no ax to grind. Peter Byrne gives a higher "rating" to footprints found by people closely associated with his Bigfoot Center; my practice would be to do the opposite.

Few of the photographs of Bigfoot prints meet professional standards of quality: they are seldom shot from a variety of angles, with notations on exposure time, aperture, time of day, date, the exact location, and so on. For this reason the majority of such photos are unreliable as evidence.

Finally, there is the question of fecal matter, or droppings. Reports of hair, blood, bones, and other matter have been few, but as for droppings, also called "scats," there are many alleged specimens. These are of little use, however, for a variety of reasons. For example, the scats of a bobcat are easy to identify within the bobcat's typical habitat, when relatively fresh, and especially when found in the vicinity of other signs of bobcat. If the scats are analyzed in context a biologist can ascertain details of diet, state of health, approximate size, and so on, but the same scats sent to a laboratory without detailed notes on their original location and their estimated age might easily be taken for those of a domestic cat, a fox, or another small mammal whose diet approximates that of a bobcat, especially in the absence of internal parasites. Scientists are understandably reluctant to make positive identification of the source of any unspecified fecal matter, especially if they are informed in advance that the material is from an "unknown" species. To paraphrase a respected zoologist who has had enough unsolicited and unwelcome packages sent to him in the mail, one would need high boots to wade through all the piles of shit that are put forth as evidence.

Nearly two decades ago Ivan Sanderson consolidated what seems to be an impressive array of Bigfoot evidence into three impressive-sounding but purely arbitrary categories: 1) "Intrinsic" (matter such as hair, skin, and blood); 2) "Cognate" (tracks and fecal matter); and 3) "Corollary" (a general grouping that includes noises, cries, odors, and reports of the creature's throwing rocks or moving large objects). Perhaps because he felt he had to give minimal allegiance to the profession he had once served well, Sanderson admitted near the end of his book that the evidence within his first category was paltry. In the single known case in which a thorough on-the-spot investigation was made by a team of qualified experts—the famous Hillary expedition to the Himalayas in 1960–61—various pieces of hair and skin alleged to belong to a yeti were proved to be the result either of mistaken identity or of falsification.

On the other hand, Sanderson said that the evidence within the "Cognate" category was persistent. Even if most of this proved false, the quantity of the footprint and fecal evidence was convincing. He added that much the same could be said for the "Corollary" evidence. Still, in truth, quantity has little to do with quality or accuracy in this matter. A thousand footprints and a hundred pieces of dung are meaningless if they cannot be substantiated in some way, and the same goes for reports of strange noises in the night, odors, rock-throwing monsters, and the like.

In the meantime, there is the matter of the documented legends and myths: the record of history, as it were. Should we put

Bigfoot into the category of myth, along with legends of trolls and giants, satyrs and cyclopes? Or is the "record" of such creatures—which is certainly abundant enough—actually evidence for the existence of our creature, or of several hairy giants related to man?

1. Medieval depiction of a "wild man" fighting an armored knight. (*Historical Pictures Service, Inc., Chicago*)

2. Bob Gimlin with casts of the fourteen-and-a-half-inch tracks left by the creature that he and Roger Patterson allegedly filmed on October 20, 1967, at Bluff Creek, California. (*Photo courtesy of René Dahinden*)

3. Zane Gray's 1977 cast of the Lake Ann Bigfoot print. (*Photo courtesy of Kenneth Wylie*).

4. René Dahinden and Roger Patterson with the Bluff Creek castings, made in October 1964. (*Photo courtesy of René Dahinden*)

5. Dr. John Napier holding a Bluff Creek cast, 1971. (*Photo courtesy of René Dahinden*)

6. A hoax Bigfoot suit, 1977, in the tradition of the "Minnesota Iceman." (*Photo courtesy of René Dahinden*)

7. Bald-faced grizzly bear. (*New York Zoological Society Photo*)

Two large mammals, standing characteristically on all fours, as opposed to Bigfoot, reputed to be bipedal.

8. Lowland gorilla. (*New York Zoological Society Photo*)

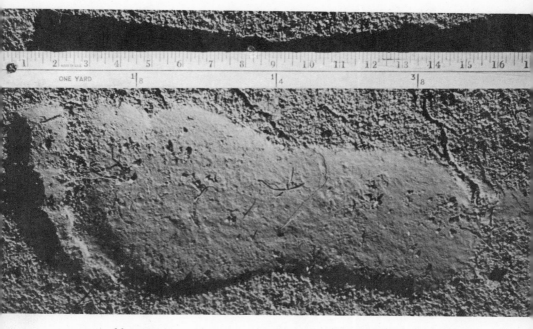

9. A fifteen-inch track in the ground discovered in September 1967 at Blue Creek Mountain, California, which is only about five miles by air from the site of the Patterson-Gimlin film. (*Photo courtesy of René Dahinden*)

10. A freeze frame from the Patterson-Gimlin film. (*Photo courtesy of René Dahinden*)

3. Giants in the Earth

There were giants in the earth in those days.

GEN. 6:4

But the race of man then . . . was much hardier . . . and built on a groundwork of larger and more solid bones within, knit with powerful sinews throughout the frame of flesh; not lightly to be disabled by heat or cold or strange kinds of food or any malady of body. . . . Then too as they ranged about they would occupy the well-known woodland haunts of the nymphs . . . and as yet they knew not how to apply fire to their purposes or to make use of skins and clothe their body in the spoils of wild beasts, but they would dwell in woods or mountain-caves and forests and shelter in the brushwood. . . . And trusting to the marvellous powers of their hands and feet they would pursue the forest-dwelling races of wild beasts with showers of stones and club of ponderous weight. . . .

LUCRETIUS, *On the Nature of Things*

There is nothing really new about the Bigfoot lore of recent decades in North America. Legends about near-human creatures are as old as human culture, and they conform to a pervasive traditional concept that is found in folklore the world over, and widely represented in literature and in art. From the rain forests of West Africa to the highlands of central Asia, from the sylvan glades of Mediterranean Europe to the high Alps, from the equatorial jungles of South America to the dense montane forests of North America, diverse peoples have believed in the existence of strange humanoids covered with hair.

These legends generally share a common theme: the existence of subhuman creatures with such human traits as erect posture and bipedal locomotion, manual dexterity, exceptional cunning, and perhaps a preference for face-to-face copulation. They are inhuman, nevertheless, because they appear to lack speech; also their behavior is described as "bestial"—directed by instinct rather than volition, this behavior often includes overt sexual tendencies with humans as their object—and their physical characteristics include extreme hairiness, great size, and superhuman strength. Sometimes the creatures are only vaguely humanlike, erect and bipedal but with heads more like those of carnivorous animals, and with fangs, manes, and the like. Some of the legends portray beings that seem completely human in physiology except that they are covered with hair. Also, they do not live in large groups in regular shelters, cultivating crops and hunting with typical weapons like the spear or the bow and arrow. In their most ancient and most persistent mode these legends usually carry a message of fear. The creatures are to be avoided because they bring bad luck, abduct and ravish maidens, destroy livestock and crops, and even eat human flesh.

These creatures should not be confused with other, perhaps more familiar mythological monsters—the half-human, half-animal beings such as centaurs, mermaids, manticores or the several kinds of sphinx (usually half man and half lion, jackal, or wolf, often with wings). In folklore these "unnatural" human crosses fall into a separate category. Even the most gullible person wandering in the woods behind his farm in central Greece or northern Italy two thousand years ago did not really expect to encounter a sphinx or a centaur. He might hope to spot a faun or a satyr, but the more obvious crosses were legendary creatures even to the folk who believed in them; that is, they were thought to have existed in former ages—perhaps in the Golden Age, when the Gods moved freely among men, or in the age before man was himself fully reduced to mortal form. Like the Titan, the Chimera, and the Gorgon, they were generally believed extinct in the world of men, or at least they were assumed to exist only in faraway places where civilized men rarely traveled.

The presence of these far-out creatures in the consciousness of ancient peoples is similar to contemporary belief in ghosts, or perhaps to the folklore among many primitive tribes regarding the ability of certain people to transform themselves into animals, or part-animals. It is taken for granted among some peoples that shamanists, sorcerers, and holy men are capable of such feats, so completely altering their outward sensory vibrations that they are perceived as beasts. Carlos Castaneda says that his Yaqui sorcerer can somehow alter his corporeal nature while in a state of trance. Perhaps such mythological beasts were akin to the werewolves and other products of evil transformation once believed in by Central Europeans and Amerindians.

Even in ancient times educated people disbelieved in such creatures—Lucretius pooh-poohed the possibility of anything like a centaur existing in nature—or put them into the fairy-tale category, to be described for children, perhaps half believed in but certainly not worried about.

Humanoid creatures are, however, often portrayed in literature as more believable beings, possessing no obviously unnatural characteristics. They have only one head, for example, one nose, one mouth, two legs and arms, two eyes, and so on. In other words, they conform more readily to commonsense knowledge of the natural world. Interestingly, it is probably easier to frighten a child, or to pique the interest of cynical adults, with stores of a humanlike creature or a bogeyman— perhaps a member of an alien tribe or an inmate escaped from an asylum—than with stores of a weird man-horse or human-headed lion.

It is understandable that the impressive body of lore regarding humanoids is taken by apologists for Bigfoot as proof of the existence of "relic humanoids," or at least of subhumans of some kind. It is assumed that the humanlike beings that crop up so persistently in folklore might be quite real, that the legends might contain a germ of truth. If so, there could be a link between such legendary beings and our Bigfoot. It goes without saying that if there is such a thing as Bigfoot, the existing species would have to have an evolutionary history. And logic dictates that a creature so closely related to mankind would have coexisted with humans on this earth in prehistoric as well as modern times, unless, of course, one is prepared to accept a theory of spontaneous generation, or some kind of outer-space connection.

The outlines of this theme in mythology are fairly clear. The Bible mentions "giants in the earth" that coexisted with man in the time before the flood, and there are references to the *se'irim* (in Hebrew, the "hairy ones") in Isaiah and elsewhere, although the expression has been variously translated as "satyr" and "devil." For the Latin Bible, St. Jerome used the word *pilosi* in place of *se'irim,* and in his own commentary on Isaiah he wrote, "When in the following it is said that the 'hairy ones will dance here' (*et pilosi saltabunt ibi*) we must understand this to mean either incubi or satyrs or a certain kind of wild men whom some . . . regard as of the nature of demons." St. Jerome could hardly admit to the natural existence, even in Isaiah's time, of near-men, since such were apparently not of God's creation as described in the Bible, and they certainly could not have survived the flood. If they were not God-created beasts, they had to be incorporeal demons. Some biblical scholars have interpreted the *se'irim* as "sons of Esau," who was, of course, exceedingly hairy. But the original meaning of these obscure references in Hebrew is lost to history. The *se'irim* might simply refer to humans more hairy than average.

Perhaps because of Judaism's hatred of idolatry and because of the anthropomorphic nature of the one God of the Hebrews, the Bible is not a very fruitful source of references to ancient Near Eastern legends about hairy humanoids.

Even older than the Bible is the Mesopotamian *Epic of Gilgamesh,* the story of the hero-king of the city-state of Uruk more than four thousand years ago. Although considered one third divine, Gilgamesh is himself wholly human in physical aspect. But his opponent, Enkidu, whom he later tames, is quite different:

> Shaggy with hair is his whole body,
> He is endowed with head hair like a woman. . . .
> He knows neither people nor land. . . .
> With gazelles he feeds on grass,
> With the wild beasts he jostles at the watering-place,
> With the teeming creatures his heart delights in
>   water. . . .

Confronted with Enkidu's overwhelming strength, Gilgamesh civilizes him by confounding him through the sexual favors of a harlot of the city, hence exorcising his bestiality, so that when the tamed Enkidu tries to approach his former wild-beast companions, they run away in fear. He has become human through the sensuality of that most human of pleasurable acts. Gilgamesh has no trouble besting Enkidu in the ensuing fight, and they become friends.

Greco-Roman literature is replete with examples of legendary humanoids, some huge but most man-sized. Most notable are the elusive but ubiquitous satyrs, those hairy creatures of the woods who possess goatish sexual capacity and a human sense of mischief. Some versions of satyrs are interesting because they are portrayed as human in body, although covered in hair, with pug noses and beetle brows. Only in middle-to-late ancient times do these gamboling creatures take on the familiar goat hindquarters and horse legs and hooves affixed to a human torso. In some versions the satyr's human body was usually depicted with only goat feet, or perhaps with goatlike sexual organs, sometimes with the penis erect. Very often the satyrs wield huge clubs or tree trunks as weapons. They were divinities of woodlands, protectors of animals and lovers of music, but also inclined to take lustful advantage of any maid who wandered unawares into their midst.

The fauns and sylvans, lesser sprites of the forest, were also portrayed as hairy humanoids with their animal characteristics barely visible. Faunus, the Roman god of animals, although usually portrayed as goat-legged and horned, was also portrayed only with shaggy hair or an animal skin thrown over his human body.

It is interesting, too, that the first representations of centaurs show them as giants with hairy bodies. Their definitive appearance as men with the bodies of horses from the waist down seems to date back only to the time of the great sculptor Phidias, whose work adorns the Parthenon. Before that they were depicted as half human and half horse, but with human forelegs and sexual organs rather than equine ones.

Silenus, a god of wooded mountainsides, also was depicted as hairy and squat, a bit bestial, with a sensual face beneath a low forehead and projecting brow. Like the satyrs and the nymphs and fauns, he did not use tools and apparently had no skill in metallurgy.

Rather fanciful descriptions passed on by ancient travelers and writers may not fall within the realm of mythology, but they are curious enough. Herodotus was probably the first to place near-human creatures in a defined, although distant, geographic region—conveniently out of reach of his literate contemporaries. One such group of "wild men" he placed deep in the Libyan desert, among huge snakes, people with dog's heads, and other "people" with eyes in their chests. Herodotus was careful to add, parenthetically, "I don't vouch for this, but merely repeat what the Libyans say."

Ctesias traveled in India and wrote a book in which he suggested that hairy wild men lived in India and beyond; he thus helped to establish a belief that the East was the land of marvels, an idea that has lasted for more than two thousand years. Megasthenes, a Greek who served as ambassador to the court of the great Indian king Chandragupta, expanded on Ctesias's descriptions and noted the existence of a monster with its feet reversed. The Roman scholar Pliny said that a race of *silvestres,* wild creatures with hairy bodies, existed in India. These creatures had yellow eyes, canine teeth, and were incapable of speech, able to utter only horrible shrieks. It is possible Pliny was describing the gibbon, an ape found in the Far East.

Somewhat earlier, Hanno, the Carthaginian explorer, had described hairy creatures of near-human shape on the coast of West Africa, probably in the region of present-day Sierra Leone. He and his men killed and flayed some females of this species, which he described as hairy women. It is interesting that Pliny believed Hanno's creatures to be the Gorgons of ancient Greek mythology; today Hanno's tale is regarded as basically factual and his creatures as either gorillas or chimpanzees. The latter are found in the immediate hinterland of Sierra Leone to this day, and the gorilla's range may have extended that far west in Hanno's time.

Late in the first century, Plutarch, a Greek who admired all things Roman, described how the Roman general Sulla, returning with his army from the sack of Athens in 86 B.C., came to Dyrrachium—in what is now Albania—and captured a satyr in its sleep. This creature was supposedly taken to Sulla and interrogated in many tongues, none of which it understood; its only communication was something "between the neighing of a horse and the bleating of a goat."

The persistent quality of ancient legends about such creatures is further marked by the passing on of various words, especially from the Latin, that are common throughout Europe to this day. The word "ogre" derives from Orcus, the Italic god of death, and became *orco* in Italian (hence J. R. R. Tolkien's humanoid goblins called "orcs"). The same goes for the German *Fänke* or *Fangge*, the "wild woman" of Tyrolean lore, whose name is derived from *fauna,* the female faun.

Legends about hairy humanoids were common among Teutonic and Celtic peoples even before Roman times, though they were passed along in greatly adulterated form once they were translated and recorded by the Romans in the early Christian era. The Anglo-Saxons called the creatures *wudenwasa* or *wudenwasan,* which later become the *wodewose* or *wodehouse* of the Middle Ages. Literally, this means "wild man," a term that has long been associated in British as well as Continental lore with hairy, manlike beings that live in remote forests.

In their earliest manifestations these giants appear to have been more believable, more mortal—a counterpoint to the dwarfs, gnomes, and other, smaller humanoid creatures that inhabited woods, mountains, and out-of-the-way places.

In Anglo-Saxon literature there is the *Beowulf* epic, with its humanoid monster, Grendel, who is hairy, huge, and carnivorous, and whose very gaze is paralyzing. Grendel is an example of the archetypal carnivorous biped of the ancient north, the legendary monster whom no one but the pure in heart can withstand. A far more satisfying creature, with his human attributes, than the disembodied and ectoplasmic organisms of the traditional ghost story, Grendel is at once horrific and yet misunderstood. A recent retelling of the myth from Grendel's point of view, by novelist John Gardner, re-creates a sympathetic monster, altogether human in his fear and rage, his loss and loneliness. This theme has become quite common in Bigfoot lore.

Among the Celts, wild humanoid creatures were usually seen as guardians of the forest, charged with the safety of animals, full of wisdom and secret lore. Brittany, especially, was a center of such tales, with its enchanted forest of Brocéliande where the hairy wild men were believed to reside well into the Middle Ages. Such stories were also common to Wales, Cornwall, Ireland, Scotland, and to much of Western Europe before the Germanic migrations. The earliest such beings were humanoid giants, such as the legendary Fomorians, who fought the hero Partholón when he and his twenty-four men and women invaded Ireland, and they had to be overcome before the land could be peacefully occupied. The mythology of Ireland describes humans interbreeding with wild Fomorians, which has led most scholars to assume that the Fomorians represent an earlier population that was conquered and displaced by the invading Celts.

The Arthurian legends also embody survivors from earlier Celtic myths, including woodland giants who capture maidens or threaten farms and villages. In *Gawain and the Green Knight* there is reference to the stone crags where wild men dwell, and the Green Knight himself is a transformed giant. These wild men are typically represented in human form, although they usually possess less than human intelligence, little or no speech, wooden clubs or tree trunks in place of weapons of steel.

During the Middle Ages these wild and woolly creatures were central to a remarkable lore that is represented in some of the most striking literature and art of that period. As described by Richard Bernheimer in his *Wild Men in the Middle Ages,* they were a curious combination of animal and human traits, "without, however, sinking to the level of an ape." They were almost universally depicted as covered with a growth of shaggy hair, with only the face, feet, and hands bare and sometimes the knees and elbows, "or the breasts of the female of the species." Although Bernheimer states at the beginning of his book that these were imaginary creatures used mostly as literary or artistic figures "whose legendary character is proved by [their] appearance," he devotes one chapter to what he calls their "natural history." Indeed, he describes the mythology of the wild man in terms one might use to explain a given species, distinct in anatomy, habitat, and behavior. He notes that the wild man appears in "the clipped verses of French Arthurian romance, in the epics by German minstrel singers, and in the writings of Cervantes and Spenser." It is also widely represented in sculpture and painting, illuminated manuscripts, and on stove tiles, candlesticks, drinking cups, house signs, chimneys, house beams, the capitals of columns, choir stalls, baptismal fonts, and tomb plates. The façade of the Church of San Gregorio in Valladolid, Spain, has a "wild-man" gargoyle usurping the place normally given to saints, at the jambs of the main portal.

In most of these representations the wild man has a fully human face, not in the least simian, and except for his shaggy coat of fur, he is human in physiology. One such creature adorns a fine ivory cask from fourteenth-century France, now in the Metropolitan Museum in New York; another, shown holding a shield with a greyhound embossed on it, is in the National Gallery's Rosenwald Collection.

Throughout the Middle Ages and well into the Renaissance this wild man was, in Bernheimer's words, "endowed with the character of reality" and apparently believed to exist. There are many stories of the capture of such creatures, usually by hunters who wandered deep into the forest. In *The Faërie Queen,* Spenser gives us the typical attributes:

> Other language had he none, nor speech,
> But a soft murmure and confused sound
> Of senseless words, which nature did him teach
> T'express his passions, which reason did impeach.

The wild man's lack of language, along with his incapacity to recognize or conceive of the Deity, made him less than human.

The wild man compensated for his less-than-human nature with his superhuman strength, which made him the equal, if not the superior, of creatures such as dragons, bears, wild bulls, and boars. It was generally agreed that he shunned human contact, living only in the most remote wilderness, making his bed in caves and crevasses. He could not produce fire or even the simplest agricultural implements and was thus reduced to a fare of berries, acorns, and the raw flesh of animals.

But the wild man was not just a genuine creature that was rarely seen. To many people he was also an allegory for man in his unreconstructed state. Christianity had transformed the uninhibited sylvan creature of pagan mythology into a perfect symbol of the fallen man, outside the pale of God's law, a brute because of his descent from grace, perhaps caused by madness. In this sense the wild man was not really believed to be a different species at all. The hero Lancelot, in the throes of love-madness, is unable to cope with the reality of his forbidden love for Guinevere and becomes insane, spending forlorn years living in the woods like an animal. To be cast down like a beast is one of the wages of sin. Likewise, in the German epic *Der Busant* a prince is separated from his lover in the forest, cannot find her, and thus becomes demented, grows hairy, and roams the woods on all fours until he is found and brought to a castle as a curiosity. There he is taught to walk upright again by a kind duke, and is finally restored to full humanness when reunited with his beloved.

Obviously, like St. Jerome in an earlier age, medieval thinkers could hardly conceive of a theory of changeability, or evolution, among nature's creatures, although some skirted a concept of gradualism, whereby anything capable of existence in a transition from one species to the next could not be impossible in God's plan. But even if some medieval genius had speculated on the idea that the wild men might fit somewhere between man and some earlier and lower humanoid or ape—a "missing link," as it were—such an idea would have been pure heresy. Man was conceived of as a purely created being and, like all other species, fixed in nature. So the strange creatures of medieval lore had to be considered the result of some form of degradation or degeneration.

Similar legends among Asiatic peoples are probably not as well documented, or at least not as readily available to Western scholars. The best known is the familiar yeti, of Sherpa lore, which wanders singly in the high forests of the Himalayas, even beyond the tree line. Sanderson pointed out correctly that these legends are not confined to the Sherpas, or even to other peoples within the Himalaya, but seem to be widespread throughout central Asia. There are considerable differences in reports of the physical appearance of the Himalayan yeti. The Sherpas say that it is about the size of a large man, coated with thick, reddish-brown hair, that it has a conical head, bull neck, prognathous jaw, and a wide mouth with no visible lips. The feet are broad and flat, the second toe longer than the first, and these two wider than the remaining three. Some Nepalese lore describes a smaller type, no more than four or five feet tall, hiding in the warmer valleys below the great peaks. This is called *Teh-lma* by the natives of the region, has red fur with a slight mane, and seems to differ from the yeti in behavior, although apparently it shares the yeti's omnivorous habits.

Sanderson has reported a third Himalayan type of humanoid, a giant of rather apelike aspect. This is supposed to be a hulking creature with shaggy gray fur, a flat head, beetle brows, long, powerful arms, huge hands, and a humanlike foot with two subdigital pads on the ball of the foot below the big toe. If Sanderson was correct—and there is ample evidence that he stretched things a bit from time to time—this giant would be similar to the legendary Sasquatch of North America. Sanderson said that this creature was locally known as the *tok, kung-lu, gin-sung,* and *dzu-teh,* among other names. Legends of this giant seem to be concentrated on the far side of the Himalayas, especially in the Ta Pa Shan, Tsinlings Shan, Ta Khingan Shan, and other ranges to the north and northwest. Unfortunately, because Sanderson so mixed up native legends with recent reports, it is impossible to separate genuine tradition and local legend from contemporary stories that have become widespread since the great Himalayan expeditions began. On the basis of Sanderson's sensationalist statements, it would require extensive research into Nepalese, Tibetan, and other traditions—both oral and written—to set the mythological record straight.

It has been alleged that there is literary evidence regarding the so-called Snowman, however. A Czech physician and anthropologist named Emanuel Vlček has looked at this evidence, and his conclusion is that such a creature does exist. Tibetan books within the ancient Lamaistic tradition, Vlček tells us, are entirely realistic and systematic in their descriptions and illustrations of wildlife and domestic animals; no dragons or other imaginary creatures are portrayed along with the local fauna. Hence, Vlček accepts as compelling evidence the appearance in an anatomical dictionary of a bipedal primate, completely covered with long hair except on the hands and feet, standing erect on a rock, one arm outstretched. The creature is described in the text as a "man-animal" (with captions in Tibetan, Chinese, and Mongolian). A more recent edition of the book illustrates the same creature in an even more naturalistic manner, and includes explanatory notes to supplement the trilingual captions. In each case the translation of the name is "wild man." Vlček himself translated the text accompanying the illustration as follows: "The wild man lives in the mountains, his origin is close to that of the bear, his body resembles that of man, and he has enormous strength. His meat may be eaten to treat mental disease and his gall cures jaundice." Vlček further claims that this creature has been known "for at least two centuries" to the natives of Tibet and also to the monks "who used to meet him from Tibet to the present Mongolia and therefore included him in a kind of standard textbook of the natural history of Tibet applied in Buddhist medicine."

For some reason Sanderson and his colleagues neglect to mention other legends of apelike or near-human creatures in Hindu lore. Sanskrit legend tells of the apes who fought in the army of King Hanuman, but it is well known that these are references to the aboriginal inhabitants of India who were driven by the Aryan invaders into the hills and forests. Many Hindus still speak of their descendants, with the full scorn of superiority born of caste, as "monkey people." In Hindustani, likewise, there is the *bunmanus,* or "man of the woods." He has no tail, walks erect, and the skin of his body is black, slightly covered with hair. This description has long been accepted as applying to the darker, non-Aryan, aboriginal inhabitants of the land rather than to some kind of ape, or ape-man. Perhaps this is why Sanderson presents us with such a selective list; "ape-men" who can talk as other men do are not very good candidates for subhuman creatures, since they are nothing more than obvious examples of traditional racial stereotypes.

Within China, "wild-man" legends are common, although they have not been systematically studied. Chinese mythology is full of the typical monsters usually described as demons, including those of human aspect. The folklorist Bacil Kirtley tells us that the Chinese, like the Tibetans, traditionally believed that there was a wild-beast king who lived in the mountains, "A wild man with long, thick locks, firey [*sic*] red in color, and his body is covered with hair. He is very strong: with a single blow of his huge fist he can break large rocks to pieces; he can also pull up the trees of the forest by their roots."

Much the same goes for Japan. Of course, the Japanese have genuine experience with an aboriginal race of hairy humans— the so-called hairy Ainu—who live to this day as hunters and fishermen in Hokkaido and other northern islands where they retreated after the Japanese populated the main islands. They resemble Europeans more than they do Mongoloid peoples, and the Ainu language has never been classified as belonging to any other known family of languages. It goes without saying that they are *Homo sapiens* like the rest of us, fully human.

If humanoid monsters are the "backbone" of folklore worldwide, they are especially common in legends throughout Indonesia and the other islands of south and Southeast Asia. Many of these probably related directly to the gibbons, the siamang, or the orangutan. Gibbons are found from northeastern India across Southeast Asia and on the islands of Sumatra, Java, and Borneo. Neither gibbons nor siamangs are big enough to be confused with humans, but when, rarely, they descend to the forest floor, they prefer to walk on two legs, often holding their long arms up above their heads. And of course they lack tails like all apes.

The orangutan is one of the so-called *Ponginae,* a subfamily of "great apes" within the larger family of apes called *Pongidae,* and hence grows to considerable size and weight, approximating that of man. This big, reddish ape has been found only in Sumatra and Borneo in historic times, but it was formerly widespread through the adjacent islands, and in prehistoric times on the Asiatic mainland. Its very name *orang utan* means "man of the woods" in a major dialect of Sumatra, and for many years most Europeans believed it to be a kind of subhuman. An illustration of an orang in the British Museum, dated 1658, shows a hairy woman with a slightly simian face and fully erect posture. At that time the differences between the apes and man were not fully understood. For example, it was not understood that all of the great apes, orangutans included, do not walk erect, on two legs, but instead move on all fours, using the callused knuckles of the "hand" in conjunction with the forelimbs.

Nearly a hundred years later the great Swedish naturalist Linnaeus still classed the orangutan as a separate species within the genus *Homo,* called *Homo nocturnus* or *Homo sylvestris orangutan,* although he clearly understood that the chimpanzee was quite distinct from man and belonged to a different genus. Since eighteenth-century scientists, already well versed in rudimentary classification and observation, could make such an elementary mistake, it should not surprise us that the people of

Indonesia—or of other parts of Southeast Asia—could similarly confuse an ape for a human or near-human.

The legendary *orang-pendek* of Borneo and Sumatra, sometimes called the *sedapa,* is a smallish hairy creature of lowland forests, and is often described as having its feet reversed; this is almost certainly an archetypal creature of myth, since it is repeated in one form or another among lowland tropical folk worldwide. It is the kind of legend that might not be entirely fanciful in origin, considering the existence of the orangutan and the gibbon in those regions.

On the island of Ceylon, where no apes are found, there is a tradition of similar interest. This is the legend of the Nittawo, or the "lost people," a race of pygmies who inhabited various Sinhalese mountains before being exterminated by more recent migrants. These Nittawo were short, between three and four feet tall, erect, fully human in form, with a coat of reddish hair; they slept in caves or on platforms of branches in the trees and fed on what they could catch, possessing no fashioned weapons. The legend says they had no speech.

Indeed, this matter of size poses a serious problem within the entire body of legends about hairy humanoids. It can be resolved only if one credits the lore as even potentially factual, either by a Sandersonian theory accepting several species of hairy humanoids or by dismissing one body of lore as wholly mythological and accepting another as true. There are obvious dangers in such arbitrary selectivity.

African legends of wild men and elusive humanoid giants are in some ways comparable to those of Southeast Asia. Africa is linked to Eurasia by land, and it is the apparent birthplace of mankind and the home of the most famous and numerous of the great apes—the chimpanzee and the gorilla.

Despite his field experience as a zoologist, Sanderson was never satisfied with the provable and the known, so he devoted an entire chapter to Africa in his book on abominable snowmen. Without submitting clear evidence, he claimed that there were three areas of Africa where ABSMs (his abbreviation for abominable snowmen) were reported. One of these he described as the southern face of the Guinea massif (in West Africa), another as the east side of the Congo basin, and a third as the eastern escarpment of Tanganyika (now Tanzania).

Certainly it is true that stories about wild men persist in many parts of Africa. The obvious explanation is that the great apes are there. Until fairly recently a large percentage of Africans lived within or close to the natural habitats of one of these species. African folklore, like folklore everywhere, sometimes includes pertinent and accurate observations on local flora and fauna, just as it contains fabulous elements, beings that we in the West call imaginary. It would seem safe to say that when a great ape is present within a given region where legends of such hairy monsters exist—and apes are present in two of Sanderson's ill-defined African regions—it is probable that the one is related to the other.

The trouble is, as Sanderson noted, that hairy creatures are sometimes described in African tales as human in general form and gait, and not infrequently they are differentiated from chimps or gorillas, creatures that are understood by local peoples to be animals distinct from mankind. The so-called *agogwe*, found apparently in southern Tanzania and across the border into Mozambique, is an example. The *asye` ousou* of the Baoulé in the Ivory Coast and the *kriffi* of the Temne in Sierra Leone are among many other examples that Sanderson did not mention, although he quoted his fellow "unknown-animal" hunter Bernard Heuvelmans regarding legends of reddish hairy dwarfs in the Ivory Coast, and spoke of larger manlike monsters in the eastern Congo watershed. I've heard similar stories of these dwarfs during my extensive stays in Africa at various times between 1962 and 1975. Apparently many of the peoples of the Futa Djallon massif, at the southeastern edge of the Guinea highlands—which extend into the Ivory Coast—have similar tales.

Most of these stories are vague and not very convincing. The wild men in these tales seem mostly of a mischievous nature, probably similar to the legendary sprites of the temperate zones, elves, brownies, and leprechauns. The *kriffi* and the *asye` ousou* are really genies, or earth spirits; they may be described in legend as different from regular wild animals, but they are distinguished more by their function than by mere physical description. Many of them are believed to spirit away children and to cohabit with humans. Some are bad and will punish those who break customary taboos. Others can change their form at will, and move among people unnoticed, sometimes to do good. Some are said to live in villages of their own deep in the forest. Others are solitary and have vast wisdom, meeting with human sages to communicate their knowledge.

I saw one of these creatures in the highlands of eastern Sierra Leone in 1965, not far from the Liberian border and the wild Wologisi range beyond, whence he was supposed to have come. He turned out to be a fully human dwarf, who lived in the mostly uninhabited mountains beyond and "consorted" with various spirits of the hills. I noticed that he spoke Kissi, as did others in that area. In fact, he seemed quite eloquent in that tongue, and apparently spoke Mende as well. Some years later, near Kabala, in the Koinadugu district of Sierra Leone, I heard similar stories of mountain dwarfs, and I talked with people who had seen them. Some simple questioning revealed that these little people could also talk; presumably they were the genetically stunted humans familiar in every country but among some preindustrial folk considered to be strange, even magical.

Equatorial Africa has several groups of pygmy inhabitants. Some of them, as the anthropologist Colin Turnbull has pointed out in *The Forest People,* are exceptionally hairy, in contrast to the larger people around them, and their hair is often of a reddish hue. There is evidence that pygmies were once found throughout the Congo basin and beyond, and they probably roamed long ago all the way from the eastern escarpment of Tanzania to the Futa Djallon range in West Africa. If there must be a factual explanation for African legends about hairy wild men, one need not look very far.

Equally interesting is the fact that Africa seems to have few examples of huge, dangerous, ogre-type monsters of humanoid aspect, the kind that crop up so often in legends of mountain folk in the temperate zones. Perhaps it is enough to have a real gorilla, or even a chimp, wandering the forests beyond the clearings. One writer has said that if a creature like the gorilla did not exist, mankind would have had to invent it. In appearance alone, any grown gorilla is awesome enough, with its vast black body, great arms and hands, deep-set, glowering amber eyes, huge head, and massive jaws. Early observers of gorillas really did not observe at all and assumed a ferocity on the animal's part to match its terrific appearance. (It wasn't until the early 1960s that George Schaller finally proved how gentle these giants really are.) Almost fifteen years ago in West Africa I stumbled upon an adult chimpanzee during the onset of a noisy thunderstorm. I suppose the wind was against me as I hustled for cover about a mile away, running through a large cocoa farm. A large black ape was busily breaking open the young cocoa pods to extract the sweet nuts inside. Since I glimpsed beyond her two smaller figures that disappeared at once, I supposed it was a female. This kind of encounter is very rare, and it gave me quite a start. I have since read a good deal about chimpanzee behavior, and I know now that I was actually in little or no danger, but at the time, I had no such reassuring knowledge. In my mind to this day, that ape seemed to be as big as I was and fully capable of doing mischief.

I have since had no trouble understanding why many African people might believe that the great apes will steal and even eat human children or mate with women. There is even a "learned" article about such an incident, reported in Sierra Leone during the early part of this century, and such stories have been widely repeated by Europeans until quite recently. The famous ethologist Jane Goodall has observed that chimps will catch and eat young baboons and other small animals, and even engage in cannibalism, though there is no evidence that they have ever eaten human children. The point is that unsubstantiated stories of abduction and of carnivorous attacks on people by the great apes make up a lore all their own, though we know today that these animals are harmless to humans unless provoked.

Misconceptions about animal behavior are long lived and deeply rooted and thus difficult to eradicate. Irrational attitudes continue even among well-educated people. Once, when telling the story of my brief encounter with the chimp, I had intended to make a point about how perceptions can be deceiving. But a well-traveled listener interrupted me, incredulous: "You mean you didn't even have a gun? I'd never go into a jungle like that without a weapon. You could've shot the damned thing."

The tendency of one group of humans to label another as distinctly different in kind, even as being of an altogether separate species, is ancient and universal. It wasn't long ago in the United States that whites liked to think that blacks were a subhuman species, as a justification for slavery, among other reasons. Some even went so far as to argue that the offspring of black and white couples were less fertile, or even infertile, like the mule that results from crossing a horse and a donkey. (This analogy accounts for the word "mulatto.") Such nonsense hardly needs comment, but it is worth remembering that all folklore, written and oral, whether painted with the respectable gloss of a literate tradition or known only among preliterate folk, is by definition unscientific. If such lore bears within it the grains of fact, which it does in some cases, these grains must be sifted through the screen of scientific inquiry before they can be separated from the chaff of fantasy.

The peoples of Russia, including many of the Asiatic tribes living throughout the mountainous regions of the Soviet Union, also have their share of humanoid legends. These have been reported by the hominologists who believe, with Sanderson and others, that such stories are proof that relic humanoids exist. In the Caucasus Mountains there are tales about a hairy creature called *kaptar,* allegedly more cold-resistant than humans and with an apelike face and beetle brows and footprints broader than those of man. There are abundant tales of a similar creature in the Pamir Mountains, as well as in the Karakoram, Tien Shan, the Altai, and the Hindu Kush ranges. Porshnev and his disciples have claimed that these stories indicate specific anatomical and behavioral details that add up to a single species, variously called the *alma, albasti, goolbiyavan, yavan,* and *gool,* among other names. It is usually said to be mansized, although thicker, with heavier muscles, a short but dense coat of body hair without an underlayer, so that the skin can sometimes be seen, and without hair on the hands and feet.

Color is supposed to vary with locality and age, but it ranges from black and gray to reddish brown and pale yellow. The facial skin is dark, and the head hair is usually different from that of the body. The forehead is low and receding, with prominent eyebrows, deep-set eyes, flattened nose, heavy, strong jaw, wide mouth without lips, and a forward-projecting cone-shaped head on a powerful short neck. Of course, the creature has an upright, bipedal posture, and when it walks, the arms hang down in front of the body, making them seem longer than they are. This creature is supposed to be able to run as fast as a horse, climb cliffs and trees with ease, and take to the water readily. According to the hominologists, it has no tools, though it may use stones as projectiles and as windbreaks. It does not know fire or cooked meat. It can make many sounds—whistling, whining, and so on—but cannot talk. It eats both meat and vegetables, mostly wild, and it will opportunistically steal cultivated fruits and vegetables, or even a lamb now and then, leaving a distasteful smell behind. Apparently this strange, near-human thing will sleep through the winter in the extreme north, after putting on fat, like a bear, and it is mostly nocturnal.

The hominologists believe that this creature may be a surviving Neanderthal, as suggested earlier. The data seem to indicate a creature quite different from that of the Americas, or even the Himalayas. Nevertheless, the lore is considered significant because of a Russian scientific expedition to the Pamirs in the early part of this century. According to several published reports—though these have not been verified, to my knowledge—a member of this expedition named V. A. Khakhlov submitted a thorough report in 1913 to the Russian Imperial Academy of Sciences. The report was then shelved because it described these unknown creatures in detail and concluded they were real. Apparently the report was unearthed by Boris F. Porshnev, who sought out the then elderly Khakhlov in 1959 and proceeded to publish extensively on the subject, thus becoming the father of the hominologists. According to Porshnev, the survival of these strange beings, which occupy some kind of intermediate position between *Homo sapiens* and the apes, is proved not only by the many reports, sightings, and other evidence but also by the pervasive legends. He also claims that the survival of this relic humanoid is proved because of the "univeral taboo surrounding the relic hominoid among all indigenous populations (of humans) today." Bayanov and Bourtsev have since extended this argument, even going so far as to say that "much of the mystery and deification or condemnation of the creature in historic times is due to the fact that he has been a potential, and sometimes actual, 'diluter' of the human race." They allude to evidence of a captured female called Zana, who was tamed, trained to perform simple tasks for her master, and supposedly bore several half-human children. They do not explain how this might be possible with an animal that is supposed to be less than human and that stemmed from a different line of hominid evolution.

It is interesting that this view, although hardly in line with orthodox scientific opinion on the nature and origin of man, is entirely consistent with most traditional folklore about humanoids that abduct people and mate with them. It is really just another version of the ancient myth of the bawdy beast that ravages village maidens and sometimes produces offspring of mixed blood. Even the famous *King Kong* of the movies, an ape that needs a woman for fulfillment of its sexual needs—though obviously too large to consummate the desire—is a current popular version of that ancient tale.

The New World, too, has its share of such legends. The best known is the subject of this book—the *sésqac, cyát-ko, zamekwas,* or *soq'uiam,* known in its Anglicized version as Sasquatch. Apparently Sasquatch originated as a kind of giant mountain demon in the folklore of the Salish tribes of the Pacific Northwest coast. Dr. Wayne Suttles, of Portland State University, has closely studied the ethnographic data among these Salish groups, and his conclusion is that the cultural track of the Sasquatch grows fainter as investigation proceeds. The creature's specific attributes, claimed by Bigfoot buffs to be held in common by many of the Amerindians of the region, actually vary greatly from tribe to tribe. For example, the giant *cejatko* (se-*at*-ko) of the Quinault group is supposed to reside in woods and mountains; it is nocturnal, it whistles, and it steals food, but it is not described as hairy. It will steal women, trick and kill people, and has a spike on its toe. The *sésqac* of the Stalo group is a huge, nocturnal forest or mountain dweller; it is hairy, moves fast, and steals food, but it can speak, can produce half-human offspring, and likes to travel by water.

A close look at the traditional descriptions among the various Salish tribes, unadulterated by modern feedback, shows that they have little in common with the elaborate recent versions of the Sasquatch. The same goes for such legends among other Northwest Coast Indians, including the Tsimshian, Kwakiutl, Nootka, and Bella Coola. All of these peoples needed lore to help explain an apparent contradiction in their understanding of the natural physical world. They believed that man stands apart from nature, and they also believed that man depends upon nature. One way to separate man from nature was to show metaphorically how dangerous it is to cross that barrier between the nonhuman and the human. Another way was to define humanity through images of nonhumans, minimally different from people in appearance but clearly not human because of size, behavior, and so on. As with preindustrial peoples all over the world, who seem to have less need to *dominate* nature than we do, various humanoid giants, or dwarfs, gnomes, and the like, can provide such images. And, of course, to these peoples, such things are equally as "real" as the things seen through ordinary experience.

Farther south, the huge creature known as *o-mah* or *u'mah*—the model for what Sanderson called the "neo-giants"—is actually the Yurok name for a local creek devil that was believed to poison streams in the Blue Creek region of the Siskiyou wilderness of northern California. *U'ma'a* also means a kind of sorcerer and his bundle of poisoned arrows.

Geography may be important in all this. The Pacific Northwest is topographically exceptional and even awesome. The huge rain forests rising up the steep mountainsides are frequently shrouded in dense cold mists, as if to mark the edge of the world. The only places that seem fit for human habitation are thin slivers of coast, mostly rocky beaches, and even these seem threatened by the great loom of the firs and cedars. This would be especially so in an age before the coming of modern logging and great steel saws. Large parts of these woods are nearly impenetrable, with slippery paths snaking through the undergrowth, choked with huge ferns, rotting logs, sometimes interlaced with bogs and fungi-coated swamps. Nearly all of the Northwestern coastal tribes, who understandably preferred the known dangers of the open sea, believed these dark forests to be populated by primeval eldritch creatures, strange animal-men, giant ogresses (these were usually cannibalistic), beasts that had little in common except that they were mostly rudimentarily humanoid. Most of these creatures faded with the coming of European settlers to the Northwest, but an undercurrent of half-remembered legends persisted, and these became the basis—greatly misunderstood and widely misrepresented—for the Sasquatch legend in its modern form.

But what about the often-cited archaeological evidence, including certain carvings on totem poles, and especially on masks, that reveal puzzling apelike creatures in a world where no known apes are found?

The most famous of these is the "monkey mask" (now in Harvard's Peabody Museum) representing a creature called *bukwus* by the Tsimshian Indians. This has become notorious as an example of archaeological proof for the Sasquatch's existence. The case has been examined by Edwin L. Wade, an ethnologist and archaeologist at Harvard who specializes in North American Indians. Wade notes that among the Tsimshians, *bukwus* is nocturnal, herbivorous, semiaquatic, and antisocial, but it is also small, no larger than a man. The oft-carved anthropomorphic *dzóonokwa*, on the other hand, is an eight- or nine-foot ogress that roams the forest seeking children to roast and devour, and her face is not at all similar to that of *bukwus*. She has a rounded, thick-lipped mouth, a large jaw with a protruding chin, and wide-set eyes beneath beetle brows and a sharply rising forehead. There is little that is apelike in *dzóonokwa*, in contrast with *bukwus,* which looks rather like one of several varieties of monkey. If, as John Green emphatically argues, these two legendary beasts represent genuine creatures that are members of a single species, we would have a case of mammalian sexual dimorphism in reverse that would set the whole world of zoology on its ear.

Wade does not shy away from the problem of explaining an apelike mask, such as *bukwus,* in an area where no apes or monkeys are supposed to exist. He points out the simple fact that all of the peoples of the Pacific Northwest coast had regular contact with European and American seamen, especially after whaling and merchant ships began to visit the region in the late eighteenth century. By the 1840s several of the coastal tribes had a "booming tourist-art business," carving all kinds of exotic beasts for ships' captains, fur traders, and merchants. Many of these carvings, usually done in slate, portray peacocks, lions, elephants, and, of course, monkeys, none of which are indigenous to North America. Northwestern Indians may have hired on as crew members on whaling vessels, being expert whalers themselves (like Tashtego in *Moby Dick,* though he came from the opposite side of the continent), and so traveled around the world. Northwest Coast artists were allowed great liberty in interpreting their subjects, since their carvings were not religious icons and thus fixed in purpose or meaning. It would be easy enough for a native carver to incorporate a new and captivating "monkey" style, borrowed from abroad. This interpretation, Wade suggests, is at least as good as the one that postulates that the *bukwus* mask is based on a Bigfoot creature that exists in nature.

Among other Amerindians there are legends about hairy monsters. These creatures are typically residents of remote and uninhabited forests—Indians, like most people, preferred to stay on the beaten track—and they often abduct women. Some of them even guard animal life and possess secret skills. Sometimes a humanoid monster represents the spirits of departed ancestors, and so is potentially vengeful. The Yaqui Indians of northern Mexico believe in a large humanoid living in an unexplored canyon in the Sierra Madre Occidental. The Indians of the Chiapas in southern Mexico have a legendary *salvaje, cax-vinic,* or *fatasma humano.* There are similar legends in Oaxaca, and some of the creatures in that region are believed to be men who transformed themselves into animals *(binquizacs)* to escape the Spanish conquistadores.

In Guatemala there is the *sisimite,* a manlike being believed to steal women for its mates. Sanderson reports that this beast is thought to be both a horrible giant and a dwarf, with a body covered with long hair and with reversed feet. These creatures live in uninhabited hills and precipices and in dark streams far from villages or towns, and are guardians of remote and secluded places and protectors of animals, and will therefore attack solitary hunters along hidden paths.

The "Mosquito Coast" of Central America also has its humanoid creature: "a tailless anthropoid ape called *ulak,* or *uluk,*" according to Sanderson, "reminding [one] of the gorilla, orangutan or chimpanzee of the Old World. It is of erect position, about five feet in height, covered with black hair, and has the teeth turned backwards. It is greatly feared, as it is supposed to carry off human beings of the opposite sex."

Sanderson has also recorded stories told by the Caribs of British Honduras that describe the so-called *duendis,* or *duende* (a Spanish word for "fairy" or "hobgoblin"), small, furry men who leave footprints with pointed heels and who carry leaves over their heads like sombreros.

Space does not allow for more than a few examples of legends from South America, where many exist. The Andes have their *duende,* a creature that is supposed to live in deep canyons, where it can sometimes be heard crying like a baby. This little being is wont to plait the hair of horses at night because it is fond of horseback riding and needs to weave stirrups into the mane. Other creatures in the Andes are described as carnivorous giants, as is typical of the legends of mountain folk. The Brazilian Mato Grosso has the *mapinguary,* a vicious brute that leaves twenty-inch footprints and tears the tongues out of living cattle for sport. Von Humboldt's record of his famous expedition into the unknown jungles of South America late in the eighteenth century mentions stories of hairy wild men living in the deep woods who carried off local women.

Even the Indians of the eastern woodlands and the Great Lakes region in North America have oral traditions about ogres of the forests, rivers, and lakes. Some of these creatures are terrifying to look at, and cannibalistic. Usually, however, they are spirits, inhabitants of one of the upper levels of the world where people cannot go in this life. The Algonquin *windigo,* or *wiitiko,* is a huge, hairy creature, elusive, apparently able to appear and disappear at will. Iroquois legends describe stone giants, rather like the titans of Greek mythology, who use rocks and tree trunks as weapons, live without benefit of fire, and are ignorant of tools. ("Stoneclad," a rock giant of Cherokee mythology, is another example.) The Iroquois had three categories of sprites of humanoid aspect: strange dwarfs that lived in rocks and water, others that lived under the ground, and those that protected fish in the rivers and made vegetation flourish.

Apparently there is no region inhabited by man that lacks legends of this kind. But what does all this mean? Is it possible that some of this lore is based on fact, as Sanderson, Heuvelmans, Green, Porshnev, Bayanov, Bourtsev, Vlček, and many Bigfoot buffs believe? Is the apparently consistent detail among some of these legends, at least within certain regions, really evidence that a species of near-human actually exists, thereby explaining the sightings, footprints, odors, and sounds? Is it possible that a number of unknown primate species survive? Or do these legends have their origin in archetypes that go back to the beginning of the human race, persistent themes that might stem from the unconscious mind, creatures of dreams, related in their meaning, origin, and purpose to dragons, mermaids, unicorns, and bogeymen?

It is obvious that most of the legendary material doesn't describe anything that ever really existed in nature. The creatures in question are simply supernatural beings whose origins are blatantly fabulous and whose parallels with other imaginary creatures prove their mythological nature. I state this at once because it does no good to pretend that fancy is fact even when one might wish it to be.

Even if Sasquatch or the yeti is one day discovered, it won't mean that the legendary material is at all factual. The discovery of the Komodo dragon, a large carnivorous lizard of the Lesser Sunda Islands of Indonesia, did not prove that dragon legends are "true," as some Bigfoot apologists would have it. For drag-

ons, at least in folklore and myth, are wholly fabulous creatures, complete with fire-breathing talent, sometimes the ability
to speak, and a penchant for abducting maidens. Perhaps some
dragon tales had a minimal basis in fact, resulting from certain
distorted stories passing from Indonesia to the mainland of
Asia, and gradually to Europe. The knowledge of the one-
horned rhino, or of the Arabian oryx—which has *two* spiraled
horns—did not prove that unicorns exist. Anyone familiar with
traditional unicorn lore is aware that the fabulous creature has
attributes that bear no relation to animals in the real world.
Like dragons, the unicorn exists in mythology in order to perform another role.

At least one American folklorist, Bacil Kirtley, has taken the
trouble to list some of the parallels found within legends about
hairy hominids. Most apparent is the characteristic of having reversed feet, a feature that crops up from the time of Megasthenes, in the fourth century B.C., into our own era. This is
widespread in the New World, Asia, Sumatra, Africa, even in
Ireland, Switzerland, and the Philippines. Many descriptions of
the yeti also include this trait.* It probably derives from the
fact that the tracks of bear, from Sumatra to the Himalayas,
from Louisiana to the Cascades, often appear to point in the opposite direction of the animal's movement. This is partly because all bears walk with a "toe-in," quite the opposite of
humans, and partly because bears have their largest toe on the
outside rather than the inside of the foot.

Another recurring theme is that ill-fortune, illness, or death
will afflict anyone encountering one of these eldritch creatures,
regardless of the local name or other distinguishing characteristics. The father of Tenzing Norgay, the famous Sherpa guide,
was reported to be ill for a year after seeing a yeti. In the Pamirs the gulbiyaban challenges strong men to fight when they
cross its territory. If the traveler wins, he is safe, but if he loses,

---

*There is full documentation of this trait in Stith Thompson's six-volume *Motif-Index of
Folk Literature*. The most pertinent motifs are F4331.1; F436; F441.3; F460; F521.1;
F567; and F567.1.

he suffers long illness. Even to gaze upon an *orang-pendek* in Sumatra is said to bring death. The same is true of certain *kriffi* of the forests of northern Sierra Leone, and of various hairy dwarfs elsewhere in Africa. Kirtley writes that the kinds of supernaturally tinged creatures "to whom a meeting or seeing-tabu attaches could be enumerated indefinitely, for the faith is almost universal that human beings encountering nonhuman presences experience not only immediate fear or shock, but also a persistent and debilitating supernatural contagion."

The wild man as forest guardian is a global trait, too, not merely limited to the sylvan creatures of classical myths or the hairy wild men of the Middle Ages. Also universal is the creature's practice of abducting women. Pictures of the European wild men often show them carrying ladies off into the forest, presumably for sexual purposes. African peoples have believed that gorillas steal women for this reason, and among many Northwestern Indians the several "tree strikers," "whistlers," "cockleshell men," and other ogres of the forest, including the *sésqac* of the Stalo tribe and the *cyát-kwu* of the Puget Sound, do the same thing.

There is also the nearly universal belief that these humanoid creatures can be caught if they chance to drink wine or fermented liquor. Traditionally the creature will invariably escape after sobering up, using its great strength to break its bonds and flee. Yeti have allegedly been caught this way, and there are illustrations of medieval wild men being thus lured and trapped. In ancient times it was believed one could capture an intoxicated, slumbering satyr. In 1978 in Michigan this method was proposed by a frustrated Bigfoot hunter. It is unlikely that the man who made the suggestion was aware of the ubiquity of this idea in folklore. Had he been so aware, he probably would not have made the suggestion; for it would risk having the Michigan Bigfoot classified permanently within the realm of myth.

I am not prepared to say that the widespread existence of these parallel traits should be taken as proof that all of the hairy humanoids of legend are purely imaginary. But the pervasiveness of these folkloric themes does show that the bulk of the so-called evidence contained within myth and legend does not hold up very well. Sanderson's claim that plausible reports of encounters with humanoids are confined to certain montane regions, where the creatures could have migrated or perhaps evolved from earlier primate types, is obviously not true. Even the Solomon Islanders have their ape-men, and the Solomons are part of an area that drifted away from the Eurasian continent long before mammals had evolved. Kirtley cites several other examples in his fascinating article. His own conclusions are worth quoting in part:

> Even the most sincere and factually documented stories of Abominable Snowmen and other unknown hominids, we must conclude, are simply myths and emanate from persons who have made distorted interpretations of their own experiences, who have translated observed phenomena or evidence to accord with incidents which are adumbrated in folklore and, as are most traditional stories dealing with the extraordinary, structured to highlight effects of terror or to dramatize some ogrish singularity.

The unquestionable antiquity of man-beast legends appears to support Kirtley's tough conclusion. Even if these legends have multiple origins—stemming from experience with real animals such as apes, monkeys, and bears, and from transformed stories about other, different human types—the striking factor is that their core elements are so alike. Kirtley's suggestion that people "continually renew the fantasy through autobiographical anecdotes" is also pertinent. Anyone familiar with the patterns of embellishment in the universal human pastime that we in the West call "telling tall stories" will at once recognize the soundness of this observation. Nor should we be surprised that some members of our own population would take such stories seriously. In many parts of the world nearly everyone does.

Scholars have studied the world's mythologies for well over a century, and there are certain accepted conclusions about their functions and their "truths" that are germane. Carl Sagan, in his provocative book *The Dragons of Eden,* correctly points out that myth, rather than being pure nonsense, is really "a metaphor of some subtlety on a subject difficult to describe in any other way." Thus the archetype of the goblin, troll, cyclops, mountain ogre, etc., is often explained in terms of "ingroup" psychology; that is, the tendency of one group of people sharing a common culture to label outsiders as inhuman. This appears to be especially true when legend records a hard struggle for survival on the part of a group of newcomers who eventually overcome an aboriginal population.

Even when there is no protracted struggle, myths like this arise. Not so long ago European "eyewitnesses" claimed that the Patagonians were so tall that the heads of the Europeans came only to their waists, and various plains Indians, such as the Sioux, were seriously described as giants in some early accounts. When the Norsemen began to raid Western Europe and penetrated to the Mediterranean, the Christian Europeans and Arabs alike often described them as gigantic, though in fact the Scandinavians were only somewhat taller on average. Conversely, it is almost certain that the hairy dwarfs of the Viking sagas, the "mist monsters," often dressed in kirtle and colored cap, relate to the ancient Lapps once widely dispersed across northern Europe. Dwelling in caves, armed only with arrows tipped with stone, the dwarfs are often portrayed eating human flesh—as recently popularized in Michael Crichton's novel *Eaters of the Dead.* The explanation that they were remnants of a Neanderthal population is possible, but unlikely.

Such myths contain an original element of truth turned through time into a metaphor of compelling interest or special force. It is even possible, as Sagan points out, that some myths of humanoid monsters could be a cultural or genetic memory of the times when "gracile" Australopithecines (or possibly more "robust" ones) shared the African savannas with our hominid ancestors.

The idea that myths as "archetypes of the collective unconscious" actually reveal a dimension of reality was first seriously proposed by the Swiss psychologist C. G. Jung. Jung pointed out that whereas certain aspects of truth are revealed through scientific experimentation, and others through intellectual analysis, there is another dimension revealed through the creativity of art, music, and literature. This is of course widely understood, and perhaps it always has been, in the sense that a Shakespearian play may utilize a fantasy—as in *The Tempest*—to illuminate a great psychological truth, or in the sense that all legends of creation hold within them profound lessons about man's dependence on the earth and his ultimate origins in the earth (and, some would say, his capacity to abuse his talents). But Jung made it clear that there are many aspects of the mental life of mankind that have been constant and universal, recurring as types or motifs and expressed in a variety of historic modes, ranging from the most ancient primitive myths to the futuristic dreams of modern humans. Perhaps this is most evident in our current wave of science-fiction movies such as *Star Wars* and *Close Encounters of the Third Kind*.

It should be noted that "archetypes" are universally held psychic symbols, what Jung called "monadic symbols." These, he said, are not only part of the "natural" world for a people but part of the "human nature" of the people themselves, fully expressing their collective character. Jung firmly believed that widespread social attitudes expressed consciously are deeply rooted manifestations of various archetypes with a long history in the human psyche. He even suggested that the conscious attitudes held by modern science at any given time are subject to this principle, despite the pure air of rationality that science proclaims. Perhaps he was right, for there is really not much difference between the biblical attempt to build a tower to heaven—Babel—and our modern attempt to breach the heavens with telescopes and penetrate the cosmos with rocket ships. Maybe there is not much difference between the legendary quest for monsters—whether sought by Jason, Odysseus, Beowulf, St. George, or Sir Gawain—and the modern equivalent, whether the search is for fossil proof of man's animal origins or for Bigfoot.

In most tribal societies—and perhaps in ours as well—the underlying structure of mythology is unconscious; thus, in monster legends the important thing is not just the tale, or the narrative, but the fact of certain motifs, or themes. Most of us in the modern world remain childlike in our comprehension of nature, and especially of our place in it. In so-called primitive tribes a common leitmotiv is the fear of animal revenge. Why are we so arrogantly sure that this doesn't function among urbanized and industrialized people, especially when so many "hunt" during only one season and with such guilty and atavistic pleasure in the kill?

What, then, are we to believe about "wild man" legends, and about modern phenomena such as Bigfoot? Perhaps, once upon a time, creatures different from us, but also not wholly unlike us, shared the earth until we either wiped them out or they faded away, unable to adapt. Some legends are certainly imaginary constructions devised to explain the unexplained. Many represent stories of conflict between different human groups, in which one group is transformed into subhuman form. Certainly there is a "collective memory" functioning in the present, as it did in the past. Archetypes become part of the people who hold them and present another way of communicating, a means for people to relate and interact on the most basic level.

Yet is it possible that these stories could be not only symbols but also evidence that some unknown, perhaps near-human creature survives out there?

Before a discussion of whether such a creature (or such creatures) *could* evolve and survive into our crowded present, a word of caution. This branch of teratology, the study of humanoid monsters, is fraught with pitfalls for the simple reason that we are dealing with a potentially humanlike being. As the ecologist Paul Shepard has written in his book *Thinking Animals* regarding the similarity of apes to humans:

It needles us because the ape is uncomfortably close as an animal and disgustingly far away as a human. The ape and human images are a set of imperfect oppositions, an instrument for self-analysis. . . . And . . . the ape's behavior epitomizes our own failure to integrate our human and animal aspects, and by parallel, our limited success in harmonizing our human and spiritual sides.

What, then, might be said of a creature more akin to us than any ape? If it does exist, the prospect has to be as confounding as it is exciting.

4. A Biological Connection ?

The existence of sub-human and even sub-hominid creatures has crept steadily forward in time.

> IVAN SANDERSON
> in *Abominable Snowmen:*
> *Legend Come to Life*

[In] trying to solve the mystery of the "snowman," "wild
man," or whatever . . . with the help of existing paleoan-
thropological knowledge—let us recall another mystery,
one residing within this very body of knowledge. By this
we mean the generally accepted view that *Homo Sapiens* is
the only surviving species of the Hominidae. Isn't it mysterious, if not mystical, that we should be the only survivors
of the whole family, while the nearest family, the Pongidae, boasts of several surviving forms? And isn't it possible that by confronting one mystery with the other we
shall be able, like detectives, to unravel them both?

> DMITRI BAYANOV AND IGOR BOURTSEV
> in *Current Anthropology,* June 1976

There is undeniable romance in the search for a potential cousin
to man. The endeavor has become for its devotees much more
than just another monster quest—a modern version of the medieval search for the dragon's lair—because it is assumed that the
mysterious creature is a hominid, or at least a member of the
family of apes. Success in the search would certainly make even

the most recent discovery of yet another unknown tribe of humans seem pale by comparison. What could match the drama of that documented confrontation exposed to the full glare of the modern media? How would the National Geographic Society present a special on this? Would some captor, or wildlife zoologist, accompany the creature, caged or shackled, onto the Johnny Carson show? Would a specimen be killed and mounted? If so, where would it be displayed? In the Hall of Mammals among the apes? If humanoid, where would it belong?

Of course, most scientists hardly expect the quest to succeed, for it is axiomatic among primatologists and anthropologists that we alone survive of all the lineage of that remarkable and dominant family called *Hominidae.* The other hominid species are known only as fossils, presumed extinct, long since gone the way of the saber-toothed cats, the cave bear, mammoth, giant sloth, and other animals whose fossils echo a time when the earth teemed with great beasts, a time before the cold came and everything changed.

On what biological basis, then, do the hunters of Bigfoot persist in their search? Is there a real chance, despite the opinion of orthodox science, that one or more of the hominid or pongid lineages gave rise to a handful of creatures yet unknown? Certainly there is a chance. You do not launch an expensive search after a creature if you believe it to be extinct. But what is the nature of the evidence? The subjective evidence of the reports and the objective evidence of the tracks would not be very convincing if it were not linked to a coherent theory that fits the known fossil evidence. Is it true, as the hominologists say, that in tackling one mystery—the evolution of but one successful form of hominid—we might solve the other?

It is almost inconceivable that a large bipedal mammal could belong to any but the primate order. Among placental carnivores, for example, only one family, *Ursidae* (bears), has given rise to species large enough to fit the descriptions of Bigfoot. No one has ever suggested that the big cats can stand on their hind legs and move about—as bears do on occasion—except in circuses. Bears only among the large carnivores are found in places where Bigfoot is said to be, and only bears among these larger carnivores could be even temporarily confused with a bi-pedal creature covered with hair.

But, of course, bears do not walk on two legs; they are fully quadrupedal beasts, though they sometimes rear and shuffle on their hind legs. The fact that bears have adapted through the ages from a once highly carnivorous mode to a selective omniv-orous diet—in ways that superficially resemble the adaptations of baboons and humans—does not mean that bears share an evolutionary heritage with the larger members of the primate order. Bears, as any high-school biology student knows, emerged from an entirely different line of evolution. Their closest living relatives are pandas and raccoons.

So if the creatures sighted in our vast northern forests really exist, and if they are not bears mistaken for hominids or apes, they must be primates of some sort, members of the order that has given rise to monkeys, apes, and humans. And if the crea-tures are really bipedal, as accounts seem to agree, one would assume that they belong to the *Hominidae,* the only family among the higher mammals that has adapted to walking on two legs. If the creatures belong to the *Pongidae*—the family that in-cludes the great apes, gibbons, and siamangs—it would be hard to explain the erect posture, the apparent shape of the foot as indicated by tracks, and of course the two-legged gait, attri-butes not shared by the apes or, as far as we know, their fossil ancestors.

Most laymen understandably care little for the elaborate sys-tem whereby animals are categorized and classified, according to proved affinities and characteristics, into order, suborder, family, genus, and species. But without such a system we would still be in the Dark Ages in our comprehension of animals, their relations to one another, and their roles in nature. We would be unable to study them intelligently, and our awful difficulties today in protecting and utilizing them would be enormously compounded by ignorance. We might still believe that entirely different species can cross-breed, or that the ob-servable world of nature is in chaos. In such a world, as in the largely imaginary world of our ancestral myths, anything would be possible. Elephants might sprout wings; serpents, too, might fly or breathe fire. Men might change, by the rising of the moon, into wolves and savage their fellows in wholly un-wolflike manner. Bears might mate with mountain lions and buffalo might talk. It would be marvelous indeed.

Alas, we have to deal with the real world as it is. If Bigfoot wanders the montane forests of our Northwest—and perhaps the swampy thickets of our north-central and southern states—we cannot pretend for long that he is so out of the ordinary that he doesn't fit into the existing scheme of nature. If, as some prefer to believe, the creature is from outer space, and thus not part of our world at all; if the many reports are projections of some kind, glimmers from another dimension—perhaps from within another "time warp," along with the "lost" pilots of the Bermuda Triangle—we can only throw up our hands and abandon rational explanation. But if there really is some unknown beast out there, what kind of animal would it be? Indeed, what *must* it be, according to known zoological principles?

The primate order is one of nature's success stories. During the past several million years at least eighteen families have evolved and about a dozen of these still thrive. There have been one hundred genera, and more than fifty of these still exist, including more than one hundred species. We can trace the outlines of this order back nearly seventy million years to the end of the Age of Dinosaurs, when the earliest fossil primates appear, tiny creatures like tree shrews. These small mammals fed on fruit and other vegetation and probably lived on the ground. About fifteen million years passed before the primates evolved into five or more distinct families, which spread gradually outward from their earliest known sites in North America across to Europe. By about forty to twenty-five million years ago—in the Oligocene Epoch—the majority of the primates were in Africa, and they had meanwhile increased in size and adapted to life in the trees. These resembled today's lemurs and tarsiers, and from Africa they gradually spread through Eurasia and back again into North America—the continents being closely linked at various times during these epochs as the earth's tectonic plates drifted, collided, and drifted apart, moving toward their present configurations. Probably one of these migrants then reached South America and evolved into the New World monkeys, or perhaps the latter derived from a monkeylike ancestor that came directly from the Old World somewhat later. In any case, during the Miocene Epoch, about twenty-three to five and a half millions years ago, the two major branches of monkeys—the Old World and New World—had gone their separate ways.

In the meantime, as they moved gradually outward from the warmer parts of the world, some of the Old World monkeys gradually began to evolve into the forerunners of the apes. They lost their tails and developed larger and more powerful arms and torsos, greater jaws, and significantly larger skulls. From the Miocene Epoch we have fossils of a half dozen or more species of extinct apes called dryopithecines. These ranged from the size of a gibbon to the size of a full-grown gorilla. Fossils of these apes have been found both in Africa and Asia, roughly dated to between twenty and fifteen million years ago, and they clearly indicate evolution toward the existing species of apes.

Considerably later, about nine to five million years ago, emerged the celebrated *Gigantopithecus* of Asia. What the body of this giant ape was really like we don't know. Careful research and clever speculation indicate that it was probably similar to a huge gorilla, although apparently adapted to open upland savannas rather than to tropical forests. It was able to cope with most open-country predators because of its great size and strength, though its young might have been quite vulnerable. Careful examination of its fossil teeth indicates that *Gigantopithecus* was graminivorous, or grass-eating, rather than folivorous, or leaf- and fruit-eating, like other apes. There is no evidence in the fossil record that it was also carnivorous, an interpretation popular, for obvious reasons, among Bigfoot apologists.

A reconstruction of *Gigantopithecus* imaginatively proposed several years ago pictured it as a huge, manlike carnivore, more or less erect in posture, carrying its prey up the face of the

Kwangsi cliffs in southern China. This has since been dismissed on geological and biological grounds. For example, the present caves in the Kwangsi cliffs were once simply sink holes in a limestone plateau where these great apes once flourished, and erosion over hundreds of thousands of years has exposed these holes as cliffside caves. Fossil bones found in conjunction with *Gigantopithecus* include another robust fellow primate, the ancestral orangutan. A careful tally of these fossils has revealed that carnivorous animals predominate among the cave fauna of Kwangsi. This has led one paleontologist to suggest that the weight of the evidence leads to an unromantic conclusion: *Gigantopithecus* was more likely to have been prey than predator in spite of its estimated height of perhaps eight feet and a weight of up to eight hundred pounds.

Thus the reconstructed picture of *Gigantopithecus* most widely accepted today is as follows: Sometime in the Pliocene Epoch a very large species of ape probably evolved from *Dryopithecus indicus,* which was a robust creature with jaws almost as big as a modern gorilla's. Since *D. indicus* was found in the northern border area of India during the late Miocene and early Pliocene, the evolution of *Gigantopithecus* from this line makes good geographical sense. Likewise, it would make sense for any previously forest-dwelling ape to adapt to open country by eating grains and seeds. An increase in body size would assure a means of some defense against predation, which had to be a threat for any creature not fleet of foot, and greater bulk would enhance foraging in the lush grasslands. Nevertheless, since it evolved in the direction of enormous bulk, it is probable that *Gigantopithecus* represents an unsuccessful side branch in pongid evolution. Unlike the adaptations to open country of the hominids and baboons in Africa, the specialized adaptations in the case of *Gigantopithecus* led to eventual extinction.

It is also significant that there are no traces of fossil evidence of this creature more recent than the fossils in the Kwangsi cliffs, which date to about a million and a half to a million years ago. Nor have fossil bones of anything resembling such a large primate been found through the vast expanse of Asia that stretches from Kwangsi to the Bering Strait, or beyond into the

New World. Had such a creature adapted to the north and migrated into Siberia and the New World, one might reasonably expect some evidence along the presumed line of migration. Among plentiful fossils of the large animals that moved in both directions across the Bering land bridge, nothing resembling any primate (except man) has ever been found.

So the picture of *Gigantopithecus* is one of a huge, presumably quadrupedal ape. Foraging in open country, this hulking beast was well adapted to a particular but short-lived habitat of warm open savanna covered in lush grasses. Mass and strength discouraged its largest predators, but packs of wild dogs (dholes) might easily have taken its clumsy young or surrounded and eventually killed a healthy adult. Dholes in packs have been known to bring down bears and even tigers, and they commonly make their lair in caves or holes in the ground. Their fossils have been found in conjunction with *Gigantopithecus* teeth and jaw fossils. Other large predators might have posed a similar threat, but predation alone could not have spelled the end of this great beast. For *Gigantopithecus* the end probably came gradually, resulting from alterations in the habitat to which the huge pongid was unable to adapt.

The disturbing fact that the lineage of mankind also adapted to this open-country mode of feeding has been the cause of considerable speculation and great confusion among Bigfoot experts. Actually, hominid adaptation to this mode was an independent process, occurring in Africa at a much earlier date, during the first ten million years of hominid history. Earlier in this century, when the only remains of *Gigantopithecus* were a few teeth scavenged from Oriental apothecary shops by von Königswald, the apparent likeness of these teeth to those of man—except for their size—could easily lead a fine scholar such as Franz Weidenreich to suggest a close relationship between the hominid line and *Gigantopithecus*. Only in the last decade or so have the differences become significant, instead of the similarities. Few anthropologists or primatologists today would argue that *Gigantopithecus* was a member of the hominid line; the evidence points rather to a branch off the stem of the pongid line.

Let us return again to the time of the dryopithecines and pick up the thread of fossil evidence where we left off. Late in the Miocene—an epoch of significant evolution for all members of the pongid and hominid lines—between about fifteen and nine million years ago, another ape emerged. Fossil evidence of this rather unspecialized creature, called *Ramapithecus,* or Rama's ape, has been found in both Africa and Asia. And, more important, these fossils indicate evolutionary movement away from typical ape characteristics and toward what anthropologists consider to be humanoid traits. On the basis of this evidence, many experts today assume Rama's ape to be directly ancestral to a remarkable line of creatures that emerged in southern and eastern Africa about four or five million years ago. Usually classed in the hominid line because of their erect posture and bipedal locomotion, these sons of Rama are generally called the australopithecines.

It is generally agreed that this "southern ape" had a body remarkably similar to a modern human's, although smaller. Its brain, however, was hardly bigger than that of a chimpanzee. Were they man, or ape? Not all anthropologists agree, but the erect posture and two-legged gait—a fact recently and absolutely proved by Mary Leakey's discovery of actual footprints preserved in rock-hardened volcanic dust and dated to about three million years ago—seem to put them clearly on our side of the divide.

As with all evolving animals, nature gave rise to more than one species, and probably more than one of these australopithecines existed at the same time. The largest was the famous *Paranthropus,* more accurately called *Australopithecus robustus.* Adapted to an almost wholly graminivorous diet, this creature had a ridge on the cranium rather like that of a gorilla. This has caused a fuss among Bigfoot people who claim to detect a similar cranial ridge on the (female?) creature in the Patterson-Gimlin film.

Another creature was the more "gracile"* species usually

---

*This term is used by anthropologists to emphasize the relatively graceful physiology of *A. africanus* as compared to that of the far bulkier *A. robustus.*

called *Australopithecus africanus,* which was rather smaller and more agile than *robustus,* with a brain capacity of about 450 cc., as compared to about 1400 cc. for modern man. Although we cannot say that it was more intelligent than *A. robustus,* this nimble creature had meanwhile adapted to a more diversified diet, adding berries, nuts, birds' eggs, grubs, beetles, lizards, and other small animals to a diet of roots and seeds. This adaptability—in contrast to the dead-end specialization of *Gigantopithecus*—combined with the freedom of the hands made possible by the erect posture, seems to have aided nature in an incredible transformation. Thus the larger brain began to evolve.

Exactly how the lineage of man emerged is not entirely clear. One version is that this smaller, more nimble, more gracile *A. africanus* gradually gave rise to a later species called *Homo habilis,* and then to *Homo erectus,* a clear ancestor of modern man that had begun to appear in the African savannas—and quickly spread to Eurasia—about three quarters of a million to a million years ago.

A more recent version suggests that the lineage of man began even earlier. Richard Leakey, son of the famous team of Mary and Louis B. Leakey, who unearthed the first *Ramapithecus* and the robust *Australopithecus* types, has discovered fossils that indicate a third erect primate approximately coexisted with the two australopithecines. This one clearly seems to fit the hominid line because of its much larger brain. To the younger Leakey it seemed that this gracile-toothed creature was remarkably similar to that of a hominid discovered by his father some years earlier and called *Homo habilis,* dated to about 1.7 million years ago. The catch is that the younger Leakey's find in the Lake Turkana region of Kenya apparently lived between 2.5 and 3 million years ago, making it a rough contemporary of both *A. africanus* and *A. robustus.* Assuming it to be an earlier version of his father's find, Richard Leakey kept the name *Homo habilis.*

The point is that if the creature in question actually does represent an early type of the genus *Homo* and was not merely a larger-brained australopithecine, then human evolution was branching off on its own divergent line some three million years ago, perhaps earlier, already going in a direction separate from that of the australopithecines.

Even more recently a team of anthropologists led by Donald Johanson of the Cleveland Museum of Natural History has unearthed the fossil bones of yet another smallish, fully erect primate in the Afar region of Ethiopia. Called *Australopithecus afarensis* by Johanson, the almost complete skeletons of several individuals of this species have been found in close proximity. This indicates typical higher-primate social organization and cooperation. Since the creature existed from about 3.7 to 2.9 million years ago, it is believed by the Johanson team to be the oldest indisputable evidence of the family *Hominidae*. If Johanson and his colleagues are correct, *A. afarensis* might be the "stem species" from which *Homo habilis* arose on the one hand and *A. africanus* on the other.

From the media hype that greeted publication of Johanson's extensive research, one might think that the missing link had at last been found and that the whole question of human evolution had been finally settled. Actually there is no such thing as a missing link. The genuine mystery of human evolution does not depend upon a single find for its solution, and even if many more fossils are discovered, it is doubtful that the whole process will ever be entirely unraveled.

So what we actually have is a rather loose and often confusing collection of pieces of fossil evidence. Scientists simply do not know the full details of primate evolution as it led from something like *Proconsul* (a very early large, unspecialized ape) to *Ramapithecus* and onward to the hominid line with its several branches, and in yet another direction to the dryopithecines and the pongid line with *its* several branches. What we do know beyond reasonable doubt is that the hominid line was on its separate way at least three or four million years ago, probably much earlier. Johanson's *A. afarensis* did not spring fully erect when its ancestors left the forests behind; a bipedal gait and erect posture had to come gradually, like all other adaptations in nature.

As recently as fifteen or twenty years ago it was considered daring to suggest that the human line could be dated back to beyond a million years. Today no one is surprised when anthropologists suggest ten million years, or even twice as long. When we consider what is known of ape evolution as distinct from that of man, we are certain that the lineage has its beginnings at least as far back in time. It bears repeating that no respected evolutionist since Darwin (and including Darwin) has seriously considered that man evolved from the apes themselves, or even from an ape ancestor such as the dryopithecines. The lineage of the great apes, or pongids, probably diverged from the ancestral human line at least as far back as the Oligocene-Miocene transition some twenty-six million years ago, since the ancestral stock that led to our modern chimps and gorillas can be clearly identified in the early Miocene Epoch. Work on the comparative anatomy of primates shows that the three large apes share numerous structural and genetic similarities that set them apart from man on the one hand and from gibbons and siamangs on the other. This, plus blood research, indicates that the separation of the lines leading to the gibbons, siamangs, and to man began even before the various great apes began to diverge from one another.

The siamangs and gibbons went their separate ways toward that highly specialized mode of locomotion called "brachiation" (swinging through the trees using the forearms and grasping branches with the hands, the body hanging free beneath). The other apes evolved quadrupedal modes, using all four limbs in conjunction, whether in the trees or on the ground. Only the hominid ancestors evolved a truly bipedal mode when they ventured out of the dark forests.

Ultimately, pongid evolution gave rise to the seven existing species of gibbon and siamang but to only four species of great apes. Of the latter only three (excluding the pygmy chimp) approximate man in size: the gorilla, the orangutan, and the chimpanzee. Because of the evolutionary heritage of arboreal (tree-living) life, all the apes have extraordinarily long and powerful arms relative to their body size, much longer in fact than their legs. (The opposite is true of man.) This characteristic in apes is probably a vestige of an early developed mode of brachiation or partial brachiation among the most remote ancestors, a mode that never developed among the ancestors of man. It is interesting that among all existing pongids, only the gorilla has become terrestrial (ground-feeding), since it is much too bulky in maturity to forage safely high in the trees, and hence it descends to the ground to feed in the daytime. Gorillas prefer, nevertheless, to return to the trees to sleep at night, and young gorillas play happily in the trees until they reach adolescence.

Chimpanzees are both arboreal and terrestrial. Probably because they occupy two ecological niches, the chimps are the most successful of the great apes, and surely they are the most adaptable. The orangutan and all of the gibbons and siamangs are arboreal.

The point of all this is that the existing apes, without exception, are confined by their evolutionary specializations, magnificent but limited to tropical-rain-forest habitats, unable to adapt and survive dramatic changes in their environments, for they are wholly unsuited to open woodlands, scrublands, and plains. Having long since evolved a skeleton that cannot efficiently move about using only the hind legs (the pelvic structure, the large bones of the leg, the foot, and the backbone will not allow a free upright stride), the apes never had the chance to exploit their considerable eye-hand coordination. The fully dexterous hand, with its opposable thumb, freed for a thousand tasks, is peculiar to man and his hominid ancestors. And since in apes the forelimbs are necessary to locomotion, whether in the trees or on the ground, the potential of these higher primates to develop a larger brain was never realized. That the potential exists among the great apes has been proved in recent years by the observations of field biologists such as Jane Goodall, Dian Fossey, and George Schaller, and even more strikingly in laboratory experiments. We now know that young chimps and gorillas are capable of constructing simple sentences using either sign language or computers. (They have no means of *voicing* the words or symbols that their brains wish to communicate.) So these apes seem to be on the very threshold of thinking. Of course, they have been frozen on that threshold for a long long time, perhaps since the time when they remained within the comforting canopy of green forest, accepting its ecological parameters as their shelter, never to dare the risks of open meadows or the glare of the dangerous plains. And there they have remained, hastened only during the last century to premature decline, perhaps even extinction, by the destruction of the fragile habitats at the hands of mankind.

Thus, no species of ape known to science has adapted to open spaces since *Gigantopithecus* ranged the plateaus of southern China more than a million years ago. Likewise, there is no evidence in fossils, or in the existing mosaic that makes up pongid evolution, that any ape has ever successfully adapted to what we call a "temperate" climate, meaning those zones where four seasons follow in more or less predictable succession. The former habitat of *Gigantopithecus,* in Kwangsi, is not particularly cold in winter even today, and several million years ago it was warmer than it is now. When the great Ice Age began and the glaciers began to push south from the polar caps, perhaps that huge primate successfully retreated for a time to the south, or to warmer valleys. Perhaps it could not adapt quickly enough and passed from the face of the changing earth. Perhaps, against all odds, *Gigantopithecus* did survive in small numbers, making a new adaptation to remote montane forests, evolving in the Himalayas and other mountains into a species that still exists, a relic, the legendary *me-teh,* or yeti.

Speculation about what might have been, or what might be, when there is no proof to the contrary is not typical of biologists whose primary concern is focused on what *is.* Sometimes paleontologists engage in careful speculations about what might have been, but they prefer to stay within the outlines of known and accepted evolutionary patterns. Among the Bigfoot fraternity such inhibitions are rare. Even to accept the existence of such a creature requires imaginative speculation. Thus, as there is no proof that the creature doesn't exist, there is none that it does. In the absence of a physical specimen, in the absence of fossil or other evidence, there is a great uncharted ocean of possibilities. This is probably one reason why the pursuit of Bigfoot is so attractive to so many people. The range of possibility allows for any explanation that can be shaped to fit within known scientific principles. The fact that possibility can be a long way from probability is easily dismissed or conveniently forgotten. So there is no shortage of elaborations and theories, some of which make elementary sense, although the majority are often absurd.

Is it possible that some kind of ape, despite the contrary evidence of bionomics and evolution, might have made a hard adjustment and migrated north to survive in the remote mountains and chill forests, eventually to cross over to North America and likewise to survive there furtively in giant form?

It is just possible, though the odds may be a million to one. Nature has a way of filling its niches, including those that man has not yet noticed. Such uncharacteristic adaptation in a tropical species would demand many qualities not shared by any previous—or existing—species of ape. Obviously a thick coat of fur would be necessary, quite different from the rather coarse and relatively sparse coat found on existing apes. It would have to be layered with dense, fine hair close to the skin and longer hair on the outside. A deep layer of subcutaneous fat would help, as it does with bears. And if the ape in question remained large, it would require huge amounts of food. Thus it would have to develop an omnivorous diet similar to that of a bear, with emphasis during summer on green deciduous vegetation, berries, and other edible fruits, supplemented in other seasons by small animals and fish.

But, as most people know, bears hibernate in winter. Even among polar bears, which can easily catch fish, seals, and other meat year round and need no vegetation, the female dens up in winter and emerges only in late March with its young. The American black bear, found in a range that extends from the subtropics to the boreal woods, has adapted within these varying habitats by means of semihibernation, which is shortened or lengthened according to the severity of the winter. Wherever the snow stays through the winter it is simply impossible for such a large omnivore to get enough to eat during the winter months. In Michigan, Minnesota, and Ontario the black bear is not seen from November to April. For about six months it is asleep most of the time, living off body fat stored during a long spring, summer, and fall of lusty eating.

No one to my knowledge has ever suggested that any ape or any large higher primate might hibernate or even semihibernate. It is a concept alien to what is known about the order. Primates of all kinds are, and always have been, exceptionally active species, needing less sleep than many animals, typically diurnal rather than nocturnal. Only a few lemurs and some other very primitive primates are nocturnal. A few primate species have adapted to the lower fringes of the temperate zones, but the list is small. A few macaques, those short-tailed or tailless monkeys of Japan, North Africa, Asia, and formerly of Mediterranean Europe, and, of course, the advanced hominids have done so by means of extraordinary flexibility rather than by means of specialized physical adaptation. The hominids did not adapt to northern climes by means of luxurious fur or a thick layer of subcutaneous fat, and certainly not by hibernation. Rather than becoming less active in the bitter months of winter, the hominids learned effectively to extend their warm-weather activity throughout the year, wearing the skins of other animals for warmth, utilizing tools to extend the range and efficiency of their hunt, organizing their collective energies so that a band of hunters could effectively slaughter large game in great numbers, collecting and storing ripe autumn fruits, and mastering fire. In other words, they have adapted by using the full potential of the growing brain.

Thus, *Homo erectus* fossils, found at the most remote dates only in Africa, have been found at later dates in Java, northern China, the Mediterranean, and Europe. During the interglacial periods *Homo erectus* reached latitude 49° north. No one has seriously suggested that these early men migrated simply by pulling up stakes and moving hundreds or thousands of miles to new locations. Instead expansion into new habitats was carried out by means of *budding,* a process in which a few individuals would hive off from a prospering band and create independent bands in nearby territory. If these groups were successful, the process would continue for as long as each new group could adapt to adjacent marginal zones. The fact that this budding continued and indeed accelerated during a time of dramatic change in the earth's climate (the series of cold waves that we call the Ice Age) is perhaps the most eloquent testimony to hominid flexibility. It could not have been done by means of mere physical adaptation. It was accomplished because these ancestors of man were becoming highly intelligent. They were already on the verge of shaping the natural world to their needs rather than merely adjusting to the natural world.

Thus, to assume that an ape might have adapted and migrated into the Asiatic north, thence across to the North American mountains, there to survive in the form of a giant up to eight feet tall or more, weighing perhaps five hundred to a thousand pounds, is to stretch the odds almost beyond reason. Despite their adaptation to small grains, insects, and certain kinds of seafood readily collected on the shores, the macaques of Japan and the Mediterranean did not move into temperate forests or plains. They established a precarious foothold in the range just beyond the subtropics. Even the langurs of southern Asia, which adapted to relatively cold seasons on the southern Himalayan slopes, did not really venture from their traditional habitat; they remain confined to dense belts of mostly deciduous vegetation where a variety of plants still flourish in what amount to evergreen subtropical forests.

For the moment, let us assume that some kind of ape did make the move. Without the benefit of organized hunting for larger game, such a large primate would have to hunt alone, like a tiger or brown bear, and it would need an exceptional range of plants and animals to support its bulk. If it did not hunt or confine its meat intake to smaller animals, it would require a diet that is at once highly selective—according to season—and broad in scope. In temperate zones, even in the best conditions, edible greenery is not comparable to what is available in a tropical forest. And what of winter? If the ape did not somehow adopt semihibernation, in the manner of bears, what kind of stomach would such an animal need? When people say, "Well, it could browse like a deer," are they aware of how specialized a deer's digestive system is? Deer, like elk, moose, bison, and our domestic cattle, sheep, and goats, are ruminants. They have the potential to survive a northern winter because they have a complex fermenting vat inside their bellies, evolved through thirty million years. It is a system that allows these large-hoofed animals to flourish on green roughage such as grass and twigs that are converted to energy, flesh, muscle, fat, and bone by means of a four-part stomach, composed of the rumen, reticulum, omasum, and abomasum. The food is torn loose or grazed, chewed briefly, and swallowed in a great gulp into the rumen. Bacteria and various microorganisms within the rumen break the roughage down further while the stomach walls knead it gently. In circumstances of plenty the rumen will fill within an hour or less (cattle grazing in lush pasture can fill it in a few minutes). Then, during a period of rest, little cuds of the partly digested material are regurgitated to the mouth, where they are chewed and swallowed again. Further digestion progresses in the rumen and through remaining segments of the stomach. A relatively large amount of waste material, rich in bacteria, is eliminated perhaps a day or two later.

All of these ruminants are prey species that have survived largely because they can eat quickly and hide. Some, like deer and certain antelope, can run fast or leap away. Others, like cattle and bison, have size on their side. But all ruminants possess that fermentation vat that enables them to select a vegetarian diet of incredible variety, adjusted to region and climate. Deer can live on water-related plants in the Florida Keys, on crab apples and gleaned corn in Ohio, on dry grass and coarse shrubs in the arid hills of Arizona, on birch twigs, hornbeam buds, and cedar boughs in Michigan and Maine, on freshwater plants in creeks, on dense deciduous shrubbery in Pennsylvania.

What kind of adaptation within the stomach of our hypothetical Bigfoot could match this? Where would he find the equivalent of the tropic forest's thousand deciduous fruits and succulent leaves, bamboo shoots, soft vines, tree ferns, and sappy roots? Perhaps he could find enough in certain favored regions of northern California, or on Washington's Olympic peninsula. Even there, what would he substitute in winter, when the forest's autumn harvest has gone? Would he gather grubs, snails, frogs, salamanders, fish, and burrowing rodents as substitutes for his arboreal tropic vegetation? Would he perhaps gather acorns and nuts and dry berries and store them squirrellike for winter, building caches in select places, as wolverines have been said to do in advance of winter? Would he gorge on river grasses and swamp sedges in spring and summer, and eat the leaves of trees such as alder, aspen, birch, maple, dogwood, and willow? And during late autumn and in the snows of winter, would he rely on seaside scavenging or browse somehow on juniper and cedar, hemlock and yew, or an occasional rhododendron, sorrel, or laurel? Without a rumen, how would he digest these exceedingly rough leaves and needles?

I think it is safe to assume that such a specialized stomach could not evolve within a mere two or three million years, the shortest period of time required for other, related adaptations if such a large creature were to survive in temperate zones. Even gorillas have no fermentation chamber despite their almost exclusively herbivorous—to be exact, folivorous—diet. When gorillas need even such basic nutrients as vitamin B_{12}, they must turn to the occasional grub, since they cannot synthesize that vitamin. It took the known ruminants thirty million years to get where they are, and, as it is, many fail to survive a hard winter. With a stomach presumably not radically different from that of existing primates—including that of man—the diet of our hypothetical northern ape would be limited, all the more so in the north-central forests.

So, unless our creature hibernates, we are left with the alternative that he has turned largely carnivorous, at least in winter. If so, would smallish rodents, frogs, etc., be enough to sustain such bulk? He would at least occasionally need big game, in the way that mountain lions and wolves do. And, hunting big game, he would be among the predators whose presence is regularly marked by their kills, including—almost inevitably—the occasional domestic beast. Yet there seems to be no great hue and cry among stockmen to number Bigfoot among the hated varmints to be trapped and killed, or poisoned. Nor is there evidence within the supposed ranges of the creature that it has adopted a primarily carnivorous diet for even part of the year. The assumption is that our Sasquatch remains omnivorous, probably almost duplicating the foraging habits of the larger bears. This, of course, brings us back to the necessity of hibernation to get through the winter.

The more one investigates the probabilities, the less likely it seems that some kind of ape could have successfully adapted to the northlands, survived through the several ice ages, and crossed into North America.

What about the relic-humanoid hypothesis, then—that Sasquatch and his Eurasian counterpart(s) are members of the hominid line, of either fairly recent or very ancient divergence from humans?

Our hominid ancestors managed to adjust to northern Eurasian habitats because they learned to clothe themselves in furs, to huddle around fires, cook meat, fashion deadly tools of stone and bone, seek the shelter of caves, and construct their own shelters. Hunting and gathering became efficient because of increased cooperation in larger groups to assure a high-protein diet necessary to keep an active diurnal primate alive amid the freeze. This provided necessary fat, iron, calcium, and the undigested vitamins that are stored in the innards of prey animals (which we moderns foolishly throw away when we butcher). Without the increased abundance of meat, killed in many varieties and by means of an astonishing range of techniques, our hominid ancestors would hardly have made it through one glaciation to the next interglacial period. We must remember that agriculture is a recent invention. Our ancestors would surely have become extinct without the hunt, as did many large mammals in the ice ages.

Furthermore, many of the adaptations that allowed the hominids success were cultural and social, stemming from intelligent action rather than from changes in the body. Except for relatively minor changes, the body of *Homo erectus* was the same as that of *Homo habilis,* and, for that matter, almost identical to that of *Australopithecus afarensis.* The posture remained erect, the stride perhaps improved a bit, and *Homo erectus* might run more efficiently or carry objects more easily over distance.

Modern man is certainly an efficient walker and runner, as any Olympic competition proves. In fact, no mammal except for certain canines—such as wolves, coyotes, wild dogs—can cover greater distances in less time without rest, or without stopping to feed.

And what a marvelous advantage to use the insulating blanket of another animal's hide and hair, while at the same time consuming its flesh. In physical comfort and efficiency alone the payoff had to be enormous. Pity the zoo polar bear in the summer or the common dog in its yard with only a tongue to regulate body temperature on an August afternoon.

With *Homo erectus* and Neanderthal man there was an increase in body size, but the form did not change much. From the fossil evidence of *Australopithecus afarensis,* the hand has scarcely changed at all; nor have the foot, pelvis, and backbone. The bodies of the early hominids were thus preadapted to a remarkable future, fairly well worked out in nature's scheme before we developed our large and troublesome *sapiens* brain.

So the greatest physical alteration was the brain itself. Between *afarensis* and *erectus* the brain size approximately tripled to a late average of about 1200 cc. Neanderthaloids averaged 1500 to 1600 cc., just above the norm for modern humans of 1330 cc., though there is no evidence that they were more intelligent, since they failed to invent the bow and arrow, apparently did not construct artificial shelters or carve and paint from nature.

With the evolution of intelligence and communication by means of symbols that can project not only concrete but abstract ideas, the hominid had presumably become human. So it is probably not merely our use of tools—which several species of animals, including certain birds, use—that distinguishes us from all other animals. Nor is it our rather puny, unspecialized bodies. It is our intelligence that makes the difference. For with this capacity we can *extend* tool use to manipulate the very environment around us, which no other animal can do, and we can cooperatively plan our endeavors and focus our characteristic primate energies to the larger end of alleviating the struggle for food. Thus we have increased our numbers in geometric proportions. This is our triumph, and of course it might be our downfall.

But to return to our question: Is it possible that another species of hominid survived into the present, since we know that at least one species has done so? There are enormous problems of biology, geography, physiology, and ecology attached to this question. Our hominid ancestors, including those that have become extinct, such as the Neanderthaloids, did *not* adapt by means of growing a thicker, more luxurious coat of hair. Neanderthal, like his Cro-Magnon successors, apparently used animal skins to protect his body from cold. He certainly had fire and sophisticated tools fashioned with great precision from bone, wood, fiber, and stone. It is, of course, possible that Neanderthaloids retained thick body hair. The fact that many Caucasians have a thin but visible mantle of hair covering most of the torso, the outsides of the arms, the legs and buttocks, the backs of the hands, sometimes the feet, and all but the upper part of the face might be taken as evidence that certain of our ancestors had extensive body hair. But this is characteristic only among males and is uncommon or nonexistent among other races of man. Besides, such hair is hardly thick enough to serve as insulation. In other words, there is no reason to assume that Neanderthaloids, early or late, possessed an insulating coat of hair akin to that of a bear.

It is true that Neanderthal man possessed a foot that was proportionally broader than that of modern man and one that lacked a pronounced arch. But there is no evidence that the Neanderthal was exceptional in size; in fact, the Neanderthaloid type was on average smaller than *Homo sapiens.* Fossil skeletons show the Neanderthaloids to have been more heavily built, with larger bones; at the places where muscle attachment occurred there are larger protuberances. Still, as many anthropologists have pointed out, Neanderthal man, even in his most pronounced or "classic" form, was not the shuffling apelike monster of early reconstructions. Unfortunately, one of the first fossil skeletons used for reconstruction was that of a severely arthritic middle-aged man who was stooped and bowed from his malady. Worse, the French paleontologist Marcellin Boule, who rebuilt and interpreted the bones in question, made an astonishing series of errors. He misconstructed the bones of the foot to make Neanderthal man appear very like an ape, with the big toe separated from the other toes (like an opposable thumb), thus forcing him to walk on the outside of his feet, in ape fashion. He misinterpreted the knee joint to make it seem that Neanderthal could not fully extend his leg, and he placed the skull atop the curved, misshapen spine in a forward-thrust position. For some reason Boule completely ignored the very large cranial capacity of the skull and focused his attention instead on the low forehead and large brow ridge, assuming therefore that the creature had a low level of intelligence.

It is now regarded as a great tragedy that Boule's reputation was formidable enough to allow him to shape world scientific and public opinion for decades thereafter (his research was published in three volumes between 1911 and 1913). The legacy of that mistake can still be seen in the otherwise fine display of man's evolution in the American Museum of Natural History, in New York City, where the Neanderthal's posture is incorrectly illustrated as only partially erect.

Many other Neanderthal fossils have since been found and reinterpreted. They reveal a hominid of fully erect posture, exactly like that of modern man, although the arms are somewhat longer proportionally and the neck is shorter. The skull has that heavy brow ridge, with the low forehead slanting sharply back. The general appearance, however, is that of a human. It is often said that you might not take a second look if a Neanderthal man (or woman) sat opposite you in a subway, provided that he or she was clothed. My guess is that you would take a second and maybe a third glance, for such a brow and massive head on such a short neck would be unusual. But who, even then, would doubt his or her humanity?

Let us suppose that some Neanderthaloid type did retreat to the most remote forests and mountains when more nimble and successful *Homo sapiens* arrived on the scene. Let us further suppose that these particular Neanderthalers retained a distinctive nature; that they did not interact or interbreed with their taller and more imaginative cousins; that they hid away, fearful of the growing bands of sapiens that encroached on their ancient hunting grounds. In the process they somehow adapted to a life in which instead of hunting large game with neatly fashioned tools, as they had done for thousands of years, they learned to rely on small game, fish, uncooked vegetation, fruits, and nuts. Let us assume a pattern of degeneracy: away from the proficient use of fire; away from the organized and conspicuous family unit or the larger kin-related band; away from the facile and rapid communication of ideas over considerable distances* and toward a more solitary, primitive, constricted existence. What is required is some kind of unheard-of evolutionary reversal.

Given such unlikely degeneracy, there could perhaps be some kind of relic humanoid surviving in remote regions where conditions favor the survival of other relic species. But, if so, how can we account for the fact that the fossil evidence points in the opposite direction—to a situation during the middle- to late-Paleolithic period of Neanderthaloid types coexisting with early *Homo sapiens?* And how do we account for the fact that Neanderthaloids appear to have moved away from specialized forms toward a more *sapiens* type; indeed these fossils are nowadays labeled *Homo sapiens neanderthalensis* and accepted as members of the human species.

Orthodox interpretations of Neanderthal man's place in evolution are so much at odds with the theories of the hominologists that just about the only way we can give credence to the latter's ideas is to accept the possibility that Neanderthaloid fossils represent a species distinct from the line that led to humans. We would have to accept Neanderthalers as creatures with little or no powers of speech, few or very primitive tools, no use of fire, yet surviving even now in the remote parts of two or more continents. Given a certain amount of mental gymnastics, this theory can be made to seem coherent. One would have to assume that the "separation" from the line that gave rise to *Homo sapiens* occurred at a very remote period, making possible a "presapiens" family of which Neanderthal man is a major ex-

---

*We know Neanderthal man could do this because certain stone-chipping techniques were spread across vast expanses of territory.

ample, and of which the unknown hominids today are relic survivals. According to Porshnev, the genera that led to these relic humanoids began with an australopithecine. Porshnev does not say which, but his disciples Bayanov and Bourtsev reject *Paranthropus* as an ancestor to this line, so presumably he means something like *Australopithecus africanus.* Other genera in Porshnev's new line include *Meganthropus* ("giant man"), a name given to fragments of an outsized lower jaw by von Königswald in the late 1930s, though now generally classed as belonging to a slightly smaller kind of *Gigantopithecus.* Also in Porshnev's line are *Pithecanthropus* (the group that includes Peking man and Java man) and the so-called troglodytes, which include the fossil Neanderthaloids and the alleged modern survivals that Porshnev called *Troglodytes recens.*

This appears to be straightforward enough, but the "break" that is assumed by Porshnev between his "presapiens" and the genus *Homo* is arbitrarily based on criteria that are foreign to biological science. To exclude all of the pithecanthropines, for example, from the human family is absurd. In effect Porshnev asks us to throw out the taxonomy that has been painstakingly built up by three generations of scholars and to accept his alternative classifications, no matter how ambiguous, underdefined, or farfetched. Ultimately he asks us to accept his new system on the basis of a purely hypothetical creature.

Porshnev's hypothesis is nothing if not clever. Those who seek a cogent theory that claims an alternative evolutionary process for man *and* for Sasquatch will surely find it satisfying, at least at first glance. But there are so many problems with this hypothesis that it would take a book to detail them, so I'll just note a few. Porshnev and company do not explain what branches of presapiens—or what fossil evidence—might have given rise to our North American "neogiants," or what branches also might have given rise to his troglodytes. Are we to assume that the largest evolutionary manifestation of a presapiens branch to emerge in North America somehow retained an occipital ridge on its skull, making a gorillalike crest on the head, while the smaller, more humanoid troglodytes of Eurasia developed a smooth large skull with a cranial capacity on average larger than that of modern man? And what of the yeti, with its presumed simian foot, so radically different from that of Sasquatch, or that of man? Which putative branch of presapiens did this creature evolve from?

With clever work almost any educated person could concoct a theory that makes some sense, but such an exercise would be nonetheless egregious. Isn't it better simply to say, "Yes, let us by all means search for a specimen, living or dead, but let us not classify it prior to finding it"? I think any thoughtful person who has studied the fossil record—and I emphasize that this is a "record"; these fossils are *physical* evidence—will recognize the fabulously speculative nature of the above formulations. If you have an *a priori* theory to which you must arbitrarily fit the fossil record, you can go on forever, but will any but the most intrepid Bigfoot devotee readily accept all these somersaults through the stony fields of fossil evidence?

Ivan Sanderson seems to have recognized that it would be impossible to explain all of the reported variations in size, location, habitat, behavior, etc., by means of evolution in one family, one line. So he suggested that the creatures have evolved from several different lines, including the ape and human families, and gave us his four separate putative species. As hard as this is to swallow, it at least makes sense in terms of the thousands of reports. Nevertheless, anyone who has plowed through the turgid prose of Sanderson's tome on abominable snowmen will seek in vain for clarity. Facts are mixed with near facts; incredible interpretations of basic zoological principles are interspersed with scores of inconsistencies as Sanderson tries to explain exactly how his four creatures fit into the fossil record. As one reviewer has said, it is as if Sanderson deliberately tried to be disbelieved.

Again, there is only one *known* species of hominid in existence, and that is man. So why does the relic-humanoid hypothesis, in one or another of its elaborations, retain such nagging persistence? I think the answer is evident. With so many reports whose only real consistency is that they describe a hairy creature walking erect on two legs, and with the more or less humanoid shape of the giant footprints in North America and central Asia, some variant of this theory remains the only explanation that makes biological sense. Otherwise we have to seek an explanation within the pongid line of evolution, and we are educated not to expect any surviving ape, known or unknown, to be bipedal.

In fairness, I must admit that within a larger "humanoid" category—leaving out the "relic" part—there are many unexplored possibilities. For the present, one hypothesis will be as good as the next as long as it has internal consistency, imagination, and as long as it fits neatly into the admittedly sparse fossil record. I remain amazed, after having read Bigfoot literature for years, that no one has come up with a better theory than the examples cited. I am tempted to do so here, but of course it would prove nothing.

There is, however, yet another possibility that demands more attention. I have noted that various species of large monkeys have successfully adapted to the forested slopes of the Himalayan massif, sometimes venturing for short times in summer high into the mountains above the tree line. The existence of these langurs in such a habitat (the lower reaches of which, I must emphasize, are nearly tropical) and the indisputable fact that both the ancestral orangutan and the huge *Gigantopithecus* once lived nearby, on the edge of ecological zones that are barely subtropical, would make it possible that a yet-unknown species of ape might survive in the most isolated mountainous canyons. Perhaps such an ape has adapted to an omnivorous style, alternating between the cloud forests and their lush vegetation and the more open alpine region, rich in mosses, lichens, flowers, small shrubs, and small animals. Biologically, most of the Himalayan massif is *terra incognita.* Such factors as the range of edible plants that flourish along the southern flanks of the Himalayas—a range that exceeds even the most favorable of Pacific Northwest habitats—and the relative isolation of the region until only three or four decades ago might account for the survival of such an ape. Perhaps it is related to the ancestral orang, or perhaps it is a smaller and less specialized offshoot of *Gigantopithecus,* or even a descendant of one of the larger dryopithecines.

One might expect, if an unknown ape survives in such a habitat, that it would be of modest size, rather than huge, and exceedingly nimble on all fours, but also able to move rapidly for long distances on its hind legs, thus possessing a characteristic primate sense of balance but with adaptation in favor of scrambling over rocks and crags as well as through the trees. It would almost certainly have to be a terrestrial ape, so in certain circumstances it might resemble a human, with somewhat shorter arms relative to the torso than a gorilla, chimp, or orang. It might leave broad, rather apelike footprints in the snow of high passes in summer. And it would certainly be hairy.

As Peter Matthiessen suggests, the fact that all expeditions in pursuit of such a creature have failed "may only prove that [the] habitat is virtually impenetrable, and that after long centuries of hiding, these rare creatures are exceptionally wary." During his expedition with George Schaller to seek the snow leopard in the Himalayas, Matthiessen had a brief glimpse of a dark creature that jumped behind a boulder, a creature too big for a red panda, quicker than a bear, too dark for a wolf or leopard, too covert for a musk deer. Eventually he settled for the unsatisfactory explanation that it was a musk deer after all, but, he adds, "it is hard to put away the thought of yeti."

Certainly it is harder to put away the idea that an unclassified ape lives in the Himalayas than it is to accept Sanderson's theory about so-called "proto-pygmies," members of the hominid line.

Still, there are problems. Yeti tracks apparently indicate bipedal locomotion and do not suggest alternation between a two- and a four-legged gait, which is what one might expect with such a mountain ape. Could nature have given rise to a large primate that does not properly fit into either the hominid or pongid families, walking entirely on its hind legs? Are we indeed prejudiced against this latter possibility because we do not want to admit the possibility of *another* bipedal primate besides ourselves? And if such a creature could survive in the Himalayas, can we entirely discount the possibility, however remote, that it, or a similar creature, also migrated to North America, where Bergmann's rule might account for its greater size?

We seem to have come back to square one. What we must remember is that the most sensible, most biologically cogent, most consistent theory regarding but *one* of the many alleged hairy creatures, within only *one* geographic and ecological zone, is still only a theory. We are faced with the fact that we lack physical evidence. Yet when all the pros and cons are laid out and debated *ad infinitum,* who would deny that the mere idea of the existence of Bigfoot, in whatever form, whatever variation, has inherent possibilities that go beyond mere curiosity or adventure?

5. Conundrums and Controversies

꘎ ꘎ ꘎ ꘎ ꘎ ꘎ ꘎ ꘎ ꘎ ꘎ ꘎ ꘎ ꘎ ꘎ ꘎ ꘎ ꘎ ꘎ ꘎

All controversies have arguments to support both sides; whether these ... seem plausible depends, crudely, on whether one has made a prior commitment to any stance. All members of our society agree on the rules of reasoning; disagreement ... generally stem[s] not from faulty reasoning but from differing premises. The ideal of a scientist as a dispassionate observer is not realistic: we all reject massive amounts of sensory data which we class as irrelevant.

BILL HARVEY
in *The New Scientists,* March 1978

You ask me, there's nothing to it. Most of these Bigfoot people have got to be a bunch of crackpots.

HUNTER
in Benzie County, Michigan, January 1979

꘎ ꘎ ꘎ ꘎ ꘎ ꘎ ꘎ ꘎ ꘎ ꘎ ꘎ ꘎ ꘎ ꘎ ꘎ ꘎ ꘎ ꘎

Seeking information on Bigfoot, I have come to the unlikely setting of Michigan's populous and fertile thumb. Wayne King's neat house is set well back from a paved highway not far from the nondescript village of Millington. To me this farmland is familiar country, as I grew up not far away in Genesee County. Now in late September only stubbled fields mark the recent harvest. There are scattered woodlots, low on the wide horizon, and warm, shallow lakes off to the northeast. Once this unprepossessing landscape was dotted with prosperous small farms, but now most of the good land is leased or owned by a handful of large-scale farmers or huge conglomerates. Most of the people in the region work in factories in nearby Flint or Saginaw. King himself does so, but I am with him because he has widely advertised himself in the state's press as the director of the "Michigan Bigfoot Information Center."

King greets me in the warm light of the morning sun. He is a heavyset middle-aged man, good-humored, stolid, with thinning dark hair. He reminds me of some of the men I grew up with; his manner is respectful but also solicitous, with perhaps a hint of suspicion regarding this stranger who has come asking questions about Bigfoot. Apparently the Bigfoot Information Center is in his house, for he directs me at once to his large basement, where an office is located. It is an enclosed space taking up a whole corner, neatly appointed. A small leatherette couch faces a desk angled across a corner. The desk is uncluttered, but the walls are covered with an array of clippings, photographs, drawings, maps—all Bigfoot paraphernalia. There are several file cabinets, and against one wall in deep shadow is a glass case of some sort. I notice a huge plaster cast of a Bigfoot track, displayed near a row of books about the monster.

King brings coffee. He is happy to chat for a while about the unremarkable fact that I grew up not so far away. We are of the same generation but apparently share no mutual friends. We are both eager to get down to business. Soon King flips on a tape recorder.

"For my own protection, you know."

He does not want me to make my own tape; nor can I take any photographs. King asks for proof of my identity and background, my reasons for investigating the Bigfoot matter. I produce my driver's license and explain myself. His manner changes perceptibly. What I have said about my education and background obviously does not please him. A knowing smile appears as I explain how my publisher commissioned me to research this fascinating subject without bias. Quickly King explains his own credentials, how he began to study the creatures many years ago, only gradually becoming the expert he now is. He notes that he is associated with an organization headed by

John Green called the British Columbia Information Service Exchange, a clearinghouse for Bigfoot data collected all over the continent. There are few people in this business, King warns, who can be trusted.

Why? I want to know.

Too many people, King explains, are out only for themselves or for money. I must be careful in my investigation to listen only to the genuine experts, those, like John Green and René Dahinden, who have proved their worth.

I say that I am a bit nonplussed by this, by what appears to be deep factionalism within the ranks of the Bigfoot experts. What are the criteria for an independent investigator? How can I distinguish between one group and the next?

King is more animated now. The room is dim, the light just adequate near the couch for my note-taking. As he talks, King holds a small pointer-light in his hand. From time to time he directs its beam to a picture, a clipping, a letter tacked to a bulletin board, a file drawer ("In there are hundreds of validated depositions about sightings right in this state"), a photograph of a huge Bigfoot carved in wood. I am myself a little ill at ease because of his increasingly defensive manner. Perhaps King sees me as a potential critic, not to be trusted. He is taking pains to speak carefully, and I am uncertain whether he will continue to cooperate. And there is something undefined but keenly felt about this elaborate basement office, this Bigfoot Information Center; it is almost as if I have been there before.

I will learn soon enough, King says, whom to believe.

"Do you know where the name Bigfoot got started?" he asks suddenly.

I see at once that he is testing my basic knowledge, feeling me out. He has already expressed strong views against the establishment critics, the "university people" who help keep people in the dark about the Sasquatch. A lot of information is suppressed. But now people are learning the truth and coming forward with their own stories.

"Especially in the last year and a half," King adds, "people feel that there is somebody to rely on." He has scores of depositions on tape, carefully validated, that prove this. Some newspapers, such as the *Midnight Globe* and the *National Enquirer,* have helped, too. They will print truthful stories about what is really happening.

I remark that the press coverage of the phenomenon intrigues me. For example, there is the recent incident in Byron, Michigan, in which a reported sighting of a Bigfoot, widely covered in local newspapers, was discovered by the sheriff to have been a prank perpetrated by a fellow in a gorilla suit. Newspapers have also widely printed this information. My intention is to make a point about the basic unreliability of newspaper accounts, especially if published in sensationalist papers. Even local newspapers seem to enjoy playing a game with the phenomenon. But King wants to make a different point. That Byron story, he says angrily, is a deliberate attempt by the authorities in Shiawassee County to "keep down the pandemonium." Having worked as a youth at a summer camp near Byron, I know the town fairly well and can scarcely imagine that sleepy place being the scene of pandemonium of any kind. But King goes on. He intimates that it is obvious to those privy to the "facts" of that case that no human being in a monkey suit could have escaped so easily, wading in the night up the Shiawassee River, eluding the sheriff's deputies. Actually, I had often canoed that very river during the early 1950s when its drainage was greater and the river had fewer subdivisions and paved-over regions. Even then it was shallow enough for one to easily wade through most of its upper reaches between Linden and Shiawasseetown, including Byron. But King gives me no chance to express my misgivings. He produces a map of Michigan Bigfoot sightings and points out that there have been similar sightings at other spots in Shiawassee County, and in nearby Ingham and Livingston counties. King assures me that he has personally screened many witnesses and there are depositions in his possession, all validated. King indicates his file cabinets, and explains that he and his associates have devised new techniques to determine whether people are telling the truth or lying. Further intrigued, I ask his permission to study some examples. It would be fascinating to compare notes, since I know of no specialized nonelectronic technique, beyond my own sense of veracity and my training in the use of oral traditions, to tell when people are lying. Any new method that goes beyond independent corroboration would be immensely useful to scholars, IRS investigators, parents, and cops. Besides, the depositions sound fascinating.

"Sorry. Only association members have access to these," King replies. He hastens to explain that until I have been "in the business" of the Bigfoot search for many years, I cannot really be considered an expert. People are tested for many years, he says, before they are accepted.

"We must beware of self-indoctrinated, self-ordained 'investigators,'" King continues with a pointed glance in my direction. "When I began my own investigations, unbeknownst to me, Mr. John Green was watching from BC, and as I made public statements about the creature being carnivorous in the winter season, etc., with fish as a major part of its diet, with rodents especially, etc., I was accepted into association."

My thought is that Mr. Green out in British Columbia must be perspicacious indeed to keep such close tabs on Mr. King's activities from afar. I inwardly resolve to find out more about this apparently far-flung network of Bigfoot investigators who exchange arcane information that cannot be studied independently by scholars. Cautiously, I again request to see the relevant files, at the very least to be allowed to look at those pertinent to the Byron incident. Without access to these how can anyone accept the implication that perhaps the local authorities in Shiawassee County have deliberately engaged in diversionary actions in order to make an allegedly "genuine" sighting appear to be a hoax? King stands firm. His files are not open to just anyone, he explains. He ticks off more names and repeats his opinion that the sighting in Byron was genuine as originally reported.

But what about Bigfoot information, generally, in Michigan? I inquire. Surely it is an extraordinary thing, even one such sighting in such a populous state, especially in the southern industrial region.

"There are upwards of three hundred Sasquatch in the Lower Peninsula of Michigan alone," King states with emphasis.

He waits for this to sink in and launches a detailed exposition on the important differences between what he calls his own "contentions," which are not yet proved, and "known facts," such as the existence of Bigfoot. On cue I express surprise at such a figure. Wouldn't one expect more in the Upper Peninsula? Yes, he agrees, there are probably more there.

"Michigan is surrounded by water," King says, to my surprise. "And there are ninety-seven varieties of edible plants and trees that are identical to those in the Pacific Northwest, plus the range of dampness and soil conditions are similar, plus all the shoreline and the conditions that prevail on shorelines."

Wondering how much he knows about the complex subject of littoral ecology, I withhold the obvious questions. King is talking rapidly now. I am clearly being instructed. At one point, while discussing the distribution of Sasquatch in Michigan, he abruptly adds, "They are everyplace else, also."

This I find even more extraordinary. But since I have an expert before me, I ask him what he means by this—everyplace in the United States, or North America, or the world, or just Michigan?

King leans toward me across the dim room, engaging my eyes. Clearly I must play the pupil role and not interrupt so freely.

"The population of Sasquatch is on the rise, sightings are increasing every year, every month, and they are being sighted in zones where none were seen before."

This rising population of Sasquatch, he explains, is connected to an increase in their ranges. The vast increase in validated reports proves this, especially in the years since true Sasquatch experts like himself, John Green, and others have begun validating reports, eyewitness accounts, and footprint evidence of this "*Gigantopithecus* ape."

King leans back. It is obviously appropriate now to ask another question. I wonder if perhaps the Bigfoot creature might belong not to the pongid line but rather to the hominid line. Without hesitation he replies, "No. It isn't human; like I said, it's some kind of ape." I ask a few more questions along this line, but I sense again that a different tack is in order. King needs no prompting; he is ready to explain how the creatures survive in Michigan.

"Mr. Wylie, if you are any kind of outdoorsman, you will admit you've seen many strange rock piles in the middle of nowhere; maybe you thought it was from some earlier farm, but not with all those old trees around. Didn't you ever wonder what they were? Well, they are moved there by Sasquatch to trap rodents, snakes, and small edible animals."

Furthermore, he explains, the creature will even attract beavers in special traps set in riverbanks. Seeing my eyebrows raise again, King adds, with asperity, "This can't be denied. We have proof."

King sits back, waiting for my inevitable question, his hands folded across his stomach. So I ask for an example of the proof. Finally, I am becoming accustomed to the rules of the game. I restrain a tendency to grin. But King does not: His broad face breaks into a brilliant smile.

"What can you offer us in return?"

And it doesn't take long to find out what I might offer. There is a great need of money so that King and his associates can buy a "sniper scope," an infrared night detector like those used in Vietnam by the army to detect the movement of enemy soldiers. Such a device, he explains, "would be a most valuable asset to our research operation and progress." With it he and his colleagues might be able to spot and shoot a specimen.

King says he has himself been close to Sasquatch many times. He has sound recordings of one near Lake Ann and some from near Lansing. He has seen two, near Kingston, in September of 1977—a mother and offspring. There was plenty of physical evidence, too, since the two creatures were feeding off apple trees, using two sixty-pound boulders for "leverage, to reach up from and get apples." He had been called to the scene as an expert; he had seen their eyes as he arrived. He also recorded the sounds of these specimens.

Did he then have a chance to shoot? I ask.

"At that time I didn't have my rifle, so we couldn't shoot. And at that time our intentions were different; we weren't yet ready to kill one."

He points to a rifle case in the corner of the room. In the course of our conversation King has alluded to what he calls the mistaken policy of many Bigfoot hunters not to shoot a specimen if the chance arises. Along with John Green, he has changed his mind. Now it is necessary, he says, to prove to the skeptics that the creature is there.

But what about conservation? I wonder. Couldn't this set a bad precedent? Peter Byrne, in Oregon, a former big-game hunter himself, has argued persuasively against acquiring a specimen by shooting one. At least one major government body, the U.S. Fish and Wildlife Service, has acted to require protection of the Sasquatch, should one be discovered, fearful that undisputed evidence of its existence would encourage curiosity-seekers or hunters who might endanger its continued existence.

King is not impressed.

"Man is domesticated to the point of almost putting himself out of existence," he proclaims with gusto.

I wonder what this means, so King explains further.

"Folks just won't look at the truth objectively, so we may be doomed."

I am at a loss for words. King has become progressively restless during these hours. So have I, but I have moved from my couch only a few feet to take a closer look at certain clippings and other displays. King's pointer-light is in frequent action now, and though the day has progressed past noon, in the dark basement it seems to me almost as if night has fallen.

Suddenly I realize why this basement office has given me a sense of *déjà vu.* While growing up, I had often seen similar basement arrangements, nicely paneled, well appointed, everything in its place, where workingmen pursued their hobbies. But King is not making chairs, or tying flies, or polishing stones. He is obviously embarked on a quest.

He is also steeped in the stories of Michigan's Bigfoot, and he begins to regale me with some of the most significant incidents. Michigan, he proclaims, is the only place where an account of bodily attack by a Sasquatch has been reported, documented, and corroborated, by himself. Well, not exactly a successful attack, but at least an attempt. The incident, he says, involved three National Guardsmen from Ohio who were chased into an armored personnel carrier. The Sasquatch, trying to gain entrance while the men huddled inside, broke off the antenna, so outside communication was impossible. Finally the men escaped and they had to tell a civilian to call for help. A deputy sheriff of Crawford County responded and interviewed the men.

King cannot, of course, reveal the names of the men involved, or allow me to see the relevant depositions. I'd have to pay for the use of such important data, but the incident, he notes, is a matter of record.

More important, in King's opinion, is an incident that took place in the spring of 1977 in Benzie County, near Lake Ann. This involved the former state trooper with the memorable name of Zane Gray, who discovered unmistakably genuine tracks of a Sasquatch behind his new house, and who also found real physical evidence—namely, a large dropping. King says he has himself interviewed and validated this case, as he has many others, and he has also talked to a woman named Mrs. Browning, who lives just down the road from Gray, who has seen a Bigfoot.

Furiously taking notes, since King does not want me using my own tape recorder, I suggest tentatively that the Lake Ann case seems exceptional in many respects; I have, of course, heard of it previously. He brightens perceptibly. Yes, it is a very good example.

"Look, you keep saying the scientists and all them people keep asking for physical evidence. I want to show you something."

King's pointer-light moves in a sweep across the room, coming to rest on a letter pinned to the bulletin board.

"Go on, read it. It is self-explanatory."

I rise and move to the wall. King's dot of light directs my eyes. It is a letter on Michigan Department of Natural Resources stationery, signed by a Dr. John Stuht. The letter makes it clear that the sample of fecal matter investigated contains horsehair, and possibly deer hair. I want to know what the implication of this is. Still not fully accustomed to the nature of such evidence, I add that it seems to me a very inconclusive letter, since it falls short of identification.

Triumphantly, King smiles.

"How can they identify an unknown creature that they know nothing about?"

I am quite at a loss for words.

King leans back in his chair again, fiddles with something, and the room begins to grow brighter. No, not the room itself. The glass case behind and to the right of his desk begins to glow. Soon it is brilliantly illuminated. King motions me to move to the dome. His gesture is expansive.

"There! You asked about physical evidence. There it is."

I am gazing in wonder at a rather large brown pile of shit, sealed within a glass case. The room is bathed in the reflected glow of the shrinelike display, and the circular pile of fecal matter is unmistakably there, all right. I am inwardly pleased that the deposit is inside the glass. It looks dry enough, however, very much like a cow pie.

The interview winds down thereafter. Over three hours have gone by and King has regaled me with a torrent of alleged details about Bigfoot. He has revealed his contention that the creature's eyes vary in color as a result of differences in the sexes. He has told me he is studying Sasquatch sounds, including a presumed "language"—an ancient dialect, according to King, allegedly understood by Bigfoot as well as by various Indians. There are revelations about the relationship of the Michigan Bigfoot to the southern skunk ape of the Bayou country, which, King assures me, has three rather than five toes. Furthermore King has informed me that Michigan has led all other states in validated sightings of Bigfoot during the first third of 1978, with more than six hundred in the last twenty years—of which King claims to have checked out sixty—and more than six hundred "confirmed" tracks and print specimens. As I prepare to leave, I wonder what Michigan's active zoologists would make of this extraordinary information. Wildlife ecologists capable of keeping track of the fluctuating population of the elusive and endangered fisher, or the timber wolf, would presumably be falling all over themselves at King's evidence of several hundred gigantic bipedal apes.

King is again cordial as he walks me up the stairs and into the sunny September afternoon. There is a red-tailed hawk soaring off to the east, in the direction of Otter Lake, where I swam as a boy so many years ago. We pause to shake hands. King has a final word as I get into my car.

"You tell your publisher to help us with financial support, and you will get your money's worth. Without our help and our information, you won't get far in your investigation."

It is high autumn in northern Michigan when I find Zane Gray at his busy John Deere dealership, a few miles south of Traverse City. Gray is a soft-spoken man of unassailable reputation in the county that he now serves as sheriff. Like his famous namesake, he is an experienced outdoorsman and a lifelong hunter. And, with twenty-six years of distinguished service behind him in the Michigan State Police, a high-quality outfit, Gray is one of the northland's better trackers. Behind his tall, well-muscled frame and handsome face there is obvious and unadorned intelligence. Gray is helpful by nature, sincere, an active born-again Christian whose language is straightforward and blunt. The impression one gets in his presence is one of quiet rectitude and competence. Gray is not the kind of man who would conceive of a hoax, let alone carry it out. He lacks the poverty of spirit for such foolishness.

Nevertheless the strange events that occurred that dry May in 1977 have created an unsolved puzzle, and Gray's instinct to bring things out into the open has resulted in unwanted and surely unwelcome publicity for him and his family. He greets me in his busy office with just enough diffidence so that I will know the relative degree of importance that he attaches to the incident.

Almost at once he points out, in chuckling good humor, that he had once been sent on a panther hunt when he was a state trooper. Several people were scared to death, he recalled, by reports of a "big panther" running around in the woods. Eventually he and other troopers flushed out a medium-size tomcat, thus ending the scare. "No more panther hunts after that," Gray says, and laughs. But then he adds, seriously, that these huge manlike tracks behind his son's house were something else again.

His experience was clearly genuine. Within minutes I am reasonably convinced that Gray, his wife, and his family could not collaborate to perpetrate such a hoax. At the end of perhaps an hour of close questioning and note-taking, studying the neat plaster cast that Gray made of one of the huge footprints and talking with two of his sons, I am convinced that this Lake Ann incident is indeed typical of the most celebrated Bigfoot reports. By itself, the evidence seems compelling, even persuasive, at least at first sight. I have already read through several newspaper reports of the incident, so I know already that one of the major sources of information was Wayne King. I have also concluded that this strange story nicely illuminates the most common aspects of the Bigfoot phenomenon, in terms of the nature of the evidence itself and of the participants, and because of its contradictory, almost paradoxical impact on the surrounding community.

The case has all the necessary ingredients. It occurs within one of Michigan's "hot zones" of reported Bigfoot activity, according to King and his associates. It is "backed" by the testimony of a local man of high reputation for honesty and reliability. Several people have seen the tracks, and more than one good casting has been made. There is even a short color film of the tracks, made right after their discovery. There is apparent independent testimony, by an unconnected person not far away, regarding strange odors. There is a reported eyewitness, who saw a Bigfoot in the region during the same period. There is a span of time between the first event, the strange noises that woke the Gray family, and the last relevant event, the finding of the large dropping.

As our interview proceeds I discern that Gray—although quite certain about what he has seen (tracks and fecal matter) and certain that his wife and family have heard something in the night—does not in any way fit the true-believer category. He is not even a Bigfoot buff. He is openly puzzled by many of the problems connected to the several events, and he professes skepticism about the entire matter. Why, he asks, has no one yet found positive proof, not a single carcass?

Yes, his son Dave explains, entering the conversation briefly, how is it that within a matter of a few days, Michigan's Bigfoot expert, that fellow named Wayne King, arrived with two companions to question all the participants—all of the Grays, Mrs. Browning, and others. King, he notes, had also attempted to lure the creature from behind Dave's house, which was still without a roof at that point. The weather that night was awful; since the spring rains had finally come, King and his compatriots claimed the next day that they lured the creature to within about fifty yards, and also said they had tape recordings of the weird sounds the creature made. Dave thinks King used rotten fish as bait. The rain supposedly washed away any tracks.

I see that Dave and his brother Bill are almost scornful of the incident. Such attitudes have certainly not been represented in the press accounts, and are at odds with King's version of events. The Grays are excellent witnesses, but I am not surprised to discover that their witness is not necessarily supportive of the viewpoint popularly represented in the media.

Meanwhile, Gray has pointed out that only three people outside his immediate family even knew where the new houses were being built, and the houses are invisible from the backcountry road that leads to their driveways. The tiny road, he notes, is rarely traveled, even in summer, though in deer season there are hunters. The cross-state "horse and hiking" trail cuts through the huge state forest along the same road, so there are also occasional backpackers and a few riders, but the region is very private and secluded. This, Gray says, is one of the reasons he and his son have built new houses there. How could a prankster know about the new houses? No outsider even knew they existed.

Then Gray interrupts his own narrative. "I remember that previous to the events of May 22–23 and May 28, there had already been talk about Bigfoot. That fellow Wayne King had an article about it in the Traverse City paper [the *Record Eagle*]." Furthermore, King had interviewed Gray's uncle, the Rev.

John Bare, a lifelong resident and respected "old-timer" who had presumably heard strange noises. Reverend Bare, who lives on Upper Woodcock Lake, is a towering woodsman of enduring reputation, a man whose reaction to all the hullabaloo was to point in humorous mockery to his own very large feet.

This seems important to me, so I wonder whether the fact of King's previous visit to the area, plus his interview with Bare, combined with the fact that the Gray family had been staying in the "Bare's Den" cabin shortly after, might at least raise serious doubts. Gray agrees at once, noting his many years of police experience to back up my point. But he adds, "Those tracks came by the corner of the house past a pine tree at the northwest corner of the new foundation and went about half the length of the house, and then over the bank to the northeast and down into the woods again. A big step came up the hill, up about two feet in a matter of five feet. No human could have done it, not even on stilts, and a branch of that pine tree angles there toward the house, and that would have made it impossible for a man on stilts." This, Gray explains, is what bolstered his opinion that it would be "extremely difficult if not impossible to fake such tracks. Whatever made those tracks was on them."

Yet when I suggest that no matter how convincing the evidence of the tracks might seem, we still have no good physical evidence, Gray agrees amiably.

"Like I said, that manure surprised me, but I'm bothered with all these hunters, too. Nothing unusual is ever identified, photographed, or shot, or any rabbit dogs or coon dogs, or rabbit hunters, or the like, covering all that scrub, they never turn anything up. Even the bodies of missing people are found, usually by dogs. They find carrion quickly."

Our conversation is broken by business matters, and Zane Gray busies himself with a customer. Outside, the October wind is blowing the rain at a sharp angle against the huge windowpanes. Traffic on the highway in front of the John Deere building is sparse, and passing cars leave a billowing wake of water. I am in no hurry to go out into that weather again, so I sip my second cup of strong coffee.

Zane's strapping son Dave rejoins me.

"How come King is always rumored to be around before or during the period of the sightings?" he asks rhetorically.

Dave's large frame is relaxed. He looks at me with that same keen and penetrating gaze his father has. Slowly his serious, handsome face breaks into a grin. He shrugs his large shoulders; again his actions are a mirror of his father's.

Like his father, he has work to do. Enough time in a busy workday has been spent on tales and speculations. There are more serious matters to attend to.

Before I leave, it is agreed that I will call and come back later. The Grays are curious about what I might find, and I resolve to follow up as soon as possible.

My talk with Gray and sons would normally be enough to satisfy most investigators of impartial bent. The seed of doubt regarding the whole Lake Ann incident has found fertile ground. It seems to me clear enough that certain Bigfoot hunters dedicated to the proposition that the creature exists in Michigan had ample motive, and plenty of opportunity, in this case. But there are nagging problems still. For one, King himself happily suggested that I contact Gray. Why would he direct me to a hoax?

So I come back for another interview, this time to the Gray residence. It is a cold and rainy day again, the woods drenched under a dark November sky, not the most pleasant of conditions. Gray is helpful and at once directs me to the site of the tracks behind his son's house, showing me the pine tree, the projecting branch, the steep slope, and the place where the tracks descended and disappeared down the brush-choked hill that falls away to the creek bottom. Later I hike through the area, drenched through jacket and jeans, before returning to the warmth of the Gray house and more coffee.

Much of the forest is indeed rough. A quick survey of the flora reveals it to be typical Michigan secondary woods with stands of beech maple, mixed with basswood on the higher ground, and a few ancient pines towering above. I note a few great vestigial hemlocks farther down, nearer the bottom. There are scattered cedars and some tamarack in the low, swampy creek bed, but nothing I cannot hike through or by-pass. In early November there is considerable browse for animals like deer; an occasional wild cherry in a clearing, though the tiny fruit is gone; a raspberry thicket near some dying slippery elms, their ghostlike trunks huge and white; also supporting woodbine and wild grape, their fruits gone, too. There is a sparse understory near the little creek, of mixed tag alders and some willow, and lots of big-toothed aspens are scattered on small mounds where the stream sweeps around. Even where growth is clustered close you can see directly through. I walk up to a few clumps of stunted juniper and see plenty of hornbeam saplings; their buds are being cropped already by the deer. The darker green of a few ground-hugging yew can be seen where the slopes rise into the higher woods. On the forest floor it is mostly open and wet. I have difficulty traversing only in a few places, because old wind-blown trees have fallen in random fashion. I can see that a good tracker would have little trouble in winter in this terrain.

I was to return later to the same region on a clear day in December, between the first melting snowfall and the final onslaught of winter, to try to take advantage of the brief but pleasant thaw that bares the earth for the last time till April. This time I hiked in from the west and sought the old railroad grade. There, much of the woods is very tumbled and rough, the kind of secondary scrub that hunters love because it shelters so many animals but the kind of terrain that hikers avoid. It is soon obvious, this second time, that access to the Grays' houses would not be enormously difficult for an experienced woodsman with a compass or a minimal sense of direction. There is cover in abundance for a large animal, but certainly not the kind of extensive and impenetrable cover that a creature as huge as Bigfoot might readily use. White cedar swamps are usually virtually impassable to humans, but certainly not to dogs, and only the largest swamps will discourage a determined hunter who knows local topography. On this clear December day my impression is that the region might conceivably hide such a giant creature, but not for long. Like any large omnivorous mammal, it would have to range widely to survive. Its very bulk would surely demand a range exceeding that of a black bear.

Furthermore, most of the greenery and autumn color is gone, except for the scattered evergreens and the thick cedar swamps. In most places the line of sight extends for yards without major obstruction, a typical condition in the winter woods of the area. Benzie County is too far north for even the occasional buckeye of my childhood, or for wild plum, or for those big crabapple thickets with their swaths of little autumn apples, though you might find a single crab, or maybe a hawthorn. Rather far north, too, for hackberry, and I search in vain. A few stubby oaks are clustered in sandy places, unimpressive. Some currant bushes and bearberry and other flowering shrubs are scattered in low places, but the fruits are gone. Of vegetable food there is an abundance of evergreens and the roughage of deciduous branches, bark, and twigs. But there are few leaves in December, and soon the dry grasses will be snow-covered. Small, nonhibernating, omnivorous mammals might find forage here. With luck and a good "yarding" area in dense cedars, deer will also do well enough; perhaps two thirds of them will survive a hard winter. Yet it seems no mystery to me that a bear cannot survive the winter in this land without denning up in semihibernation, to live off its stored fat.

I reflect that most of Michigan is quite "new," geologically. The patterns of drainage are recent and ever-changing. The faunal and floral communities are also new in the sense that it has been only a few thousand years since the last glaciers retreated. In fact, at least since the last glaciation, man too has been present—albeit in limited numbers, until the coming of the European settlers—among other established animals. Winters in this land are long, and summers last scarcely three months at best; there is hardly a spring at all. The interval between summer's harvest and the first lasting snow is scarcely ten weeks. Still, this habitat has supported large ungulates in abundance and—until very recently, when industrial man wiped them out—the carnivores that prey on them. A few coyotes roam the woods of Michigan's Lower Peninsula (they are abundant only in the Upper Peninsula), having apparently occupied the niche vacated by the timber wolf. But among the larger, browsing, omnivorous mammals only the black bear is found this far north. There are no wild boars, as in parts of the Appalachians and the southland where they were introduced years ago, and no feral pigs, either. An omnivorous adaptation, among the larger mammals, would not seem to be favored in this region.

Still, I am aware that there is a fairly narrow belt extending up Michigan's western coast, along Lake Michigan, where the growing season is longer, even as far as the extremity of the magnificent Leelanau Peninsula, where fruit trees, especially cherries, thrive well beyond their usual northern boundary. This is because of the moderating effect of the lake, which holds off winter's worst cold for a few miles inland and which likewise prevents any premature flowering in spring. But this pleasant corridor has long been haunted by humans. For many hundreds of years, perhaps thousands, it has been occupied by corn-planting Indians, whose most dangerous enemy was not the climate but the raiding hunter-gatherer Indians (of related tongue and custom) who descended on their cornfields from the north and from other less favored regions, coming down the dune-fringed shores of Lake Michigan in war canoes during the glorious harvest time. If Bigfoot lurked in the woodlands of this more favored zone, he must have been crowded indeed; surely he, too, would have raided the fields and provoked memorable, bitter legends.

I cannot claim that my hikes lead to any firm conclusions. But Ivan Sanderson's heroic attempt to equate what he calls MLF (myths, legends, and folklore) about abominable snowmen with the science of ecology, and especially with phytogeography—the science of plant distribution—seems to me very difficult to apply in these northern woods.

At the moment, however, my major concern is not the probability of Bigfoot's existence in the region; my concern is focused instead on the increasing possibility of an out-and-out hoax. The honest skepticism of the Grays and their willingness that I pursue the case further has been greatly encouraging. I am not surprised a few weeks later when I receive a lead by phone from Mrs. Gray, who has casually discussed the matter with an old friend. This man professes to know another person who claims to know the very fellow who "laid down those phony tracks."

Such indirect sources are altogether characteristic in the Bigfoot search, but I am intrigued enough to start telephone interviews. After several wild-goose chases I finally net an interview with a young man from Beulah, a lifelong resident who is completely candid in his smiling disdain for the whole flap. From the beginning he claims no knowledge of any connection between the "guys who laid down the fake footprints" and any downstate Bigfoot expert, but he unhesitatingly states that the youthful pranksters in question had planned the whole thing, had got together in a garage to build the contraptions and went out to make the tracks. Presumably inspired by earlier talk about Bigfoot that resulted from King's earlier visits and interviews and the ensuing newspaper stories, the boys set out to pull a prank, nothing more, and none of them expected it to become such a big deal.

I wonder out loud if my informant might himself be one of the young fellows in question. He only grins quickly and says that he would have told the newspapers it was a hoax had he been a party to it himself. He has no doubt that those responsible have had a chuckle over it, anyway. He is obviously rather bemused by my interest; he had assumed that everyone knew it was all a joke, though some local merchants might have reasons to perpetuate the hoax as a way to attract tourists. It is a fact that Bigfoot T-shirts have been sold in nearby shops.

Can he give me any names, so I might check out his information? I ask. This he does at once. I will not use these names here, but they fit neatly with the basic outlines of the case as I have investigated it. The fact of the prank is now self-evident. Only odds and ends need to be checked out. It is hardly worth the effort to pursue the case further.

There are other aspects of the Lake Ann incident that show the evidence to be unreliable. There are discrepancies between what witnesses say and what has been so widely reported in the media. Mrs. Browning, for example, willingly came forth with her account of a strong odor in the night, and her experience some years before of seeing the large, dark creature on the road near Charlevoix. But she is adamant about having seen nothing whatsoever in the region of her home, which is not far from the Grays'. She is equally unwilling even to use the term "Bigfoot" to describe the dark shape that she had glimpsed so long ago. Her view is that her experience has been blown wholly out of proportion.

"When that man, King, got wind of it and came over to visit, then it got all distorted," she says, careful to make certain that I get it right. She does not want to be portrayed again as a witness to something so specific as a particular animal, whatever it is called. She repeats again that what she saw that night was unidentified. She is very suspicious of any attempt to force her admittedly strange experience into the mold of evidence that Bigfoot is out there. She repeats that what she saw might well have been a man in a costume. "I just don't know," she states flatly.

Even accounting for the possibility that such eyewitnesses might not be ready to believe what they see—perhaps because their experience somehow numbs their faculties of discretion, observation, and comparison, or because they are worried about the disbelief of their peers—one cannot pretend that information like this is evidence.

The further the investigation goes, the more slippery, the more ephemeral, the data becomes. Expectations of direct testimony wind up being flitting shadows, impressions, uncertain opinions. The only connection in the maze of information is the fact that negative evidence increases at each stage. The probability of fraud becomes inescapable.

For many weeks, I have sought an elusive fellow of contradictory reputation through at least two counties, a man widely reported to have seen Bigfoot in the woods near Lake Ann at about the time of the Gray footprint. His name has been provided by the Bigfoot hunters, by the Gray family, who know him well, and finally by a bartender some twenty-five miles from Lake Ann who was present when the fellow told several drinking buddies about his strange experience. Scores of others, I am told, have heard the same story. The man is also known to be a self-proclaimed expert on the creature.

Finally I locate his girl friend, but she is wary. The man simply cannot meet me, but a phone call is arranged.

From the first he claims no special knowledge. Yes, he has read about Bigfoot, and has an interest in the subject. He was intrigued by the footprints found by the Grays. But, no, he has never seen the damned thing himself. He doesn't know where I got that idea.

I ask whether or not he has spoken to friends. I note the names of certain taverns.

No. They are mistaken. Maybe people misunderstood what he was saying. He has never seen any Bigfoot, though he thinks the creatures exist all right. They are out there for sure. He has known and talked with King and associates.

Has anyone, especially one of the Bigfoot hunters, talked with him recently about this? Did he know, for example, about my own investigation, the book I am writing?

No, he repeats. No one has talked to him. This is the first he has heard of my research. He cannot be of any help. He hasn't seen any of the Bigfoot crowd for a long time. And there is no point in my trying to see him. It would just be a waste of my time.

The Lake Ann incident has proved to be typical. Eventually, in case after case, incident after incident, the tendency of the information, usually offered freely by people who have no ax to grind—and no motive to deceive—leads to the probability of fraud, or at least to ample opportunity for hoax. Much of the vaunted evidence, which seems so hard, so real, in newspaper stories, fades away the closer one gets to it. Much of the information that the public acquires appears to be the consequence of pranks, of practical jokes without profit or other intent behind them. But, of course, this information is grasped by the Bigfoot people and thoroughly exploited. And most newspapers are only too willing to print the stories, often with a hint of levity, to avoid any charge of exploitation on their part.

Another pertinent case in point is the attack on the armored personnel carrier in Crawford County reported to the police in 1976. This is the case that King claims as proof that Bigfoot is potentially dangerous to people. My initial inquiry is directed to the Crawford County sheriff's office, where the sparse details of the incident are contained in an official police report, dated August 21, 1976. The deputy who answered the call is no longer in Michigan, but I am able to obtain the name of the civilian who originally made the call to the sheriff that early morning when the frightened young Guardsmen came to him for help.

John Howe is happy to talk about the incident, which he well remembers. Like most northwoods residents, he is an outdoorsman, a hunter. The whole strange event has long intrigued him, he says. But what is most important, in his opinion, is not the stuff that appeared in print, not even the details about how frightened the young men were. It is what was *not* reported that is interesting. For example, immediately after the incident, when the sheriff's deputy had gone and the scared Guardsmen had returned to their unit, he and some of his friends went out to the site where the personnel carrier was attacked. They knew that a very large bear sometimes moved through that region. Howe had seen it once.

"I hunt that area, and I've never seen any unusual tracks, except what's supposed to be there. And only four or five examples of bear. It's typical that I've only seen a bear, that big one, once."

But Howe and his friends did not find bear tracks at all, or any sign of bear, or any Bigfoot tracks, either. Instead they found a lot of tanks and large military vehicles, all parked, all cordoned off, and guarded by MPs.

"This just wasn't typical or normal," Howe continues, "so I asked what's the matter. Well, somebody siphoned a lot of diesel fuel from those tanks."

Thus the vehicles sat there unable to move until more fuel was brought in.

"Y'know"—Howe chuckles—"all that fuel stolen, and that so-called attack by a Bigfoot, well, we made a kind of local joke that Bigfoot runs on diesel fuel."

Howe is very careful not to confuse what he knows as fact with personal opinions about the incident. He will not go so far as to suggest that the reported attack was a diversion organized by thieves. But, he adds, it does seem strange—the coincidence of the attack on the personnel carrier and the fact of that stolen fuel.

Then Howe adds, his voice taking on an edge, that he is not happy at all about the way Bigfoot hunter King handled the incident. King and his companions, Howe explains, acted almost rude and disdainful, making it clear from the start that they did not like what he had to say. His impression at the time was that his testimony, his own experience with the young Guardsmen and afterward, did not conform to what King and his associates wanted to hear. King kept casting sidelong glances at his partners.

"He acted like I was full of crap. . . . He tried to twist my words around. He'd try to get me to change my words on the tape recording . . . to rephrase statements to make it sound entirely different. But I wouldn't go along with it."

And there is one other strange thing about the whole story, Howe says. Why weren't the names of those young fellows, the National Guardsmen from Ohio who were allegedly attacked, included in the police report? It is Howe's opinion that the Guard knew more about the incident than they wanted to let on, and not because there had been any Bigfoot running around out there. Those stories that went around about MPs shooting at something with glowing red eyes: Well, Howe says, that makes no sense. He knows for a fact that they don't let those kids, those MPs, run around with live ammunition in their weapons.

Perhaps it is in the nature of the Bigfoot phenomenon, despite ample evidence that even the most believable incidents are probably pranks or hoaxes, that these and similar events continue to spark comment. Among the dedicated true believers, any attempt to classify these incidents as phony seems to evoke defensiveness bordering on irrationality. This is not to say that all reports are phony, or that all tracks are faked, but for those who want to believe badly enough, no amount of explanation or examination will suffice. Some will persist in believing that the shaky evidence in support of their faith is superior to the strong evidence, usually of a circumstantial nature, in support of a hoax. And for those who are less adamant, but who still wish strongly to believe, it is easy enough to accept these examples as phony, and yet argue persuasively that *all* of the reports could hardly be false. In the final analysis the fact of a few hoaxes, pranks, or alleged hoaxes cannot prove that Bigfoot does not exist; thus, faith is sustained.

It is important to remember, despite the high incidence of hoax, that most of the people who see hairy monsters or who discover tracks are honest. The majority might be victims of hoax, and some may be confused or mistaken as to what they saw, but they are for the most part neither liars, fools, nor crackpots.

6. Scientists and Bigfoot Buffs

꼭 꼭 꼭 꼭 꼭 꼭 꼭 꼭 꼭 꼭 꼭 꼭 꼭 꼭 꼭 꼭 꼭 꼭

I have no prejudice against such a thing existing. That would be scientifically absurd, even irrational. But we don't run off looking for something for which there is no evidence. . . . Bring me a specimen, or a good skeleton, then I'll believe something is there. Bring me *hard* evidence.

> DR. RICHARD W. THORINGTON, JR.,
> of the National Museum of Natural
> History, November 1968

If you establish at any point that even *one* report is accurate, then you have an animal. And, if you have an animal, then you have literally thousands of animals.

> JOHN GREEN,
> June 1979

Something has got to be making them goddamned tracks.

> RENÉ DAHINDEN,
> June 1979

꼭 꼭 꼭 꼭 꼭 꼭 꼭 꼭 꼭 꼭 꼭 꼭 꼭 꼭 꼭 꼭 꼭 꼭

The Scientists

The great gray heap of the American Museum of Natural History is catching the slanting rays of the November sun; its massive, ornate façade glows magenta above the fading greens and golds of Central Park. Inside the huge main portal, I wait for my pass to ascend to the inner sanctum. I am to interview an imposing man who holds an imposing title at an imposing and powerful institution.

It is essential that I come here, to this great museum, to talk with this respected authority on mammals.

In his spacious office, high in a cul-de-sac within the vast museum, I am warmly greeted by Dr. Richard G. Van Gelder, curator of mammalogy. He is a large, bearlike man of sardonic mien, blunt and witty. His robust frame has been visibly battered by the worst that four continents can offer, yet he projects an aura of energy and interest. In the course of more than a quarter century of study of the classification of mammals, their origins, their behavior, and, not incidentally, their protection, Van Gelder has encountered many unusual animals, all of them quite real. This does not mean that he is uninterested in my subject, a phenomenon that may prove to be ephemeral.

Through extensive correspondence I am already aware that Van Gelder has more than a casual interest in the Bigfoot phenomenon. We had met more than two years before through research I had been doing on the ivory trade and its impact on elephants. So I know that Van Gelder is not the kind of man to make up his mind in advance of evidence or to allow himself to be frozen into a position merely because it is fashionable. In my mind he represents something close to the model of open-minded scientific objectivity. The care with which he had chosen his words in our previous association had been early tokens of his caution. But I also know Van Gelder to be capable of bold and original ideas, not fearful of venturing across the rigid and arbitrary lines that divide the various branches of the sciences.

Van Gelder has thought long and written eloquently on subjects of anthropological interest as well as on the most diverse and arcane aspects of mammalian systematics; he has studied everything from human evolution to the morphology of domestic dogs as compared to that of their wild relatives. I had originally come to him because of his interest in the larger mammals. He knows the larger fauna of the Americas thoroughly and has had extensive experience with African mammals. To me he is logically the first zoologist to interview in this Bigfoot search, not only because of his encyclopedic knowledge of mammals but also because I know he will never hedge; he will say exactly what he thinks.

Despite our correspondence and our previous association, I have not yet talked about Bigfoot with Dr. Van Gelder. I know that he has an interest but do not know what form this interest takes. Will it be negative, in my terms, or positive? I am relieved almost at once.

"You'll have no trouble with me or with any reputable zoologists," Van Gelder begins, "since you obviously profess no preconceived theories. What I mean, for example, is that the late Ivan Sanderson only lost the serious attention of his fellow biologists when he advocated entirely new and unsubstantiated classifications of 'unknown' species within wholly unproved evolutionary lines. That goes against everything we've learned since Linnaeus about the scientific method."

Furthermore, says Van Gelder, his colleagues rarely have prejudices against the possibility, however remote, that such a creature as Bigfoot might exist. If such an animal is actually found, regardless of which primate line it belonged to, its survival in North America, or even in the Himalayas, would certainly require a fresh look at primate evolution. But, he adds in a cautionary tone, the widely publicized idea that the scientific establishment is opposed to the Bigfoot search because it might somehow constitute a threat to their cherished concepts is pure bunk.

"What I object to," he says emphatically, "is the elaboration of pseudoscientific explanations about an alleged creature, its nature, behavior, ecology, and even its systematics, in advance of any physical evidence that it exists." Until such evidence is forthcoming, Van Gelder will withhold judgment. This does not mean that he believes that ninety percent of the junk published on Bigfoot or the abominable snowman will stand up to investigation.

"I've had occasion to go through much of the material myself," he says. "Maybe I can even add a few pertinent references to your biblio. My interest in this goes back for several years."

Perhaps I am unduly intimidated by Van Gelder's surroundings. His huge office, hidden within this grand and serried
structure—redolent of legendary and distinguished names,
from Margaret Mead to George Schaller—is filled with remind-
ers of nature's abundant experiments. Maybe for this reason,
despite our friendship, I find myself reacting with a small degree of defensiveness.

"Isn't it true, though, that the scientific community has not
acted decisively to support serious research into this quesion?"
I ask. "Why, if zoologists are really interested in the phenomenon, have they avoided any association with it? Haven't a
good number of searchers and advocates expressed willingness
to cooperate and begged for help, aside from the obvious
cranks? Many of these people have professed a faith in the creature's existence, a faith presumably based on a body of circumstantial evidence gleaned from hundreds of sightings and
perhaps thousands of footprints and other signs."

Van Gelder nods knowingly. Yes, he explains, it is true that
he and his colleagues are reluctant to commit money and repu-
tations to an endeavor based on faith and little else. But, he
adds, this has always been characteristic of research zoologists.
Caution and methodology are all-important. Only the rare genius, a man like Darwin, for example, has the imagination combined with the profound knowledge of the principles of his
science that can lead to a genuine breakthrough. And even
then, the creative imagination of the visionary is constrained by
proved and careful processes. Darwin's most provocative ideas
were put forth only after decades of painstaking, almost superhuman research. And in the end Darwin's faith in the theory of
evolution was based on a bedrock of demonstrable fact, and his
supposed arrogance in challenging accepted formulas was really
nothing more than confidence that the evidence would prove
him substantially correct. And it has.

"You know," says Van Gelder, "it was not a scientist or a
scientific expedition that discovered the gorilla, or the orangutan, or the okapi. That was done by explorers. Zoologists
spend a lot of time collecting specimens, but this is normally
done after a particular species in known to exist. Today, when

we find an unknown animal, it is usually something like a divergent subspecies, like the pygmy chimp, or maybe a tiny creature, a new kind of bat or shrew, for example, that has evolved in a remote and unexpected ecological niche.''

"So you prefer to leave it up to the amateurs to search for Bigfoot or the yeti?'' I cannot resist this.

Van Gelder's face breaks into a smile.

"Right, and I think you know why.'' The reason, he explains, is simple enough. His institution, or the Smithsonian or any other large museum, would probably get involved and perhaps even support an expedition if anyone, after all these years, could produce genuine physical evidence, such as identifiable bones, a good skin, better yet a whole specimen—anything in decent condition that could be clearly identified as an unknown primate or other animal, extant or extinct. "Frankly, after all this time, I don't expect any such evidence.''

But, I point out, is he aware that many Bigfoot buffs argue that various kinds of physical evidence *have* been found, only to disappear when sent to museums, or to be summarily dismissed as fake after inadequate and cursory examination? The treatment of the Patterson-Gimlin film, which is considered to be convincing evidence by some experts, is an example. What does he think of this?

"You know,'' he replies, "certain people have been saying these things about established scientists since science in its modern sense began. It is the simplest way to get a segment of the public to believe you *have* got something; you claim that the 'establishment,' or whatever, is suppressing the truth. You claim that people must be incredibly gullible to believe the scientists, who after all do have rather exclusive membership associations and specialized language and methods, and who seem to have rather mysterious communications networks. And yet, on the other hand, you expect incredible gullibility on the part of your readers, and, I might add, considerable ignorance, for the most part.''

So, Van Gelder explains, the old charge of suppression of evidence or willful avoidance is patently absurd. Why, he asks, would any reputable museum or university department do such a thing? There is no motive. Any department of anthropology or zoology would be delighted to have a real specimen of a new and previously unknown primate in its hands. It would mean enormous opportunity, exciting new research, major expeditions, unquestionable expansion of funds, new publications—the very elements that make any such institution thrive.

As for the Patterson-Gimlin film, Van Gelder has seen it, during a special viewing in company with several of his fellow mammalogists. To a man they considered it to be a human being in a cleverly constructed costume. Such things, he adds, tend to depend for their effect on the inexperience and wishful thinking of their intended audience. You see what you want to see. All films have that potential. They depend too much on interpretation.

"That's why charlatans can get so far in this business," he says.

"A version, on a small scale, of Dr. Goebbels's 'big lie'?" I ask.

Van Gelder is not willing to generalize quite so loosely. He retreats to his considered, rational position. Apparently, he suggests in tentative tones, most of the Bigfoot experts simply want to believe in their critter so badly that the wish has become a matter of conviction, a commitment. "But you know that already," he says quickly, smiling. "You've planned a whole chapter on it."

There is indeed a pattern. If an alleged piece of physical evidence can no longer be produced by its "finders" for serious examination by scientists, a common charge is that it had been deliberately destroyed by a museum or other institution. Or it has been lost for some reason, usually unexplained. Thus, popular suspicion of science, which has appreciably increased since the beginning of the nuclear age, is exploited, probably without malicious intent, in order to support the view that the authorities are in cahoots to suppress the evidence.

Since I have already looked into one of the most celebrated instances of allegedly "lost" evidence—the so-called "Minnesota Iceman" case*—I mention this to Van Gelder. At once he suggests something I have already determined to do. I must get down to Washington, D.C., he says, and visit the Smithsonian so that I can properly follow through on that case. The chief primatologist there, Dr. Richard Thorington, will surely be helpful, and all the files on that incident should be in his charge.

Dr. Richard W. Thorington, Jr., holds the official title of head primatologist in the Department of Vertebrate Zoology at the National Museum of Natural History in the Smithsonian Institution. As Van Gelder has predicted, he is at once open and helpful, and I soon have access to more Bigfoot material than I can handle in only a few days.

One of the first things I want to know, however, is whether the Smithsonian has continued even the most informal and quiet interest in the ongoing Bigfoot search. It seems to me apparent that after the incident of the Minnesota Iceman, the museum's former openness toward the issue—largely a product of the willingness of Thorington's predecessor, Dr. John Napier, to listen to the arguments of the Bigfoot cognoscenti—would have been replaced by a hands-off policy, or at least by open skepticism.

I am not off the mark. Thorington confirms my guess with cool emphasis. He is Van Gelder's physical opposite, a slight, fair man of genial manner and quick, cutting intelligence. He at once explains that regarding the so-called Bigfoot, he has no interest in examining evidence that is easily falsifiable—footprints, for example, and hair, and scats so old you cannot identify them. Hair, he points out, can become so embraided that it loses its outside surface and cannot be positively identified.

"Many people submit such evidence," Thorington says ruefully, "and the fact that it cannot be identified often assumes undue importance. Fecal matter is another good example—because really all you can do with fecal matter is say what is in it.

---

*See Chapter 7.

True, certain parasites are carried only by certain groups of families [of animals], and this can sometimes be determined if you are willing to take the time. But, again, results are often inconclusive, especially for a supposed animal I don't know anything about."

Understandably this leads us to a discussion about the nature of the evidence. Since he has followed the various controversies closely and has kept abreast of the several theories, none of which he considers to be convincing to any primatologist with field experience, Thorington suggests that perhaps after so many years of allegations and no hard proof, we have reached the point where the whole phenomenon needs to be viewed in perspective.

I reply that this is what I am trying to do, to research the whole matter from a historical perspective in order to get a handle on it that might not have occurred to most biologists, or to other interested parties who might be bound to synchronic methods because of their specialties.

"This way, if there is anything to it, my work won't impede potential research, and if there isn't anything to it, my findings will help explain at least part of the mystery."

Thorington, however, has something else in mind. He explains.

"Perhaps working within a hypothesis that cannot be falsified would help, versus one than can be falsified. For me the best hypothesis is that it—the creature—does not exist. After all, falsifying a thousand others still doesn't prove that Bigfoot doesn't exist."

"So where does that leave us?" I respond in mock despair, though for a moment I feel almost as if the bottom has suddenly dropped out of my own assumptions for research.

"I guess that leaves us where we've always been," says Thorington, "at least those of us in the scientific world. As Van Gelder says, I have no prejudice against such a thing existing. That would be scientifically absurd, even irrational. But we don't run off looking for something for which there is no evidence."

"So, here we go again. It comes down to hard evidence, then? Evidence that cannot be faked or contrived, or imagined?"

Thorington nods, with an expression of benign impatience. I wonder how many times he has been asked this question.

"Bring me a specimen, or a good skeleton. Then I'll believe something is there. Bring me *hard* evidence."

Isn't it true, I ask, that certain respected astronomers, Carl Sagan, for example, do not shy away from probabilities, from intelligent speculations on what *might* be, given certain known scientific assumptions? What about speculation that an unknown primate *might* exist, despite no hard physical proof? After all, the gorilla was not classified until fairly recently, and it wasn't until Carl Akeley and his associates began to send carefully chosen specimens out of the Congo early in this century that primatologists knew much about that particular ape. And it wasn't until the early 1960s that George Schaller's field research revealed even the most basic facts about the gorilla's natural behavior, feeding habits, mating, social structure, and so on.

Thorington is well prepared for this and plunges at once into a learned discourse on the history of the discovery and classification of the anthropoid apes, animals with which he has great familiarity. The pygmy chimpanzee, *Pan paniscus,* was indeed not classified as a separate species until 1929, he notes. But unsystematic knowledge that a smaller form of chimp existed goes back much further, well into the nineteenth century. The only real question in that case, Thorington says, was not the "discovery" of a so-called unknown species but rather its classification as a separate species instead of merely a smaller variant form.

And, of course, the orangutan was known to Linnaeus in 1760, only two years after his system of classification was developed. The name *Homo* for the human line dates only to 1758. All the great apes were properly classified in the brief period between the late eighteenth and the early twentieth centuries. The last were the gibbons, in 1903. The idea often bruited about by Bigfoot hunters that the anthropoid apes were unknown until very recently is nonsense, Thorington adds. The point is not that the apes were unknown but rather that they were not properly understood or classed in terms of their genetic relationships with one another and with man. That process is still going on with many of the most common animals. The anthropoid apes were unfamiliar to Europeans, but various descriptions of the Asiatic apes had been passed on to the West in adulterated versions for centuries—no doubt accounting for many of the legends of hairy men of the woods. The gorilla *was* unknown to Europeans until 1847, but the chimp had been known to the ancient world, and it had been properly known to Western science since Blumenbach's description in 1779.

"So you think we've found all the existing primates?" I ask. My curiosity has been piqued again. How can anyone be so certain?

Thorington hesitates for a moment. I suspect that like most research scientists, he does not like bald statements that rest on analogy any more than he likes suppositions based on conjecture.

"I'd prefer to put it this way," he says. "The existence of a large primate such as Bigfoot, especially in North America, is almost an impossibility, biologically speaking. The discovery of a new *mouse* is big news these days."

I can well imagine. But I sense that the interview is coming to an end. We have talked long and candidly, right through a congenial lunch in the museum's cafeteria, and for some time after. I have been greatly entertained by Thorington's marvelous stories, reflecting his wide experience in the field. I delay my leave-taking for a while longer, hoping for some possibly unexpected insight. Shortly I will proceed to dig through the Smithsonian's files on the phenomenon. Meanwhile, Thorington has meetings to attend.

"Look," he says, leaning forward slightly. Perhaps he senses my slight discomfiture. "I'm just out there studying the animals that exist, and there are lots of them. And I've also been very much involved in conservation work, to make sure that our fellow primates, the ones that we *know* exist, survive into the twenty-first century."

There is little I can say to that.

⊄ ⊄ ⊄

Several months later I have occasion to return to the nation's capital to complete unfinished research in the Smithsonian's files. Thorington remains helpful and considerate in every respect, though he is amused by much of what he has heard and read about Bigfoot and openly scornful of the majority of the tales associated with the phenomenon. As one of America's leading primatologists, Thorington hardly fits the image of the narrow-minded, opinionated academic snob, isolated from the real world in some ivory tower, unwilling to consider possibilities that do not neatly fit into some theoretical model of conformity. Like Richard Van Gelder and most of his fellow scientists, Thorington is an active and resourceful naturalist, as familiar with the wilderness and its creatures as any hunter (actually much more so than most) and no more isolated from the worldly realities of our civilization than a teacher in an inner-city college. Indeed, the atmosphere within the great museums, like that within the great universities, is palpably one of involvement with the controversies of our time. There is nothing pure or isolated about the work going on in such places; zoologists, like everyone else, are subject to contrary viewpoints, to disputes, to passionate disagreements. If the pressures to conform were as strong as many laymen seem to believe, little genuine work would get done.

The Bigfoot People

Many months later and thousands of miles away, I am sitting on a hot afternoon in a motel in Yakima, Washington. Far off to the west, shimmering in the heat waves, is the snow dome of Mt. Adams. Coming down into the arid valley of the Yakima River, I had a glimpse of the huge loom of Mt. Rainier to the northwest. But here, in this garish town of Yakima, once a pleasant town in a lovely valley, now, through unplanned growth, one of very few unattractive places in an otherwise magnificent state, it is oppressive. There is nothing to see from the door of the motel room to relieve the sense of oppression, nothing but the endless strip of fast-food places, motels, dealerships, hardware stores, and shopping malls. After the cool beauty of the Oregon Coast Range, the spectacular panorama of Santiam Pass through the Cascades, the impressive cleft of the Columbia River gorge, the evergreen vistas near Trout Lake and Glenwood beneath the southern slopes of Mt. Adams, this town seems to me like a descent to the edge of Hades. It is very hot.

I am pleased to be here, nevertheless. Already I am deep in conversation with perhaps the most persistent if not the most famous Sasquatch searcher of them all. Fully expecting to be cast in the role of outside meddler—an Easterner horning in on a close-knit club of oldtime experts, without proper "credentials" among the believers—I am pleasantly surprised that René Dahinden is ready to talk, so willing to tell it all from his point of view.

Already this quick, intelligent, eccentric, and rough-edged man has led me through labyrinthine paths of Bigfoot lore, the highs and lows of his personal teratological obsession. Clearly nothing in his life is as important as his search for this unknown creature, his desire either to find it once and for all or to lay to rest forever the many speculations that alternately infuriate and intrigue him. Nothing Dahinden has done or might do will ever occupy him as does this quest. For he is the only one, I think, among the entire group of searchers, hunters, buffs, and self-appointed experts whose life *is* the search itself and the struggles associated in his mind with that search. I have already read a good deal about Dahinden, since his presence as a dedicated Bigfoot hunter has often thrust him into the fore in the two decades since he first began his search. But I have no way of knowing in advance of our meeting whether this ultimate searcher is a visionary, a con man, a serious, honest investigator, or a self-deluding fool.

Indeed, it would be easy to make snap judgments about this man, to portray him as a figure of ridicule, and hence to dismiss him—as many so-called authorities have done, unfortunately. But in fact René Dahinden is not a ludicrous figure, despite the obvious romance of his position. He has a sharp and often bitterly satiric manner—for in truth he is rather a bitter man, having received so little for so much effort—but he also has a hard-won sense of the ridiculous and a capacity to see his own role in a humorous way. Bathos is not alien to him; it is intrinsic to this search that has almost consumed him. His hard and lonely choices and his life-style as an independent investigator have forged an already strong man into a truly inner-directed personality. He is a classic loner, an outsider. In another life or endeavor he night be a model for a novel by Camus or Bellow, unforgettably and absolutely an individual.

Perhaps because he has learned to be suspicious of people's motives—especially those of his fellow Bigfoot researchers and buffs, so many of whom have proved to be petty frauds—Dahinden has developed a tough-minded, critical approach to the subject that he loves. This is remarkable because he seems far more emotionally committed to the quest for the creature than any of the others. Indeed, given his faith that the creature will be found someday and proved to exist even to the satisfaction of the Doubting Thomases of science, it is all the more remarkable that Dahinden himself is not really a true believer. He skirts that position perilously closely, but he does not go all the way. He has held a little back, just in case. And though he maintains a powerful proprietary attitude—as if to say "This is my thing; don't tread lightly on it"—Dahinden has cultivated a tenacious sense of veracity and a hard-nosed skepticism regarding the evidence.

Physically Dahinden is not an impressive man. But he is not forgettable, either. He is short and stocky with a rugged, weathered face that reveals the many trials of his rough life. But his normal scowl turns readily to a dazzling grin, his growl to an explosive laugh, and his small, intense blue eyes light up quickly with pleasure. His ash-blond hair is worn close-cropped. At forty-nine he seems physically strong. There is nothing of the armchair expert in this man. He is the searcher through and through.

In her interesting book *Sasquatch Apparitions* Barbara Wasson states that Dahinden either attracts people or repels them. I soon discover why this is true, for Dahinden is driven and outspoken, given to hard judgments about others. Willing to risk

the label of crackpot through his unabashed quest, he nevertheless suffers fools badly. His likes and dislikes are up front.

It is not hard to understand why. René Dahinden was born
an illegitimate child in Switzerland in 1930 and placed almost
at once in an orphanage, from which he was soon taken by various foster parents, briefly by his own mother, and by a farm
family who apparently used him as a child laborer—allowing
him into their living room only once in three years. At a tender
age he took off on his own, and after some years at several jobs
in Switzerland, he restlessly roamed Europe, mostly doing construction work. In 1953 he immigrated to Canada and eventually made his way to Alberta, where he worked on a farm near
Calgary. There he learned, almost inadvertently, when making
a remark to his employer about a *Daily Mail* expedition that
had just set out from London to search for the Himalayan yeti,
that similar creatures had been reported for many years in nearby British Columbia.

This was just what Dahinden had been looking for. He had
experienced the dull laborer's life of routine and harsh domes-
ticity, and although soon married to a girl he had met in Swe-
den, he chose eventually to turn his back on conventionality.
Maybe something was really out there, and if it was, he determined to find it.

Apparently from the first his search was an obsession, and
eventually he was a single man again. During the first years of
his quest, Dahinden surely fit the definition of the unquestion-
ing true believer. By his own account, during the first decade
or so he developed few critical skills, accepting most reports at
face value, running hither and yon without selectivity. But he
has long since left that early phase behind. Today his position is
one of intense skepticism tinged with hope. Though he fervently claims not to care whether or not Bigfoot exists, his desire to
know the truth of the mystery has obviously reinforced an earlier obsession to find the thing that he once fully believed in.

My interview with Dahinden in Yakima is revealing of his
often compelling personality, as well as his sometimes contradictory opinions. He is too honest with himself to allow the
seductions of rhetoric to carry very far. Inconsistencies in his

views seem to spring more from his lack of formal education than from self-deception. Thus Dahinden's personal story of his quest is illuminating in itself, and in his testimony one can perhaps find kernels of a larger truth about this elusive phenomenon, even if one is disappointed by the predictable nature of the lesser details. Mostly Dahinden's story is a narrative of frustration, of hopes dashed, and of undisguised hostility.

When I finally ask Dahinden to talk freely about his feelings, he jumps at the chance.

"When I started, I was maybe like all the other beginners. After a couple of years in it I had an answer for everything. I knew exactly where the Bigfeet crossed the Fraser River, their migration routes, and ten thousand things. And the longer I'm in it, the more I realize how little we know. Because nothing seems to fit. Not as we thought it was, you know. Maybe I liked the publicity, yet I didn't know about publicity.

"Afterwards it got to be more like I *wanted* to know. Today sometimes it gets to me. It's exciting; you meet so many people, all this intrigue. It can also be a pain in the neck. And, sure, I would like to be the one who finds it. Yet in a way it would be a real pain in the neck if you are the one, you know. Yet I would hate like hell to see some joker going out in the morning to hunt deer or something and knocking one over. And the scientific community, all the jokers from the Smithsonian Institution down, getting this thing for nothing. So they can sit at home and write their learned articles!"

This last phrase is uttered with such passion, each word spaced and hard, that I interrupt.

"Isn't that likely what would happen if—"

"Not if Dahinden finds it!" he replies with equal force. "Because the scientists would be the *absolute last ones* who ever would get their sticky hands on it, and every time they opened their mouths I would say, 'Now, look, this time, do you know what you're talking about? Because you sure as hell didn't know before.'"

Such hostility toward people who represent authority seems to me important, so I press the issue further. Dahinden says that he considers scientists to be akin to high priests in previous times. They are asked their opinions not because they "know" anything in particular but because they are assumed to know by virtue of their being scientists.

I ask Dahinden if he is suggesting that in contemporary science there is a kind of orthodoxy, as in religion, whereby any deviant theories that don't fit the orthodoxy are declared heresy.

"Not that," he responds with considerable sarcasm. "Scientists today *are* the high priests. They are all-knowing. They know the answer to every damn thing. To the ordinary people. Well, maybe some of the scientists realize that they really don't know it all. If they are honest. But the ordinary people think so."

Perhaps Dahinden is voicing a widespread feeling. Perhaps the ubiquitous faith in this phenomenon, akin in sense to the "reality" of UFOs, stems partly from a sense of impotence among ordinary people, those not versed in the arcane procedures and complicated rituals of modern science. Faced with an increasingly complex world, one may have a powerful impulse to thumb one's nose at the opinion of established authorities, especially when those same authorities cannot prove, with all their elaborate methods and specialized jargon, that the phenomenon *doesn't* exist. Obviously, if the object of that faith is one day proved to exist, the authorities will be proved wrong, made to look foolish. Surely this is at least partly behind Dahinden's hostility. But in his words there is contradiction. Every year that passes without his finding Sasquatch surely tends to winnow away his once-powerful faith. Deep down, René Dahinden is a skeptic in temperament, an iconoclast instead of a pious follower, probably incapable of wholly irrational belief. And yet every year without success has increased his sense of frustration and anger.

Also significant are Dahinden's repeated statements that he doesn't need the help of the scientific community, because so much of his search is aimed at proving to them that he has been right all along. There is certainly an element here of the rejected child who hates the authority that has cast him out and at the same time wishes desperately to prove his worth to that authority. Perhaps this apparent contradiction is as much a part of Dahinden's makeup as the inconsistencies revealed in his persistent faith in the existence of Bigfoot, a faith that survives despite his exceptionally rigorous skepticism regarding the evidence.

And it is in this, the analysis of alleged evidence, that Dahinden's testimony is most useful. He is quick to doubt. Through many humiliating experiences he has learned that too many of his fellow Bigfoot hunters are mere con men, and many of them are not even very clever at their games. The fact that Dahinden may crave notoriety, through honest and legitimate means, accounts for a kind of paradox: In the face of potential fraud he is alternately tough and gullible. He is capable of calling one of the most famous of Bigfoot hunters "a two-bit con man" and labeling another "a sneaky little crook." Yet Dahinden is capable of explaining in almost the same breath why the film in question is genuine and impossible to fake. He is capable of saying that the famous Bossburg tracks, the so-called cripple footprints made internationally famous by Napier, could not have been faked, despite the fact that these Bossburg tracks were first brought to Dahinden's attention by a man whom he has called a "cheap faker." He will elaborate favorably on the analysis of an anthropologist who is rare among his fellows because he argues in favor of the existence of Bigfoot, and then turn around and say that the anthropologist ought to "stay home and scribble his papers" because he is so gullible. He will passionately argue that the main thing holding up successful research that might prove the existence of Bigfoot is the unwillingness of the scientific community to cooperate, and yet he scornfully rejects the scientists as arrogant, narrow-minded fools who just get in the way, whom he can do without.

After many hours I have become keenly aware of this. I ask Dahinden what kind of treatment he might expect from the scientific world if a Sasquatch is found.

"If the scientific community ever decided that there are Sasquatches, Dahinden and all these other jokers will be standing back there watching the expedition take off down the road, well financed, well equipped, with jokers who couldn't spell the name Bigfoot or Sasquatch if their life depended on it."

I agree that he is probably right.

"Let's put it this way," Dahinden responds. "I hope they *never* believe the damn thing exists. For my own damn protection. Because I think we would be shuffled aside in the whole thing. So, therefore, for my own protection, I hope the bastards *never* believe."

In the face of these contradictions it would be easy to dismiss Dahinden as just another confused true believer, yet in spite of the unsystematic nature of his investigations, his approach is too rigorous for easy disdain. In the course of this long interview in Yakima, it becomes apparent that Dahinden has parted company with his old friend and colleague John Green, precisely over the use and interpretation of the evidence. Dahinden believes that the vast majority of the material put forth as evidence is useless.

"I would need a sixty-ton truck to collect all the junk this guy thinks is evidence. And I'm not talking about interpretation. I'm talking about the basic evidence. If John Green says this creature is more apelike than human . . . I couldn't care less. You'll never hear me make a statement that this creature is either *Gigantopithecus* or something else, not until we find it. . . . I have no views on [its nature]. The more I hear the less I *know.* I'm really very simple. I wonder if the damn thing exists, and if the people who tell us they see it really *see* what they say they saw, and if the footprints we find are real or not, and if the Patterson-Gimlin film is real or not. I'm still worried about evidence from twenty years ago, where other people seem to be what I call the 'collectors.' They just keep on collecting without worrying that what they collected twenty years ago is of any value. They just keep piling it up. Some researchers say, 'Look at all the thousands of reports we have. That proves beyond any question that there is something there.' I'm going in exactly the opposite direction. The more reports we are getting, the more unlikely it is that the damned thing exists. Because if we have that many reports, then we should have collected the damn thing long ago.

"If the creature is only seen here, or here, or here, only very seldom, okay. But if you've already seen sixty thousand running through Michigan and standing behind every stop sign, you know, then one starts to wonder. The longer it goes on, I think, the more unlikely. If you have that many reports, over and over? Finally, one argument against the existence of Sasquatch, and that's the *only* one. Never mind their food supply and all that junk, and reproduction; the only legitimate argument against its existence is, if the damn thing exists, how come we haven't shot one, and tracked it down? You know, *how come?"*

Against this cry of puzzlement, the following exchange, which took place the same day, in Yakima, is pertinent. Barbara Wasson was present throughout my interview with Dahinden, quietly, patiently absorbing the torrent of words. Obviously fond of Dahinden, an admirer of his deep integrity and passion while thoroughly aware of his rough edges, Wasson had already written perceptively about her friend and his search. Wasson is a professional psychologist who has independently become a student of Bigfoot lore. Her analysis of many of the leading Bigfoot investigators is, as I noted earlier, quite useful, and her evaluation of the evidence is often penetrating. It is rather surprising, considering her strong orientation toward a logical view of reality, that Wasson still prefers to include herself among those who believe that the creature "is there."

In person Wasson is plump, quiet, and gentle, with an apparently naïve manner that belies a keen analytical mind. She presents a striking contrast to her effusive and domineering friend Dahinden. Wasson also has the born psychologist's capacity to listen quietly and let the other person reveal his thoughts, motives, and needs. Though she is a robust and attractive woman of cheerful manner, I sense during the interview that she does not entirely approve of the way I phrase my questions, though I have explained from the start that my questions are neither planned in advance nor intended to be comprehensive. She nevertheless responds with pertinent observations.

I ask her first what she thinks of the possible psychological needs behind paranormal phenomena. I point out that many people would look upon those associated with Bigfoot as crackpots. People are familiar, at least on a vague level, with the kind of *National Enquirer* sensationalism that deal with such far-out phenomena, so they assume that Bigfoot also fits this category.

Wasson replies firmly. "No! In my experience meeting people interested in it, I think I've found some of those . . . but not on the whole."

"This represents a minority among the serious people involved?"

"Yes, I think so. The estimated number I don't know. My thrust is certainly to try and tie in with reality in terms of whether this is misperception, a mistake on the part of the witness . . . or whether there really *is* something out there. Y'know, it is really interesting. You can't lose. Either way, it's fascinating!"

"In your book, in terms of the delineation of types of witnesses, you also go through a detailed explanation about the veracity of witnesses and how this can be determined and so on. What proportion do you think fit into your characterization of obvious veracity, instead of obvious fakes or people who are deluded, and so on? Can you possibly answer that?"

"No, I can't, because I haven't really made a rigorous study of this and I wouldn't have the numbers. I haven't had an organized approach [to this question]. What I'm advocating . . . is that someone do that."

"That is the next stage?" I ask. "In separating evidence from what isn't evidence, for example?"

"Yes. I'd love to answer that. I think the answer would be very interesting."

Nagging doubts about evidence do not seem to trouble John Green. As I've suggested, Green is the kind of man who compiles things. Since he is the premier gatherer of such information, he probably knows more about the data of Sasquatchery than anyone else. But whether or not this vast quantity of data can be corroborated as valid or reliable is apparently no longer Green's concern. Early in the game he studied the bulk of the evidence and concluded that there were too many things he could not explain through conventional scientific theory or knowledge. So Green came to his firm conclusion and has held firmly to it ever since—namely, that a gigantic animal lives in the Pacific Northwest's forests and mountains, and almost certainly throughout most of North America. Although he rejects the label, Green is a true believer.

Green's faith is at first disconcerting, because he is strikingly different in every way from the obsessed Dahinden. In person Green is almost diffident, yet brusque, too, and plain-spoken. He is middle-aged, looking somewhat older than Dahinden, very tall and exceedingly thin; his height accentuates his lean frame and his angular, large-boned face. Sometimes his manner is almost English. A controlled reserve seems to lurk beneath a tendency to make abrupt and absolute pronouncements. He is also helpful, polite, obviously well bred, even gracious. In most respects he appears to be a normal man of professional manners and aspect. When speaking, his blue eyes are often fixed directly, unwaveringly, on the listener. He is at ease with his often startling statements, and he is ready to defend them. There is an air about him of controlled impatience. Obviously he has so often answered the questions of scornful skeptics that he seems to have withdrawn partway behind a carapace, a shield of tautology. What remain speculations for others have become facts for him. Doubt is not present. Green's firmness in his belief reminds me of my grandfather's nineteenth-century Methodist convictions. His consistent good humor through a long afternoon and evening of hard questioning also reminds me of the patience of the seminar-trained clergyman when confronted by a misguided atheist.

I have found Green in a pleasant house on a pleasant street in what must be one of the nicest towns in all the world. To get to Green's home I have put my car on a huge ferry earlier this perfect June day and sailed across the awe-inspiring Strait of Georgia, a huge inland waterway that separates British Columbia's Vancouver Island from the mainland. Even after days camping in the high Cascades of Washington, in the snow-capped Wenatchee range, and in the Gifford Pinchot National Forest, the passage through the myriad rocky islets from Tsawwassen to the tiny port near Victoria is rejuvenating. I have fallen in love, like thousands before me, with this vast land of blue sea and green-clothed forest. And I am surprised at the fine weather, the high, clear days. In the distance I can see the snowy peaks of the Olympic Mountains, south across the Strait of Juan de Fuca (lucky the man to see it first among all Westerners), and directly to the east the snow dome of Mt. Baker shimmers, as if magnified by the luminous light. So I am high on the country when I drive into Victoria, a quaint and comfortable town. Only the heavy smell of the big lumber mills mars the perfection of the day.

Green is happy to escort me in my rented car for a look at the surrounding landscape. We drive for several hours, up to the edge of the Seymour Range, a spine that runs most of the length of the huge island, and high above the fjordlike inlet called Saanich. We view the towering firs, the lush and tangled undergrowth, even within a few miles of Victoria's thoroughly urban hub. We talk about Bigfoot, the Amerindian legends, and about more modern lore, the sightings, footprints, and other signs.

I wonder aloud how such a creature might have crossed long ago to such an island, and Green patiently explains that to the north the passage is often narrow enough that it could be spanned by a large bridge. And, he adds, Sasquatch is at home in the water, being apparently a partly aquatic animal that browses along the rocky shores in winter.

Later, in his house, Green is more definitive. Unlike Dahinden, Green is willing to make sweeping generalizations about the habits of the creature, even its morphology. He has long since ceased to be bothered by questions about how it might survive unknown, uncaught, unkilled, in this wilderness, or even in less likely habitats. And though apparently a little concerned by the discrepancy between the bulk of information he has collected—which he considers evidence—and the lack of physical proof, Green has grown impatient with the skeptics, especially with the scientific critics and "armchair analysts." I wonder if I am perhaps being included in this. By the time I turn the tape recorder on, he has moved into the routine of formulae.

When I ask him how, after his twenty-year search, he separates sensationalism, the profit motive, and so on, from genuine investigation, Green replies that it all comes down to the credibility, the truthfulness, of the witnesses. He admits, however, that it has long gone past the point where he has any way of checking credibility in even a small proportion of the cases reported; this is because of the enormous increase in reports in recent years. Earlier, Green notes, he could check up on many of them, when there were only two hundred or three hundred in all, but now, with about two thousand on file, just collecting the data is enough.

"I'm not claiming to have any opinion as to the validity of most of the material that I've accumulated," Green says. "However, I'm assuming two things which go to two sides of the thing. One is that there's a lot more either outright fakery or wishful thinking today than there was when the subject was virtually unknown—anytime up to the Patterson movie. In the early years of the investigation it was almost certain that if you got a lead, there would be something solid to it, because if there weren't, there wouldn't be a lead. Now it's reached the point where, with people like René and myself, you have to say to yourself once in a while, 'I damned well better go . . . check on this thing.' But you've been on so many wild-goose chases that you don't have the same enthusiasm anymore.

"There was a time," Green continues, "when I listed all the people whose names I had who reported seeing these things, and I remember I once had thirteen names. I don't remember how many years I'd been involved at the time, but it was several years. Well, now I'd accumulate thirteen names in the average month, perhaps double that."

I note that this is a large number.

"Yes. I would say—with this exchange of information, I could give it all to you exactly—we're probably running around two hundred reports a year. However, the majority of these are from east of the mountains. And . . . there *is* the possibility, as you've suggested, that there isn't a one of them that's true.

"But to get to the other side of the argument. If you establish at any point that even *one* report is accurate, then you have an

animal. And if you have an animal, then you have literally thousands of animals. Or you wouldn't have *one*. And therefore the
preponderance is that, just as with any other animal that does
exist, if somebody said they saw one, they probably saw one.
Therefore, numerous reports of an existing animal are not so
mysterious at all. Once you've got the real animal, then you
don't any longer have reason to disbelieve all the reports."

Green takes considerable pains to explain his view that even
if there isn't an animal, even if it is assumed that the Sasquatch
does not exist, then there is something strange going on.

"We have the manufacturing of tracks, which can be traced
back a long way in many areas, and we have the telling of stories of encounters with such things, disappearing into antiquity,
and in all directions. Okay? Why are people doing this? Now, it
has to be one or the other. . . . It makes no difference; both are
phenomena of tremendous importance."

With growing vigor Green explains that in his view the
whole thing should not be compartmentalized the way it is. At
least one major institution of science and research ought to get
someone influential to direct the efforts, to assign the responsi-
bility for research to the appropriate discipline, and get to the
bottom of it all.

"Because whichever of these explanations is at the bottom,
we've got something of tremendous significance. But they
don't. Absolutely not. Nowhere!"

"What do you attribute this to?" I ask.

"This is where it gets fascinating. The question that *really*
interests me at this stage of the game is, why do they take this
attitude? I think there's a good case to be made that we have a
built-in hang-up on this subject. That they are acting
irrationally."

"You mean a deep-seated prejudice or something?"

"A deep-seated something that causes irrational behavior."

"Or avoidance?"

"Or avoidance. Yes, absolutely."

Still, I remain skeptical that there is any kind of unconscious
avoidance in this matter. Too much attention has in fact been
directed to the subject by reputable scientists and scholars, to

no avail, for doubt to be so easily dismissed. Green continues to argue that not one in thousands of institutions has come to the obvious conclusion that there might be something significant in the phenomenon itself, one way or the other.

Though he is correct in his view that the subject has been strangely relegated to the back room of contemporary phenomenological research, I point out that there have been some important studies on the Sasquatch, written especially from the angle of folklore. I suggest that the work of Kirtley, Bernheimer, and my own research indicate a modern manifestation of traditional patterns, often complete with classic motifs. I note that anthropologists doing similar research would not use the word "real" at all in the way that a zoologist might, for example. Among various African peoples of my acquaintance, what is "real" to them isn't necessarily "real" to an educated Western outsider.

But Green is adamant. He refuses to accept such a classification for his data, with the possible exception of certain early material derived from Indian legends. I attempt to pull back to the point by suggesting that Green has boldly speculated in his book on the supposed behavior, size, habitat, etc., of the Sasquatch, despite the fact that no specimen has been found.

"No," Green replies, "not boldly at all. I think it's obvious. There are two possibilities. There is either an animal or there isn't. If there is, what's your grounds for rejecting a report? If there is, suddenly you have a vast store of information about it. So assume there is an animal and study the information. And if you find the animal, you'll find the information was accurate."

Admiring Green's logic, if not his premise, I inquire about the supposed internal consistency, the alleged coherence within the hundreds of reports, that has led him to his conclusions. I point out that if one does not arbitrarily select the data to eliminate reports that do not support a consistent description of the Sasquatch, there is much less internal coherence than most Bigfoot experts like to admit.

"I'm not saying that every speculation of mine will be proved correct. Not by any means," Green says.

Finally I wonder if it is true that Green has stated that the Sasquatch is probably a member of the pongid line.

"No, I haven't." He is certain in his answer. I sense that he has begun to bridle a little at my questions, perhaps by what is implied as much as by their content. But Green is accustomed to this.

"I'm not dealing with what taxonomists would do with it. What I am saying is that to the ordinary person, animals are animals and humans human, and by that definition this thing is an ape. Because it isn't in the middle . . . with the animals here and the humans [over] here. It's right over there with the rest."

Most of what Green has written falls into this speculative class, no matter how cleverly he has interpreted his voluminous data. His conviction remains stubbornly firm, and since he appears to be unwilling to limit his research to a workable analysis of the evidence—of tracks, for example—since only a few of these can be considered even remotely verifiable, Green has allowed his fertile mind to range widely and imaginatively across mountains of information, most of which cannot be tested by any accepted scientific or historical standards. It is a fact well known to historians, and certainly not unknown to newspapermen, that there are no valid criteria to determine the objective truth of things claimed by eyewitnesses when their testimony is not backed up by independent evidence from other sources, including the most recent electronic gadgets, lie detectors, and voice prints. The veracity of any witness, or even of several witnesses, depends ultimately upon separately verifiable evidence, and in the case of Sasquatch there is precious little such evidence, if any.

Regarding Green's claim—a claim repeated by all of the Bigfoot buffs—that science ignores the question, one inevitably wonders how Green can expect a trained scientist, historian, or even a reasonably critically minded layman to take these speculations seriously. For example, he arbitrarily discards all data that doesn't fit his conception of what the creature must be like or should be like—matters such as eyes that glow in the dark, evidence of three rather than five toes, and so on. No reason is

provided regarding the selection of "acceptable" evidence beyond the rather lame explanation that it "makes sense." Green
uses a biased sample, relying on his definition of common
sense. This might be well and good if there was some *other*
good evidence to fall back on. Green is convinced, for example, that his Sasquatch is a "gentle giant," rather similar to a gorilla in its harmless, benign nature, and he simply discredits any
reports contrary to this view. Yet, of course, there are reports
that the creature is violent. Why should any less credence be
given to these reports than is given to the kind Green accepts as
valid?

One could perhaps collect great heaps of data from the alleged reports, submit this data to painstaking computer analysis, and come up with correlations supporting one or another
hypothesis about the creature, its movements, its preference for
wet (or dry) habitats, its size in relation to its distribution from
north to south (or east to west), its penchant to hole up (or not
to do so) in winter, its diet, its social organization or lack there-
of. Interestingly, Green has recognized the danger is this, pro-
fessing scorn at attempts to predict migration patterns—indeed,
he claims that there "are no discernible patterns of migration"—and rejecting statistical analyses of the creature's size in
any given region. Yet he makes repeated assumptions of exactly this nature. The argument that the creature shows no sign of
mental ability is an example. As Wasson has pointed out, the
only way to put it accurately would be to say that Sasquatch investigators have been unable to observe any sign of advanced
mental ability in the reported data.

Certainly the absence of data in support of a theory regarding an animal's behavior is not proof that it does not behave in
a certain way. For a long time gorillas were assumed to be violent and dangerous to man, and in fact there was plenty of
"data"—later proved erroneous—to that effect. Only recently
has the opposite been proved true. Hence, all the data showing
the gorilla's dangerous nature had to be thrown out, along with
ancient traditional lore that it enjoyed carrying human females
off for sexual purposes. One can only suppose that Green's
speculations—for they are nothing more—about the Sas-

quatch's nature are romantic projections of his own hopes. One cannot deny him the right to make such speculations, but to mistake hopeful guesses and overgeneralizations for evidence or proof would be an error.

Earlier I examined theoretical possibilities regarding the potential existence of a large unknown primate wandering parts of North America and/or the remote mountains of central Asia and the Himalayas. Nowhere did I suggest, nor should any investigator into this mystery accept, that such speculations ought to become a springboard for an entire hypothesis regarding a creature whose very existence remains questionable. I fear this is the trap into which John Green has fallen. The result is a superficially convincing mass of pure conjecture, which is presented as if it were based on a mass of evidence. In the long run, I suspect that Green's hard work can only result in more confusion. Even if, by some unlikely chance, certain of his guesses are one day borne out, the body of his work will surely fit into the realm of fable.

7. More Buffs and Some Boffola:
An Abominable Snow Job?

¢¢ ¢¢ ¢¢ ¢¢ ¢¢ ¢¢ ¢¢ ¢¢ ¢¢

Among the majority of the people in the field suspicion
and animosity is a minimal issue and is confined for the
most part to a mediocre few.

PETER BYRNE

The cross-currents of good guys and bad guys in local Sasquatch circles ebb, flow, and change so rapidly that I doubt
anyone can keep up with them.

DR. MARJORIE M. HALPIN
Curator of Ethnology
University of British Columbia

¢¢ ¢¢ ¢¢ ¢¢ ¢¢ ¢¢ ¢¢ ¢¢ ¢¢

Peter Byrne is probably the best-known Bigfoot hunter in the
English-speaking world. This is largely because he has successfully advertised himself. He distributes an attractive brochure
outlining his lectures and describing him thus: Explorer, Lec-
turer, Himalayan River Guide, Wilderness Survival Expert,
Author. A large photo is included showing a strikingly handsome man in his late middle years, graying at the temples, booted foot thrust forward on a hillside, keen eyes gazing into the
distance, binoculars in hand, a sweeping vista of river and valley behind. Byrne seems a bit larger than life in this picture,
and so he seems in the biographical blurbs contained within the
brochure.

Perhaps inevitably, Byrne has attracted some enmity from
other Bigfoot hunters, though he claims that he has many asso-

ciates in the business who refuse to be "taken in" by the misguided people who oppose him. Whatever the cause, the leading Bigfoot hunters and investigators have sadly been split in recent years into warring camps. Dahinden particularly has been active, initiating lawsuits, most recently charging Byrne with plagiarism.

In defense of his practices Byrne is careful to state that those who suggest that he is out for himself or careless with facts have never confronted him face to face, or even in writing. He pays little attention to these attacks, preferring to marshal his energies in the search. His organization, he adds, is too busy with serious research to waste time on these disputes.

Unfortunately, my personal experience with Byrne is limited to a few telephone conversations, to our correspondence over nearly a year, and to his publications. Months before I traveled to the Northwest I had made arrangements to interview him in person, and I hoped to meet with some of his associates as well. In the spring I scheduled a greater amount of time with Byrne than I allotted for the other meetings, as I considered him, on the basis of his publications, to be the most careful investigator. I informed Byrne in April, and again in early June, of my itinerary but received only brief postcards in response (the last arriving after I had flown to the Northwest). When I tried to settle our meeting plans from Corvallis, Oregon, where I attended the annual convention of the American Society of Mammalogists, I discovered that Byrne's business phone, at the Information Center, was out of service. His listed residence phone was also out of service. I could not, of course, obtain his unlisted number. Nevertheless, to keep my schedule, I drove to Hood River in late June, but I was unable to locate Byrne, having neither his private address nor unlisted number. From people in the region I heard that Byrne had "closed down" his Bigfoot activities, and this in a way proved to be correct. So I moved on to other interviews.

When I returned from my travels, I wrote Byrne, and he called at once, expressing his chagrin at the mix-up. He said he had no idea that I lacked his unlisted number or his address, but since these had not been sent to me, this statement seemed to be disingenuous. He was also sorry that I had not been informed about the closing of the Information Center. It was all just an unfortunate misunderstanding. Perhaps so. Byrne is a persuasive man; even over the phone I could sense the charm of his personality. He is smooth and articulate in the classic manner of the self-assured Briton: his explanations are coherent, almost convincing. He takes time to praise his coworkers, to refer to his association with the Bay Area group of Sasquatch hunters and to the Sacramento group, all dedicated people, many of whom have spent "thousands of hours" in research and in coordinating information through the center.

In this and in another longer interview by phone a few days later Byrne was modest to a fault; he played down his own role and rarely used the first person singular. What a refreshing change this was, after the previous interviews; what a contrast to the often defensive, sometimes obsessive preoccupations of other Bigfoot investigators. Byrne's answers to my questions were clipped, concise, precise. He explained that over a period of twenty or thirty years he has reduced perhaps three or four thousand reports to a "credible" list of no more than 101 or 102. But, no, he is not getting out of the Bigfoot search. It is true that the "first phases" of his operations are at an end. According to Byrne, the first phase of his operations began in 1960 and lasted only a year; this concentrated on research in California. The second concentrated on the Pacific Northwest for a period of nine years and was now terminated. The third phase, which he did not explain, would follow in due course. Byrne adds that he is not at liberty to explain why the second phase had ended and why the center closed.

I am chagrined. What an unfortunate coincidence, Byrne's closing down his public operations just at the time that I am researching the Bigfoot phenomenon in the Northwest. These telephone interviews are highly unsatisfactory. It is impossible to follow through with questions over a period of hours, and one needs the eye contact and body language of a personal encounter in these matters. I am left with contradictory impressions.

I try to get to the core of this obviously intelligent and attractive adventurer. Why is he still involved in the search, I ask, after so many years without success?

Byrne is almost eager, his mellifluous voice dramatic.

"Why? It is such a tremendous challenge. To me this was a hunt ... the most exciting challenge I've come up against. Also, perhaps what we have here is some form of primitive man."

Byrne refers to his history as a former big-game hunter in India and Nepal following his war service in the East and a brief stint as a tea-plantation manager. He explains how he gradually came over to the field of conservation, how he worked with the government of Nepal to build up that nation's first tiger sanctuary in the Terai jungles. As a former hunter of big game now dedicated to protecting wildlife, he says, what better endeavor than to help find this animal, and to protect it if possible?

As for the search for Bigfoot, Byrne emphatically adds, the supporting evidence is enough for him. The footprints, of course, and especially the eyewitness accounts have been convincing. He has interviewed many impressive witnesses himself. He has devised an elaborate rating system to separate credible information from unreliable reports.

I return to the problem of the in-fighting between Bigfoot experts, which seems to me unnecessary, even ridiculous. This impression, Byrne archly replies, is mostly the doing of Dahinden and, to a lesser extent, of Green. He says he is sorry this is so. In his opinion such vindictiveness is a form of fear—fear that others might get there first. In his opinion such an attitude suggests territoriality. He adds, "They are really silly, running around with guns in the backs of pickups, trying to get a million dollars if they shoot a Sasquatch. This is a minimal issue, largely confined to the mediocre few."

Later, via correspondence, Byrne admits to having made a few errors in his work. Who, after all, fails to make mistakes? he asks rhetorically. But he and his associates have been as careful as possible. They made an unfortunate mistake regarding the 1967 film footage from Bluff Creek, which they now believe to be of dubious authenticity. Byrne also cites examples of success, including instances in which his "credit-rating system" has enabled him and his helpers confidently to declare several incidents to be outright hoaxes. He strongly defends his involvement over the years as a total and ongoing effort.

"Nonstop, seven days a week, twelve months of the year for nine years. We have been ongoing as a profession, not as a hobby, not as a part-time occupation, not as 'weekend searchers' but as full-time, nine-to-five working researchers."

Yes, he is fully cognizant of the attitude of many scientists who consider the phenomenon a "fringe science" and are therefore scared off. On the other hand, Byrne says that many scientists who have worked with him have deliberately kept a low profile, on his promise of confidentiality. For this reason he is sorry but he cannot reveal their names. They include people at the American Museum of Natural History, in New York; at the Smithsonian; at two of the nation's primate-studies institutes; and most recently at the so-called Academy of Applied Science in Boston. According to Byrne, only in the latter case is the need for confidentiality unnecessary. The Boston organization openly acknowledges its support of the Bigfoot search, just as it does for the quest for the Loch Ness monster.

Questioned about the range of the Bigfoot, Byrne adds that he gives no credence to the possibility of any large, unclassified primates living in the states or provinces outside the Northwest. He attributes reports from such places to imagination, sensationalism—which he abhors—fakery, and the psychological attraction of the Bigfoot field.

Judging from this limited contact, and from his publications, Byrne is certainly one of the better organized among the well-known hunters of Bigfoot. He is clearly the kind of man who has contacts. And unlike the others in this field, Byrne originally took the trouble to organize a nonprofit corporation to back up his search and to support his related activities. The fact that others are suspicious of his motives and methods and claim him to be a wheeler-dealer is certainly not proof that his efforts have been insincere.

A vignette of recent vintage helps to illustrate the factionalism of the Bigfoot fraternity. In the spring of 1978 a Sasquatch conference was held at the University of British Columbia, in Vancouver. Its formal title was "Anthropology of the Un- known Sasquatch and Similar Phenomena." This symposium was sponsored by the UBC Museum of Anthropology, its Cen- tre for Continuing Education, with the assistance of the Canada Council, and the UBC Press. Many scholars participated and read papers on topics ranging from the traditions of the "wild man" in Europe to "wild men" on the Northwest Pacific Coast, to "the politics of hominology." Also in attendance were many Sasquatch hunters, including John Green, René Dahinden, Bob Gimlin, Barbara Wasson, Dennis Gates, Ron Olson, and Peter Byrne.

The purposes of this conference, arranged by the academic community, were serious and worthwhile. (A publication con- taining the most important papers was scheduled to appear in 1980.) But it is what went on behind the scenes at this sympo- sium that is most interesting. The various factions, particularly the groups led by Dahinden and Byrne, began to go after one another. Old enmities were aroused and new ones engendered. Most of these arguments, and the scrambling for attention and publicity, centered around the opposing positions of "hunt and kill" and "don't kill," positions that have become attached re- spectively to René Dahinden and Peter Byrne, though they were originally staked out by John Green and the late Bigfoot buff George Hass. Soon it was obvious, to bemused scholars and reporters alike, that there was more to this bitter factional- ism than mere disagreement on what to do if a Sasquatch were found, whether to shoot it or protect it.

Personalities are obviously central to much of this angry divi- sion. At one point during a presentation of a paper in the uni- versity auditorium, Peter Byrne entered rather late, as he was wont to do according to several people who attended the con- ference. And he did not enter alone. The auditorium had been rigged with bright lights for the making of a film of the pro- ceedings; cameramen with long, heavy cords weaved through the crowd. Cameras began to grind and the noise level rose. Participating academics and the audience grew restless. Many individuals were upset because their permission to be filmed had not been asked for. Byrne, ostentatiously taking notes, had become the center of attention during this commotion. Apparently his colleague in the exploitation of the unusual and the weird, the filmmaker Alan Landsburg, had made him the star of this production. Indeed it was part of a planned documentary on the Bigfoot and yeti, tentatively to be titled *Myths and Monsters,* with Byrne, of course, playing the lead.

Soon the halls outside the auditorium and other rooms were filled with dissension and bitter argument; tempers frayed. The Dahinden faction were especially bitter and furious. Soon it was discovered that permission to film during the conference had indeed been granted by the university to the Landsburg production group. Many oldtime Sasquatch investigators seethed with disgust. Some of them, at least, were probably aroused more out of envy than for any other reason. Rumors floated and accusations flew thick and fast. Eventually the university was forced to ask the filmmakers to leave; several academics with papers to read would not agree to be filmed. Many onlookers, too, were upset at being cast as unwilling extras.

Somehow René Dahinden was identified as the central figure in this successful attempt to stop the filming. This seemed to be the case. The movie men were in turn bitter and accusatory. Byrne, stunned by the reaction, seemed upset, chagrined, subdued.

It is especially interesting that Byrne was not even on the agenda of this conference. His presence was apparently part of a design in the making of his commercial film. Several people noted that he had not bothered to attend important sessions and paid little or no attention to key papers.

On the other hand, many of the Bigfoot people at the conference seemed intent on selling their books and other Sasquatch paraphernalia. There appears to have been little in the way of a meeting of the minds among scholars genuinely interested in the phenomenon and the traditional Bigfoot crowd. This seems to have been through no fault of the academics. What the scholars had to say did not much interest most of the searchers, because for the most part the papers provided alternative explanations for the Bigfoot phenomenon. And what the old-time searchers and buffs had to say seems mostly to have aroused the curiosity of the bemused scholars. One anthropologist, wandering the halls during the worst of these disputes, was heard muttering to his colleagues, "My, my. We must find some way to study these people. They are a subculture all their own."

Dr. Marjorie Halpin, an organizer of the UBC Sasquatch conference, noted that there seemed to be a solid and consistent view that Byrne was the bad guy, and that she had yet to find anyone who supported him. More important, in Dr. Halpin's view, was the attempt on her part and that of her colleagues "to achieve a certain academic integrity . . . for the inquiry itself."

At this point it might seem that the prospects for the existence of our elusive Sasquatch are bleak indeed. Of course, the entire undertaking has been speculative from the beginning. Thousands of pages have been written and mountains of information sifted, only to come back again to that damnable and final problem of proof.

Quite naturally people ask whether the Patterson-Gimlin film isn't proof enough. This is a crucial question. What better way to approach it than to interview the only survivor between the two men who allegedly filmed the Sasquatch at Bluff Creek in the autumn of 1967.

In some ways Bob Gimlin is the most interesting of all the well-known Sasquatch crowd. This is partly because he is really not that serious about the whole matter. He is much more involved with his work, his horses, and his private life than with the ongoing search for Bigfoot. If he is a willing participant in a hoax, he has been brilliantly cast. If he is an unwilling participant, he is the perfect foil. If everything he says is exactly as he says it is, he is almost too good to be true.

I am interviewing Gimlin, at his suggestion, in a crowded restaurant in a garish shopping center near Yakima, Washington. With him is his attractive wife. It is another very hot afternoon in June. Gimlin is a smallish man, but strong and wiry. His regular, rather handsome features are tanned and lined, as one might expect in an avid outdoorsman and an expert horseman partly of Indian descent. His manner is quiet and polite; his voice can be calming in its understated tenor. He appears to be in his late thirties or early forties and he conveys an impression of youthful goodwill, as if he is determined that all this hullabaloo will not affect his sense of camaraderie or humor. One gets the impression that Gimlin would be quite happy if this whole Bigfoot thing just faded away. Yet he is outspoken in his conviction about his experience. If he is telling the whole truth, and one can only wish to extend him the full benefit of the doubt, then he is living witness to an unprecedented and extraordinary event. For when Bob Gimlin saw his Sasquatch, as nearly every Bigfoot buff in the world must know, his partner, the late Roger Patterson, was engaged in filming the strange being, in color, using a sixteen-millimeter Kodak camera.

The resulting film is one of the most controversial and important documents in the bulging file of international Sasquatchery. Watching this film, the viewer sees a dark humanlike figure striding away from the camera at an oblique angle in a deliberate but unhurried walk. Almost at the beginning of the footage the hairy figure wheels briefly to look back, turning its upper body and head, without actually breaking stride, before continuing its almost casual progress through the scrubby creek bottom. Since there are visible pendulous breasts, the figure seems to be female, but the gait has a decidedly masculine quality to it; at any rate, it seems to be masculine in human terms, with a strong suggestion of masculine size and strength. Because of the motion of the hand-held camera, details are rather blurred, and the dark shape. moving through the hard light of a mid-October day is slightly underexposed. Also, the weird figure is too far from the camera, from the first frame to the last, to discern the kind of anatomical characteristics that are basic to good animal photography, especially cinematography. Since the camera lacked a telephoto lens, the figure occu-

pies only a tiny portion of each frame. Despite repeated claims
to the contrary, this film is not of good quality. It is neither up
to the minimum standard for acceptable amateur wildlife photography nor even close to the accepted professional standard.

Even if this film really does show a Sasquatch, it will be forever impossible to prove, unless or until such a beast is found.
By the same token, if the film shows nothing more than a "man
in a monkey suit," this too will be impossible to prove, unless
someone someday steps forward and admits to a fraud. Millions
have seen this film, and many viewers have remarked about the
"baggy" appearance around the lower part of the figure's torso,
especially the buttocks. I did get this impression. It looks to me
rather like a human being, powerful and heavyset, or well padded so as to appear bulky and strong, wearing a fur costume
that fits exceptionally well except in the area of the seat. Many
people have also remarked that the figure conveys an impression of reality too convincing to be faked. To some people the
figure appears much too large to be human; to others it seems
easily within the range of a large man.

Analyses of the film have been mixed. The scientific community generally dismisses it as a fake. However, certain biomechanics experts, among others, express doubt that it is a fake.*
Of course, the veracity of the film cannot be determined by
technical analysis alone. It is actually too poor in quality to be
considered evidence in itself. Experts might argue till kingdom
come, but the fact remains that the truth rests with two men.
Roger Patterson, the man who held the camera, died in 1974.
The other participant is the man who sits before me in this
noisy restaurant, speaking above the clatter of dishes and the
intrusive Muzak. My feeling as Bob Gimlin relates his story is
that he has not contrived his narrative. He seems to be telling it
as he remembers it, sometimes without pause, sometimes halt-
ing to jog his memory. It occurs to me as it has to others that
Gimlin could himself be a victim of a clever hoax, though he
seems an unlikely man to pick for such a scam. There is no

---

*Further details of this controversy are summarized in Appendix A.

doubt that Patterson had a controversial reputation, even among Bigfoot hunters. This could be unfair, but one cannot pretend that reputation is not pertinent.

In any case Gimlin's testimony is revealing and fascinating. In spite of the questions it raises, it is a good story.

Gimlin's adventure began in late September of 1967 when he and Patterson were returning from a Sasquatch hunt in the region of Mount St. Helens, a wild region to the southwest of Mt. Rainier. Apparently Patterson received news from his wife that new Bigfoot tracks had been reported in the Bluff Creek region of California. Patterson had previously visited this region, well known to Sasquatch hunters, and knew it quite well. So he and Gimlin threw the essential gear together and drove at once down to Bluff Creek. They used Gimlin's one-ton truck and carried three horses.

Unfortunately, when they arrived at Bluff Creek, the two men discovered that heavy rains had wiped out the reported footprints, and now the creek beds were filled with new deposits of mud and gravel, crisscrossed with logjams. They decided to stay anyway, apparently stretching their whimsical search out for nearly three more weeks. As Gimlin says, "I had two weeks off, in between jobs, where I was working. So, we said let's stay down here a couple weeks and see what we can come up with, you know. Because you never can tell. There wasn't anybody else in the area."

So the two cowboys from Yakima searched through the remote canyons around Bluff Creek, using their horses by day to search the areas away from the logging roads and the truck by night to look for footprints along the roads themselves. They could not safely drive the roads in the daytime, because of the huge logging rigs that high-balled down the narrow cuts just wide enough to allow one vehicle to pass.

Gimlin seems confused about exact dates. He suggests, for example, that he and Patterson arrived in the Bluff Creek area on or about October 1. Later he states that they had searched for about two weeks before the film was taken, then he adds that it must have been around the 17th or the 19th of October. Among Bigfoot experts, including John Green and René Dahinden, the accepted date is October 20, which puts the time span at close to three weeks in the wilderness.* No explanation that I know of has been offered for this strange uncertainty about time on the part of an experienced outdoorsman. Gimlin is the kind of man who would normally be aware of the daily depletion of food supplies, fodder for the horses, gasoline, not to mention the simple passage of the days. One might assume that such an extraordinary experience would have printed the exact date indelibly in his mind.

In any case, Gimlin and Patterson found nothing for many days, nothing but tracks of deer, bear, and cougar. Both have related that they passed some time making films of daily routines, and certain random scenes of the glorious autumn foliage do indeed appear in the commercial movie that was released across the country in the early 1970s. But then, as the world knows, they rounded that small bend in Bluff Creek on that famous clear Saturday (if it *was* October 20), and the rest is history. Or is it?

Certain aspects of the experience as related by Gimlin demand further attention. According to Gimlin, at the moment when they spotted the hairy figure, the two men were in file on horseback, Patterson ahead, Gimlin behind, leading the packhorse. All the cameras, including the movie camera, were in the saddlebags. Gimlin says, "[Patterson's horse] started rarin' up and raisin' the devil. And Roger, he just kind of slid back off his horse's hip and reached down in the saddlebag. Roger was real small and agile-like. He was a rodeo rider. And he pulled his camera out. Of course, by then, even a few seconds before that, I'd seen the thing."

Gimlin's version of the moments immediately following the sighting, when Patterson tried to focus the camera on the apparition but failed to do so until the figure was already a considerable distance away, would seem to provide a partial explanation for the wild motion revealed in the opening frames of the footage, and possibly for the confusion about which

---

*This is often dismissed as a typical "minor" discrepancy, but of course the exact date of the filming is all-important. It is not clear why Patterson's testimony as to the exact date is considered definitive.

frame speed was used. But it should be noted that an earlier reported version of the event, based on Patterson's initial story and repeated by Sanderson in his *Argosy* piece, suggests that all the confusion resulted when both riders were thrown by their rearing horses. Also, Patterson must have somehow managed to set the camera to the correct F-stop, since the film's exposure is roughly correct for the location and time of day. And why did Patterson not simply check the camera after the event, to note its setting? After so many days of fairly regular use, by both his own and Gimlin's account, Patterson was surely familiar with the camera.

There seems to be another minor discrepancy. Patterson's initial story, as reported by Sanderson early in 1968, claims that the reason he finally managed to focus the camera and make the film was that the Sasquatch suddenly stopped and turned to look at him. Gimlin remembers it differently. He says that the filming had already commenced when the figure turned its head and upper body fully around to face the intruders. Gimlin is certain that this movement was in response to his own motion, as he moved up on horseback, to dismount behind Patterson. He believes the creature turned to watch him.

There are other minor variations, depending on the date and origin of the source. Apparently this vital segment of the famous tale is forever garbled by inconsistent testimony. Patterson's account seems to have changed in the years since the story was first revealed to the public.

The events subsequent to the filming are also not entirely clear in Gimlin's account. Apparently, when the film ran out and the creature had disappeared, Patterson persuaded Gimlin to abandon immediate pursuit, and the two men took time to catch Patterson's stray horse, reload the camera, and return to the tracks. Sometime thereafter they measured the tracks for foot size and length of stride. According to Gimlin, the stride varied between forty-two and forty-eight inches on the level ground, where the film was taken, lengthening to between sixty-eight and seventy-two inches beyond the bend. Gimlin recalls that he and Patterson followed these tracks for perhaps a mile up the creek bed until the footprints disappeared up a steep rocky cliff. Sometime before dark they made plaster-of-paris casts and took photos of the footprints, contrasting them with their own prints for comparison of size and depth. Then, says Gimlin, they drove out of Bluff Creek and down to the village of Willow Creek, where they spoke briefly with a Mr. Hodson at a variety store. Apparently they picked up pieces of cardboard boxes at this place, to cover the footprints in the sands of Bluff Creek. Sometime later that night the two men drove to the larger town of Eureka, where the precious undeveloped roll of film was flown out directly to Yakima, there to be handled by one of Patterson's relatives. Gimlin is careful to add that he does not himself remember the name of the place from which they sent the film but only that he is repeating what Patterson had said on several occasions.

Why this decision was made to fly the film out in this fashion has never been properly explained. Gimlin states that he and Patterson had no idea whether the exposed film was any good, and he adds that the two of them did not want to leave the region of Bluff Creek because they hoped soon to guide the Canadians (John Green and René Dahinden, among others) who had already been telephoned from Willow Creek and who might arrive at the site shortly. It certainly seems unusual that two such clever and worldly men would allow such an extraordinary piece of undeveloped film to be sent unescorted by air to a brother-in-law in Yakima, who subsequently is supposed to have taken it to Seattle for processing. All medium-sized towns have photo shops with skilled technicians capable of handling such a roll of film. If Eureka lacks such facilities, there are other sizable towns, such as Medford, not far away. Also, if the film had proved useless for some reason, the few hours of extra time would make no difference—even a child knows as much about ruined film—and if the film proved good (as, presumably, it did), there would be ample time to study it at leisure later on. One would assume that at least one of the pair would have kept the precious film closely guarded and been present when it was developed, if for no other reason than to avoid charges of tampering or fabrication. Judging from his book on the Bigfoot mystery, Patterson at least was well aware of the fact that any film would be greeted with a high degree of skepticism.

So there are clearly elements in this segment of the narrative that seem inconsistent, that appear to be quite out of character, that lead to strong doubts.

Gimlin says that he and Patterson returned later that night to their camp at Bluff Creek, apparently situated at the location of the filming. Before dawn a hard rain began to fall, one of those seemingly endless downpours that periodically drench the towering forests of that region. For a time, according to Gimlin, he and Patterson tried to cover the Sasquatch footprints with the pieces of cardboard. But it was to no avail, for the storm raged on, and soon the intrepid searchers were faced with a terrific struggle just to extract the truck and the horses intact from the wilderness. Eventually they made their way, exhausted, to Yakima.

Gimlin's saga of the escape from Bluff Creek is important in itself, and very revealing. This is because of the published statement of Bigfoot hunter Bob Titmus, which is included in *Sasquatch: The Apes Among Us,* by John Green. In Chapter 6 of Green's book, Titmus dramatically describes how he himself studied the Bluff Creek tracks and how he found these tracks to be "in good condition," along with the tracks made by Patterson's and Gimlin's horses. Titmus includes other details, claiming he found the place where the Sasquatch had sat down among ferns in the forest, apparently to watch the two cowboys below. He also claims that he found the Bigfoot tracks covered with "pieces of bark" put there by Patterson and Gimlin. He claims to have made several casts of these footprints. In Green's book there is a photo of Titmus displaying these casts.

The trouble is that Titmus states that all this was done nine or ten days after the famous incident of October 20. Gimlin's account of the narrow escape from the confines of Bluff Creek during the terrible rainstorm of October 20–21 makes it clear that the entire bed of the creek was quickly awash, quite unsafe even for a large truck, dangerous even for two experienced outdoorsmen with sturdy horses. Such gorges encourage flash floods, mud slides, and other hazards, and this is exactly what Gimlin describes in lucid detail. At one point he recalls that mud slides nearly destroyed his truck. He and Patterson just barely extricated themselves by taking a treacherous high road out of the gorge, with the aid of a construction loader that they found at the top of a ridge. The creek at the bottom of the gorge had already risen, in Gimlin's words, to a "raging river." How any Bigfoot tracks, whether covered by cardboard or bark, could survive such a storm is not explained. Did the overflowing creek somehow not wash the tracks away, leaving them in "good condition," for Titmus to find them nine or ten days later?

By now it should be clear that even the most famous and widely believed Bigfoot stories are rarely checked out for detail, including relevant events and circumstances preceding and following the alleged incidents. A thorough investigation, including interviews of all the people involved, determining where they were and when, the important dates, times, and the sequence of events, the name of the camera shop that developed the film, would almost certainly reveal further interesting problems with the above case. Gimlin's story may well be an honest account of his personal experience, but it is obviously not the whole story. And whether or not we ever learn the whole truth, it is safe to assume that few unbiased observers would wish to take the time to follow up every lead. There is simply too much about the whole episode that smells suspiciously of skunk.

Summing up the impact of these interviews and of my travels through the Pacific Northwest is difficult. I traveled on the ground through huge tracts of Oregon, Washington, and British Columbia, traversing forests, mountains, wild coastline and arid plain, with many green valleys in between. I camped in the high Cascades and hiked up into the forested slopes beneath Mt. Washington, Mt. Hood, Mt. Adams, Mt. Olympus. I walked deep into sections of several National Forests, including Willamette, Pinchot, Wenatchee, Olympic. I drove sections of the fjordlike coast of Vancouver Island and camped on the misty, rock-bound Pacific coast of the Olympic Peninsula amid huge cedars and hemlocks. I sat at dusk watching sea birds wheel over tremendous washed-up tree trunks scattered along the narrow strip beneath the cliffs. In many of the places where our elusive Sasquatch has been reported I found little to indicate that such a beast could survive, unknown, the year round, at least not without great difficulty. Even in the rain forests of the Coast Range, the overall topography, flora, fauna, and even the relatively mild climate appear to be barely adequate for the survival of a gigantic omnivorous primate of unknown natural origin, an animal that would have to coexist with man as well as with other animals.

Regarding the winter survival of such an animal, Dr. Van Gelder is even more dubious than I.

> You'd have to hypothesize hibernation, or at least winter sleep like a bear, and that would involve tremendous fat deposition and extensive feeding through the summer. No one has mentioned steatopygia [concentration of fat in the region of the buttocks] for a Sasquatch—and Gimlin's female was filmed in the autumn. . . . Therefore, if they are winter dormant, they would have to be fat, but that one was seen just before winter, and she wasn't.

I am aware that Van Gelder cannot repeatedly address his impressive skills to the Sasquatch mystery without an occasional ironic comment about the capacity for self-deception that seems to go with the phenomenon. But I also know that his knowledge of what it takes for any large mammal to survive in any given habitat, particularly those with which he has a lifelong familiarity, should not be taken lightly.

The fact that the American Society of Mammalogists held their annual convention at Oregon State University, located in Corvallis, directly beneath the shadow of Oregon's Front Range, was another fortuitous circumstance in my research during the summer of 1979. Although I had attended the meetings to participate in an elephant symposium and to read a paper on the ivory trade, many of the mammalogists knew that I was re-

searching the Bigfoot mystery. So I received many helpful suggestions and comments, not all of them solicited. I cannot begin
to summarize them but the gist is simple enough and basically
in agreement with Van Gelder. The most frequent comments
related to how such a huge animal could feed year round—a hi-
bernating higher primate seems "ludicrous to contemplate," as
one world-traveled primatologist remarked—or conduct its
mating and rearing behavior. Why is the data about young or
even half-grown Sasquatches virtually nonexistent, and how
could such large creatures consistently avoid serious injury, ac-
cidental or even natural death, which would leave ample physical evidence? (Not to mention death at human hands.)

Even if one can supply adequate responses to these questions—and the Bigfoot fraternity does so with imagination and
gusto—the questions are sobering and help keep one's feet
firmly on the ground after long immersion in the alluring
world of Sasquatchery.

Of all the places I visited, only the Olympic Peninsula
seemed lush enough in its dense understory to support and
hide a large omnivore, as big as or bigger than a grizzly bear,
year round. And, it must be remembered, the grizzly perished
in that range decades ago.

In the summer it is true that one encounters regions of abundant vegetation—scores of species of edible berries, dense rhododendrons, buckthorn, dogwood, rose hips, and so on. But in
places like the eastern slope of the Cascades, where alleged Bigfoot sightings are frequent, the landscape is covered in great
open stands of ponderosa pine, and the understory is mostly
open and sparse. One can point to plenty of places where a Bigfoot might hide, in inaccessible canyons and gorges, but for
such a creature to elude human beings successfully, with all
their devices, weapons, and dogs, seems to demand intelligence
on the part of the creature at least equal to that of man. I could
not avoid speculating about how long a determined and healthy
human, knowing the woods and woodcraft, able to live off the
land and likewise evade avenues of seasonal human activity,
might be able to survive, undetected, in those mountains in any
of the many ranges. Ten years? Twenty? It could be done, of

course. Maybe it has been done—Sasquatch searchers repeatedly point out individual tribes and individual Indians that have turned up unexpectedly from time to time—but the analogy isn't worth much. Humans are not the same as Bigfoot would have to be, and we *know* that Indians are and always have been present. Surely, in answer to the argument that Bigfoot has exceptional physical attributes, it is obvious that physical gifts alone would not be enough. The element of chance, the law of averages, would sooner or later play a role.

And what about the idea of *several* creatures? All species must breed, and among higher primates this requires long-drawn-out and risky processes of rearing offspring. Then there is that compelling process of mating—or is our creature some kind of unexpected, unprecedented evolutionary freak, a haploid perhaps, able to reproduce by inseminating itself, having within it the necessary reproductive organs of both sexes?

I did not confine my talks throughout the Northwest to scholars and Bigfoot cognoscenti; I also talked with dozens of ordinary people—ranchers, rangers, farmers, hikers, fishermen, hunters, townspeople—all who were familiar with the regions where Bigfoot has been reported. The overwhelming majority were dubious, sometimes scornful of the idea that such a huge, partly carnivorous creature could live anywhere near them without their knowledge. Even if the animal limited its kill to moderate-sized game, it would soon be known to them. A rancher who once hunted mountain lions said that people can easily go a lifetime with one of the big cats hunting nearby without ever seeing the creature, but they are aware of its presence through the normal signs. And if such a cat hits livestock, it will quickly be tracked down with dogs and killed. Among knowledgeable outdoorsmen the habits of the larger mammals are widely known in any given area, even in the most remote wildernesses. It is interesting that most Bigfoot experts claim that the same kinds of signs, or spoor, as are normal for other larger mammals are consistently available for Bigfoot, but when knowledgeable local ranchers or rangers are asked about this, they deny it emphatically. Most of these people frankly consider the whole idea rather silly. Often they will remark about the publicity that the buffs get, or seek. Since my immersion in the subject I am willing to concede that such attitudes are probably unfair, but they certainly reflect the predominant feeling among locals.

A related comment I often got from local outdoorsmen went something like this: "I'm not saying there is no such thing, all through these mountains, but not around *here*. I know this area too well. If there's such a critter here, I'd know about it. Maybe over *there*, on that eastern slope, or beyond that divide. I don't know." Invariably, when I went to the people "over there" and asked the same question, I got the same response.

Nor was I surprised at how human beings pop up in the most remote and unexpected places. The Pacific Northwest and its montane roof contain regions that are more rugged than anything in the Midwest, the East, or the South, but it is hardly the totally unexplored wilderness the Bigfoot buffs pretend it to be. At one point in my peregrinations I determined to get deep into the forest, so I hiked up under Mt. Adams late one morning into the Pinchot National Forest, north of the tiny hamlet of Trout Lake, a wild region by any standard. Below, to the east and southeast, flowed the Klickitat River, fed by alpine streams that cut their way through deep gorges that emerge from the snowy flanks of the huge dormant volcano above. This was an oft-cited Bigfoot zone. Eventually I cut off from the rarely traveled path, which was rough going itself, and blazed my way for perhaps another two hours, quite certain I was going where no human had gone before, doing my best to follow the rugged contours of the landscape. Near a large rocky bluff, above a cascading rapids surrounded by huge firs, hemlocks, and pines, I rested and used my binoculars to watch the jays and other forest birds. Soon, overheated by the hike, sweating in the hot sun, I bathed in the frigid creek and stretched out on the sun-warmed rocks to dry off, secure in my sense of being alone. Later, still naked, I sat up to eat my cheese and bread and oranges, and to drink my warm beer. Suddenly I was greeted by a cheerful "Hi there!" Four youngsters came through, two strapping fellows and two bronzed blond amazons, backpacks rising and falling as they pushed on, nodding and smiling.

Without a pause they just kept going and I just sat there in the altogether, feeling like a surprised Sasquatch. Presently I dressed, gathered up my orange peels, and tramped back down to the road in the late afternoon.

One well-publicized Bigfoot hunter once received recognition from the Explorers Club in New York, apparently for "explorations" conducted by airplane flights in the British Columbian wilderness, landing at various small strips in the bush and taking short hikes. A century ago and more, many less celebrated, mostly unknown explorers crisscrossed the same uninhabited regions on foot, prospecting for gold and other minerals, or hunting and trapping. To say that there are thousands of square miles where no one has walked is, in our era, a misleading statement.

Perhaps I belabor this issue, but reading most of the Bigfoot literature can only be misleading to anyone whose experience in wilderness regions is confined to this continent. Truly, certain of the rain forests in the Pacific Northwest are impressively dense and lush. But I have often seen, even lived and worked within, tropical rain forests in Africa that are infinitely more various in their vegetation and animal life than anything in the temperate zones, including the Coast and Olympic Ranges. Too much is made of the uniqueness of the Pacific Northwest as a potential habitat for an unknown primate. Perhaps more important, taking the region as a *whole*—since the range of "credible" sightings certainly encompasses the whole montane block of the Northwest—it is not appreciably more lush in its vegetation (either in variety or density) than many other favored ecological zones in other parts of North America. In most of British Columbia the understory is impoverished, and there are segments of Michigan's lowland forest that are more lush in their floral variety—the year round—than the majority of the Northwest's mountainous woods. The same can be said with greater emphasis about the southern ramparts of the Appalachians, or the subtropical forests of the Gulf Coast. Comments about the tiny human population in the Northwest are also misleading. The population is only small by contrast to the current and absurdly high densities in other regions. Compared, for example, to the population of medieval Europe, or even to that of Colonial America, the human population of the region from northern California to the northern reaches of British Columbia is large. There is a marked ahistorical tendency in the popular Bigfoot literature, an apparent determination to ignore the processes of history, that is almost as pronounced as the tendency to ignore the basic precepts of biology.

I will not deny that one can find really wild places where no one goes, where humans never walk. But what does that prove? There are few places left on earth where men will not or cannot go. My honest sense of the whole glorious region of the Pacific Northwest is that it would seem next to impossible for several hundred, or even twoscore, huge humanoid or apelike creatures to survive uncaptured, unkilled, even in those vast forests, canyons, and mountains.

Yet I recall an experience in the Olympic Range. It was early afternoon. I had driven west on Highway 101 from Port Angeles through a portion of the National Park. The sun was almost directly overhead, its rays like huge pillars descending through the towering canopy of trees, as if to match the giant trunks with columns of light. I sat in a mosquito-humming glade, my light backpack propped against a nearby tree, and took notes with the aid of my field guides—notes on trees and shrubs; on grasses, sedges, ferns; on insects and animals, discerned by sight, sound, and sign. The rented car was down on the road, perhaps a mile or more away. This time I was truly alone. Who would want to come here, to trace me through the tumbled and fallen firs, over the wind-blown cedars, through the thickets of spruce and alder? A small stream flowed gently perhaps thirty feet away, but the insects were worse there, so I stayed in the glade. My stomach was full of hastily wolfed jerky, nearly a quarter pound of cheddar, a third of a loaf of uncut pumpernickel, and an apple, all washed down with a Thermos full of processed cider. Sweat still coursed down my body into my shorts and down my legs. My belt was sodden, my hair dank. The effort to go even this far into the deep rain forest had severely taxed my energy. My legs no longer trembled, but I could feel the deep ache of lactic-acid buildup in the muscles.

No daily jogging could precondition the body for this; the keen stresses and sharp-tinged pleasures of wilderness hiking must be taken bit by bit.

On the way in I had seen a mule deer in a small clearing, where a giant cedar had fallen so long ago that only a long cylinder of green in the forest floor indicated its long-rotted carcass. The deer had run only a few feet and then stopped to watch, its head turned, ears erect, tail down. Accustomed to the "white flag" of the whitetail deer of home, I felt alien, intruding. Unaccountably, I had also spotted a ghost of the night; a flying squirrel, its white underbelly flashing through dappled light, silent in its gliding passage to a lower thicket beyond my line of sight. Entirely nocturnal, the squirrel must have been prompted by a predator. Earlier I had seen a circling hawk, not far above a towering dead fir. Near the stream, there were what looked like bobcat scats, unscratched and unburied in a tumble of smallish rocks, beneath an angled tree that made a mossy bridge high onto the far side. Sitting back, my notes completed, a new coat of insect repellent glistening on my arms, legs, and face, I dozed. The hike back out to the road would be difficult, maybe even a little dangerous. I had marked my way with broken twigs and simple blazes and I had learned half a dozen clear landmarks—a gigantic half-dead cedar, a cluster of almost identical firs, octuplets of perfect shape, an outcropping of rock that seemed to spring alive from a grassy hollow, a tributary brook to the larger stream. Could Sasquatch live in this place? I wondered. Or something like it? Drifting unwillingly into sleep, almost dreaming, I awoke with a start. Something had moved beyond the forest wall, beyond the glade, at the extreme-right periphery of my vision. A small breeze had sprung up through the trees. I stared into the gloom. Suddenly, in a momentary flash of half-conscious apprehension and expectation, there stood a huge creature, hulking, dark, enormous. It seemed to glower at me from beyond the inner ring of trees, its body like a tree trunk, its vast arms reaching to the earth, into the ground. The deep shadows moved very little as the wind stirred, moaning now through the towering tops of the conifers hundreds of feet above. My instant of recognition passed, and all I could see was a lightning-splintered tree, truncated to about ten or twelve feet above the ground, its upper part domed, with huge, jagged shoulders sloping from a peaked splinter to the ridged bark beneath. Gray-green moss and gray fungi coated the tree on two thirds of its surface. I had noticed it coming in, and I had wondered then what life it harbored beneath its grand decaying exterior, within its vast rotting cylinder. But I had not expected this tree trunk to turn into Sasquatch almost before my eyes. My head buzzed.

Though enormously relieved at my delusion, I was also secretly disappointed. What if I *had* seen a Sasquatch? I kept asking myself. Would I have believed it myself? Who else would believe? Like all the searchers—although unlike them, too, for I would fully expect to find nothing myself—my testimony would be quite worthless.

Or would it be?

Of course, my sense of skepticism was reinforced by that fleeting illusion, that glimpse into the psychic past of our species. But so was my sense of wonder. Had I been born several centuries earlier, or within another culture not so long ago, I might have emerged from the woods to tell my tale of an encounter with a giant. And I would probably have been taken as creditable. Today I would have been mostly disbelieved, perhaps even scorned, listened to by only a few. Would what I believed I had seen been unreal for all of that? For as the poet says, the mind is its own place.

8. Common Sense About Evidence

Of actual physical evidence for the ABSMs we have possibly one or two desiccated human-looking hands, a few piles of excrement, and, now, some hundreds of miles (in the aggregate) of tracks. We are right back where we started—with lots of reports but practically no facts.

IVAN SANDERSON
in *Abominable Snowmen:
Legend Come to Life*

Under normal circumstances, natural evidence about a given species, whether it be a huge mammal or a tiny insect, is based on direct study of the animal itself—its size, shape, diet, behavior, and so on. These characteristics are determined through analysis either of a living form or of a dead specimen, or in a few cases from the study of a skeleton or other remnants, including fossils. For Bigfoot there is no such material evidence, as Sanderson and his colleagues readily admit. All we really have is the footprints.

Knowing this is one thing, but Bigfoot writers have forged ahead with elaborate hypothetical concepts anyway, ignoring the demands of scientific methodology, in which generalizations are rarely accepted without provable data. Thus, a false impression is created in most cases, especially for the unwary or untrained, an impression that theories about Bigfoot are based on broadly known facts. Few of the Bigfoot experts have bothered over the years even to categorize the evidence they so often refer to. Only Sanderson has systematically done so, so it is convenient to fall back on his designations for a quick, unbiased look.

From the start it is impossible to disagree with Sanderson's admission that his "intrinsic" evidence (skin, hair, blood, etc.) is too paltry to be of use. The nature of such evidence is further limited—even if more of it were found—by the fact that many species of mammals have minor but wide-ranging variations in blood type, skin color and texture, and hair. Humans are a good example of this. A sizable piece of hide, in decent condition, might be readily identified as belonging to a given species, but if the sample is incomplete, degenerated, or tanned, identification becomes difficult. So why do rumors of such evidence persist? Unfortunately, any inability to get a positive identification is often taken by believers to mean that the sample in question is "unknown," and by a leap of logic they argue that it is evidence for the existence of the creature. There is no good argument against such *faith,* but no serious biologist would long consider the infinitesimal amount of material in this category as worth a second thought.

On the other hand, evidence within Sanderson's "cognate" category (excrement and tracks) appears to be abundant. If this weren't so, virtually nobody would take the Bigfoot phenomenon seriously. But, as I have pointed out earlier, there is great pretense in the argument that pieces of fecal matter or footprints constitute proof that an unknown primate exists. Napier is correct when he states that until other evidence is forthcoming, the reality of the creature stands or falls on this evidence. So we are left with the supposed impressions that these giants have made upon the surface of the earth.

Robinson Crusoe, when he spotted a human footprint on the sandy beach of his desert isle, had good reason to know that he was no longer alone. And the image that Daniel Defoe evoked with that bare footprint of man remains one of the most memorable, hopeful, and at the same time chilling metaphors in literature. No reader could doubt that soon eough Crusoe would face the end of his isolation, and great danger, too; and of course his dark companion, Friday, comes on the wings of fear. So too did our ancestors in the teeming Pleistocene watch the earth for animal signs, and their reaction, like our own, to anything unusual or dangerous was purely visceral. Even now we are primed to act on such evidence by our genes as well as by experience. A fresh bear track in the woods—if not mistaken for Bigfoot—is an alert to the hunter (or backpacker) not only to prepare himself for a possible kill but to protect himself against the same. So we take tracks seriously, as we should.

Sometimes tracks are unforgettably imprinted in certain ancient muds that later turn to stone, and we have the fossil evidence of a walking dinosaur presented to us for posterity. We even have the unmistakable humanoid footprints of our relatives in Africa of nearly four million years ago, and we see in those impressions frozen in Tanzanian stone our striking contiguity with those smaller creatures who walked, as we do, on two legs, with a foot structure exactly like ours (only smaller) even to the strong big toe and the well-developed arch.

Much has been made in some Bigfoot literature, particularly in John Green's works, of other fossil evidence, of footprints in stone, of giant humanoids dating back to the Pleistocene or beyond. None of these has been confirmed by science, however. Footprints are rare in archaeology, in any case. Apparently the only people who take these rumors seriously, aside from some Bigfoot people, are the "Creationists" who try to disprove the theory of evolution (presumably under the misapprehension that human evolution undermines or denies the truth of the Bible).

It is a commonplace that much can be learned from tracks, not only about the life form that made them but also about its behavior. For hundreds of thousands of years, the ability to do just that was a mark of mankind's special abilities, a test of necessary skills to survive. Without it our hold on the teeming natural world would have been more precarious, perhaps impossible. And even in our well-documented and much-studied present world of animals, the capacity to read tracks and to identify a species by its footprints and other signs remains a special and honored skill.

Such skills are possible partly because all species have, along with the distinctive shape of their feet, a particular mode of locomotion. The quadrupeds must move with predictable alternations among their four limbs: in a slow walk, for example, in which the hind feet are placed on the ground just behind the front feet, either in a straight line, as in the gait of a fox, or roughly parallel, as in that of a domestic dog; or in a trot, in which the hind feet might be placed at or almost at the same spot as the front feet, sometimes creating a composite print that can be confusing even to experts; or in a gallop, in which the hind feet somewhat overlap the front feet and the prints are bunched together between long leaps. Some animals do this with greater variation than others. A ponderous grizzly may "gallop" along at more than thirty miles per hour in his shambling rush, fast enough to run down any man if a strong tree or other cover is not immediately available; but even at full speed the bear's hind feet don't much overlap the front. At a fast walk most bears will place their hind feet directly in the footprint made by their front feet, and the resulting footprint is large and quite humanlike, were it not for the claw marks. A horse's hind feet at full gallop overlap the front ones somewhat more, as anyone can see at the racetrack. A cat's overlap by an even greater degree because of the animal's relative speed and the extraordinary flexibility of its backbone. Of all mammals the cheetah is the most pronounced in this tendency.

But only man among larger mammals is truly bipedal. I've noted that the ability to walk on two legs is common among certain primates and bears, but this is never the norm for these animals. They walk quadrupedally. Furthermore, they are incapable of walking with a "stride," that particular and (as far as is known) unique human gait in which the muscles of the legs, hips, arms, and shoulders are coordinated so that the body sways precariously forward until the center of gravity moves beyond the pillar of the single supporting leg. Just at the critical point of crashing earthward, the human is saved by swinging the other leg to the fore, restoring for an instant the former equilibrium. Certain terrestrial birds—the gallinaceous, or chickenlike, kinds especially—walk something like this, but they have their wings for balance. Napier, who probably knows more about human and primate locomotion than anyone alive, has said that for man disaster is never far away during the act of walking. How true. Do the young of any other mammal so often fall down or progress to upright walking through such a clumsy stage of infancy, crawling, stumbling, toddling? Even the most coordinated among us will fall on their faces more often than they can count in the course of their lives. When we grow old, the fall from our unstable two-legged stance becomes our greatest hazard, far worse than the accidents caused by cars, tools, or modern industrial life.

So nature has given humans highly specialized feet; indeed the human foot has correctly been described as the most specialized part of the human anatomy. And because of this the human foot leaves a distinct imprint, unlike that of any other animal. In sand or mud, or any soft substance, the mark of the bare human foot is unmistakable, and the shod foot is also usually unmistakable. No other known animal has such a heel and shank, and five toes stuck in front, each progressively smaller toward the outside, and with that one large, powerful toe on the inside. Thus, the way the stride marks the earth is another unique feature of human locomotion. Normal humans strike the ground first with the heel, hitting on the outside of the back. As the stride continues and the body carries forward until it is directly over the supporting leg, and then teeters far out in front, the point of contact with the ground shifts from the outer border of the foot to the inner border, moving to the inside of the ball of the foot. As the heel is lifted from the ground, the big toe thrusts powerfully to propel the weight of the levered body to the alternate leg.

All this detail is important because among humans, from heel-strike to toe-off, the entire stride leaves a unique plantigrade mark in the earth, the big toe continuous with the ball of the foot, the other toes progressively less deeply imprinted (sometimes the little toe leaves no impression at all). The narrow shank is visible where the arch barely touches the earth, and widens again to the deep heel print, canted to the outside.

In soft earth or sand the human toes will often compress a ridge between them and the ball of the foot, so the toe-off is marked clearly.

Human footprints contrast enormously with the impressions made by quadrupedal animals, including the great apes, which normally have at least two feet on the ground at any time during walking. Even at a full run most quadrupeds will strike the ground with two legs more or less together—forelegs hitting first, then the hind legs.

With these facts known, any confusion between bear tracks and presumed Bigfoot tracks would seem unlikely. Most experienced hunters are aware of the varied appearance of animal tracks and can distinguish one from another, but mistakes are made, and experts can become confused. For example, though bears usually leave discernible claw marks—because their claws are not retractable—these are sometimes not clear. In freezing weather the claws sometimes ball up with snow, creating what appear to be humanlike toes.

A great deal is made by some writers about the knowledge of wildlife that is assumed among hunters. Unfortunately this is but a half truth. Recent studies show enormous variation in zoological knowledge among those who regularly hunt, with the vast majority falling into a category of "recreational" hunters who possess limited factual information and a great deal of misinformation. This has long been true, even among the most specialized and successful hunter-gatherers, who may know their prey's behavior fairly well but at the same time believe all sorts of strange untruths. Legends of bears that can turn into men, and vice versa, might no longer carry their former weight among urbanized weekend wanderers in the woods—who have also lost a traditional familiarity with the patterns of nature— but other kinds of tall tales, many no less absurd than the stories of transformation, continue to have currency. Twenty-five years ago, when I bird-hunted as a boy in company with experienced older men, I often heard the most absurd explanations for various behavior on the part of ducks, pheasants, and other game birds. Regarding large mammals, vast misconceptions persist.

Mankind's long and legendary association with bears is complex and little understood. Plenty of ancient belief patterns survive as fragments of Indo-European or Amerindian folklore in industrialized societies. There is a kind of arrogance in the view that only primitive tribesmen from Africa or Asia or South America persist in their "foolish" beliefs while our advanced civilization has moved on to a rational, scientific point of view. The gap between the specialized knowledge of an educated elite and common lore remains enormous, even in the United States and Canada.

From this perspective some of the other explanations for mistaken identity take on greater force. There is too much assumption of scientific "rationality"—what an ironic twist in this matter of trying to prove Bigfoot's existence—on the part of those who report tracks and other evidence.

Many Bigfoot buffs also scornfully dismiss the idea that sublimation of snow (melting combined with quick refreezing) might account for many of the reported footprints. The implication is that the skeptics are stretching a possible point to its limit or beyond. But it is an established fact that animal tracks in snow, especially when the hind and forefeet are clustered closely or superimposed, may enlarge greatly as a result of the action of the sun's rays on the snow. Sometimes all four prints of a small animal will merge into a single large print, particularly if the animal has been leaping at a run through deep snow. Such sublimation cannot increase the distance between one individual footprint and the next—as Bigfoot people point out *ad infinitum*—but in the case of superimposed quadrupedal prints, even from an animal as small as a fox or bobcat, the interval between the impressions so formed may be up to five or more feet. Even the most experienced mountaineer or woodsman can be taken in by such tracks, which could easily appear to be those of a huge bipedal animal with humanlike feet.

One of the most famous examples of a supposed yeti footprint might be a case in point. Controversy will probably never be resolved regarding the "Shipton footprint" taken in 1951 on the Menlung Glacier beneath Mt. Everest by British mountaineer Eric Shipton. Shipton, as I suggested earlier, believed that he had found fresh footprints indicating a "large apelike creature" either unknown to science or not included in the known fauna of central Asia. His unquestioned reputation, combined with the seemingly clear photographs of one of the prints, acted to propel what had previously been considered a mere local legend into the realm of "fact."

John Napier has carefully studied this famous photo, and his conclusion is that the print in question is probably not that of any apelike creature at all; it is certainly not humanlike. Napier points out that a gorilla's foot has a length-breadth index of forty-five percent, compared to thirty-seven percent for a human's foot. The Shipton photo shows an index of sixty-one percent. With his profound knowledge of primate evolution, Napier simply cannot accept the idea that some form of ape or hominid could evolve with a foot so broad in proportion to its length. The Shipton print also shows an enlarged second toe, with the big toe partway down on the inside of the foot. This has been fancifully explained as a potential adaptation to rock-climbing. And most important, according to Napier, when the entire negative of the celebrated photo is studied—rather than just the part of it that shows the central footprint—there is an indication of another, rather different footprint. Napier came to the conclusion that the Shipton photo actually reveals features that showed the print to be the result of sublimation of snow. He therefore assumes the tracks to be those of a wolf or fox, or even a snow leopard. Completely discounting Shipton's theory that the tracks were fresh when he photographed them, Napier suggests that in the interval between the making of the prints and the taking of the pictures,

> the snow in the lower half of the picture had melted and re-frozen. In the upper half, the substrate is still crystalline, lying one inch deep on the glacier ice. This immediately suggests that the dark area at the outer side of the heel is not simply the heavy impression of a heel at the "heel-strike" phase of human walk-ing, as has been assumed, but an area . . . where sublimation has taken place. With this observation, the footprint loses one of its principal claims to be man-like.

Napier adds that to assume an unknown creature is walking around in the Himalayas on great, wide feet with a second longer toe on each foot "conflicts totally with the principles of biology as we know them."

Like others before him, Napier notes that many so-called yeti footprints might easily be of human origin. Pilgrims and porters often walk barefoot through the high passes, some without apparent ill effect, and in deep snow, or ice-crusted snow, people often follow in each other's footsteps, an ancient mountaineer's trick to avoid injury or a bad slip. After all, man is an abundant species nearly everywhere on earth, and humans regularly penetrate regions where they do not live, including the most inhospitable and remote zones.

Many reputable mountaineers and some scientists with Himalayan experience are more willing to credit Shipton's opinion as to the freshness of the tracks in question. It has been noted that Napier's belief that any putative unknown primate must have feet with a length-breadth index similar to that of man or the great apes is only an assumption. And other "good" tracks have been found over the years, including some discovered in December 1972 by an American expedition doing ecological reconnaissance in eastern Nepal.

I include Napier's analysis here to point out that evidence usually presented as unequivocal proof for the abominable snowman remains open to question. And even the shadow of a doubt in such cases, without further physical data to support the footprints, must be given full play.

Many proponents of the American Bigfoot argue with some justification that there are too many clear prints of obvious humanoid nature for the mistaken-identity explanation to be taken seriously, no matter how convincing it might seem when applied to the yeti. Most will admit that well over half of the reported cases are those of mistaken identity, and many are plainly hoaxes. But what about the rest?

A close look at some of the supposed "good" examples—those selected because they seem to be consistent, difficult or impossible to fake, or perhaps coincidental with a sighting—is revealing. Again Napier's analysis is useful. Of nineteen well-known examples of yeti footprints recorded in the Himalayas since 1915, Napier identifies seven as coming from at least two species of bears, two from humans, one from a langur, and one (the "Shipton print") from either a double origin or a composite print caused by snow sublimation. Of the remainder, one reportedly had its feet pointing backward; four were tentatively identified by the persons who found them as either wolf tracks; double, or superimposed, tracks; or booted and barefoot human tracks. Even the three final examples are not very convincing from Napier's perspective, because one has a step length of only one and a half to two feet, one is twelve inches long and six wide, and the other is ten to eleven inches long and five to six inches wide, thus yielding width-length indexes of fifty and fifty-two respectively. According to Napier these fall outside the range of man, fossil man, ape, fossil ape, and therefore any potential unknown primate.

Perhaps so. Napier clearly reveals a prejudice against the yeti—for which, in my view, a better zoological case can be made than for the Bigfoot of North America. He fails in his book to apply the same relentless rigor to his analysis of the North American footprints. Perhaps one reason for this is that Napier at once noted that the width-breadth index for the majority of reported examples from North America falls within his presumed range for an unknown bipedal primate.

The idea that Napier's conclusions are biased because he takes it for granted that the frame of reference must be either human or ape is slightly misleading, because his comparative base includes the known fossil record as well. More serious in my view is the fact that Napier suggests—and as far as I know was the first primatologist to do so—that the Sasquatch footprints fall into two distinctive categories: the so-called hour-glass-shaped kind and the human-shaped kind. These neat categories are entirely arbitrary. Unprejudiced study of the wide range of reported footprints—not to mention innumerable sightings—shows how selective Napier has been in his choices. Let us assume that the footprints recently reported in

Iowa, South Dakota, and other Midwestern regions—which are more akin to the Shipton print than to the more humanlike Bossburg and Bluff Creek prints—should be given equal value, at least initially. After all, they are consistent with the evidence from Asia, and any biologist would agree that it is easier to accept one genus, or one species of unknown primate, than several Sandersonian kinds. The logic for this is just as compelling if the premise is that the unknown critter has a much wider foot for its length than any known primate. But Napier obviously decided not to include any samples in his North American analysis that do not fit his breadth-length index. Certainly regarding the many footprints reported with two or three toes and rectangular or wedge shapes, Napier's selectivity is perfectly sensible.

Ultimately such selectivity serves those who are prepared to accept the probability of Bigfoot's existence. Without certain guidelines that fall within the range of pongid evolution, a systematic analysis of the huge numbers of reported Bigfoot tracks would be impossible. Napier makes an implicit assumption that any unknown two-legged creature that might exist in North America would have to possess an evolutionary pattern within a line similar to that of the known pongids or hominids. So within this frame of reference, when problems of habitat, ecology, the extent of the wilderness, human population density, etc., are considered, confining the evidence to the Pacific Northwest, as Napier does, makes sense. The point, nevertheless, is that Napier's analytic framework is arbitrary because it has to be, and given the nature of the evidence, it is also hypothetical. One wonders what Napier might have done with the same evidence of footprints had he begun from the assumption that Sasquatch does not exist?

If we look only at those footprints that fit into Napier's acceptable sample, the cumulative impact appears to be impressive. For example, there is just enough variability among the footprints in Napier's "hourglass" type from Northern California, and just enough morphological similarity, to convince even a hard-nosed skeptic. Likewise, if one ignores the above type, then the "club-foot" abnormality that Napier discovered in his study of the deformed left-foot prints from Bossburg, in Washington, would hardly seem the type of evidence the typical hoaxer might readily dream up. But, then, who is the typical hoaxer?

It is here that the worst problem in Napier's almost naïve use of evidence arises—a problem, regarding the reliability of footprint evidence, that Napier apparently did not consider. Perhaps at the time he lacked adequate information. It is true that he correctly points out that one or the other of his two types of footprints must be faked (unless there are two species of Bigfoot stalking the Northwest), but he says virtually nothing about the dubious circumstances surrounding the discovery of the tracks in question. The man who first brought the Bossburg footprints to public attention, in October 1969, was Ivan Marx, a hunting guide and legendary yarn-spinner whose involvement in the Sasquatch search dates back at least as far as the unfortunate Pacific Northwest Expedition organized by Tom Slick ten years earlier. Marx was also the man who found tracks of a similar pattern during a follow-up search in company with René Dahinden. This find netted no less than 1089 prints. Marx later made at least two controversial films that purport to show Bigfoot in nature, but even John Green openly doubts the authenticity of the Bigfoot scenes.

Of course, as I've already pointed out, the Bluff Creek tracks, which constitute the basis for Napier's hourglass type, are equally dubious. One could easily produce a scenario for the entire corpus of evidence from Bluff Creek and nearby regions based on the assumption that *all* of it derives from human agency. Most of the principals in the story, from the late fifties through to the end of the sixties, had either previous connections or opportunity and motive, and above all they had the knowledge of what would be expected by layman and scientist alike.

Of the twenty-plus reports of Bigfoot prints in Northern California that Napier included in his random sample, approximately a third are suspect because their finders had previously been involved in the search for Bigfoot or had connections with the Bigfoot-hunter network. Besides, few of the prints were studied on the spot by a qualified and impartial wildlife expert, mammalogist, or anthropologist.

Such skepticism about people associated with the Bigfoot search may seem cynical or even unfair. I certainly intend no obloquy toward any particular person, but it is a basic rule of historical investigation that anyone with a vested interest in the outcome cannot be trusted to be impartial and therefore reliable in any controversy, even with the best of intentions. In a field such as the search for Bigfoot, which obviously attracts charlatans and phonies, veracity must depend upon more than good faith.

My own experience with the Lake Ann incident in Michigan provides another illustration of the complex nature of footprint evidence when confronted directly, with both eyes open. One of the first things I noticed when Zane Gray produced his casting of one of the huge footprints found behind his son's house was that the impression seemed to lack any clear indication of a stride. The normal signs of a progression of weight along the line of the foot from heel-strike to toe-off were not visible. The plaster cast, plus a good look at the eight-millimeter film Gray made of the prints on the day they were found, indicated that the prints were strangely static in appearance, as if each footprint had been impressed—with considerable weight—almost vertically into the soft sand. Although some of the toes seemed more deeply imprinted than others, there was no visible pressure ridge in the area between the ball of the foot and the suspiciously humanlike toe marks, such as one might expect in soft sand. The more one studies them, the more the eighteen-inch prints seem unnatural, despite their superficial resemblance to giant human footprints. Like many other recorded castings and photos of Bigfoot prints, they simply do not look convincingly like the tracks of a live animal striding across the earth. In such a large two-legged creature, or even in one that walks only part of the time on its hind legs, biomechanics would require evidence of a stride.

The huge number of reported Bigfoot tracks presents another and perhaps more serious problem. How can a presumably rare creature leave such abundant tracks? Rather than being good evidence in support of Bigfoot, the quantity of reported tracks is cause for greater suspicion. In fact, fresh, clear, and identifiable footprints of such well-known but sporadically uncommon species as the mountain lion and jaguar are difficult to find. One of America's leading experts on animal tracks, Dr. Olaus J. Murie, a zoologist of unquestioned skill and reputation who authored the indispensable *Field Guide to Animal Tracks,* was forced to rely upon jaguar pugmarks obtained from a San Francisco zoo, although he had collected thousands of other plaster casts from a lifetime of field experience. This distinguished naturalist suggested that where tracks of a particular species are abundant, the species is also abundant. For example, bear tracks are not commonly found, not even by local outdoorsmen who frequent woods in which bears are known to live. Only in certain exceptional ecological regions (especially in parts of Alaska and northwestern Canada) are any species of bear really abundant. Where they are, their tracks are abundant. A common species is not by definition an abundant one.

Could there, then, be more Sasquatches than bears? Why don't we see them equally as often, not merely via unsubstantiated accounts but with ample photographic evidence and other supporting signs? I myself have two clear photographs of two bears taken in Yellowstone National Park in 1954, when I was barely sixteen years old. Years later, gazing at these two black-and-white Brownie snapshots, I was able to determine that the brown individual was merely a "cinnamon" phase of the common black bear and not a grizzly, as I had thought back then. How many hundreds of thousands have similar snapshots? Where are the photos of Bigfoot to back up the thousands of sightings? On the evidence of the tracks—supposedly so convincing—why isn't Bigfoot included in the field guides?

Furthermore, *clear* imprints of well-known, even abundant animals are far less obvious and abundant than most people realize. An expert woodsman will readily track a known animal through a *combination* of signs—that useful Old English noun *spoor,* meaning all of the signs that an animal leaves in its wake, including scats, broken branches, bent grass, claw marks or scratchings, signs of feeding, drinking, resting, sleeping, odors (of little use to humans), and, of course, footprints.

The larger primates, particularly the great apes, are difficult to track in the wild. No tracker would rely only on footprints, because tracks of wild apes are difficult to find unless clustered around an artificial feeding area where the animals are not threatened—as with Jane Goodall's chimps in the Gombe Preserve. Indeed the apes almost never leave imprints on the ground that can be followed over a long run, such as those reported by Marx and Dahinden near Bossburg in 1969 and attributed to Sasquatch.

Many Bigfoot hunters interpret the footprint evidence in quite the opposite way, but few people stop to think about it. Surely, given the huge numbers of Bigfoot tracks reported in the last twenty years over a huge range of territory, we should expect that our elusive creature has approximately the same frequency as the common black bear or, at least, that of the rare cougar.

Has any biologist bothered to count known casts of footprints of the Alaskan brown bear, which measure on average about sixteen inches long and nine or ten wide for the hind foot? Of course, there is no need to do so; the brown bear is magnificently and indisputably real.

And what about the possibility of hoax? It is one of the axioms of the Bigfoot fraternity that it would take a conspiracy of "Mafia-like" proportions to explain away the many hundreds of footprints, which seem so consistent, as manmade fakes. This might seem true at first. How could so many footprints be so widely faked in such fortuitous and remote circumstances, and with such similarity in size and appearance, over such a span of time? The fact, as I've noted, is that only a small proportion of reported footprints are functionally consistent. Many of these have been found in regions where sightings and other signs of the creature have long been reported. A wilderness region— where it is "unlikely" for a hoax to be perpetrated—is no longer so unlikely when it is publicized in the national press as a known Bigfoot area. Bluff Creek is a prime example. Also, in many cases it is not difficult to comprehend that there are thou-

sands of unconnected people in every state in the Union fully
capable of producing footprints that match an accepted pattern,
especially in a society like ours, with its high literacy rate and
wide-ranging media attention given to this phenomenon. Most
Bigfoot literature is replete with descriptions of what a Sasquatch footprint is supposed to look like, and this information
is available in almost any bookstore and newsstand.

Early reports of such footprints are so uncertain, so ambiguous (especially when read in their original form), and so contradictory as to detail that, taken together, they are almost useless
as evidence.

When put in perspective, the evidence of footprints is not
very compelling. The evidence in favor of pranks and hoaxes,
mistaken identity aside, is far more convincing in the long run.
The oft-repeated idea that the typical faked tracks couldn't fool
a village idiot is simply not so. A glance at most newspaper stories about footprints and other signs will show at once how
strong the predisposition is to believe. The reports of the investigators themselves are equally revealing. Apparently, the desire to accept all data as genuine, except the most obvious and
clumsy fakes, is strong enough to obscure rational judgment or
comparison. Although neither individual would like this comparison, there is great similarity in the way René Dahinden and
Peter Byrne have learned over the years, time and again, that
what seemed to be convincing footprint evidence has proved
on the basis of later information to be a probable hoax, or mistaken identity at best. At least these two searchers have been
willing to change their minds when faced with the obvious.
One of the more famous examples is the incident involving
Bigfoot tracks found in the Bossburg area of Washington,
which a Colville, California, citizen named Ray Pickens admitted that he faked when he was interviewed by the BBC in
1968. The scramble among the many investigators to delete
this example from their lists, and to condemn the hoax, is instructive. How many times does the "best" evidence have to be
debunked in this fashion before a grain of skepticism creeps in?

It is a simple truth that the vast majority of Bigfoot tracks
have never been investigated by trained and impartial people.

In most cases, even if good casts or photos are made, it is too late to do so.

So we are left with that tiny proportion of tracks that cannot be explained readily—tracks found in circumstances that make a hoax seem improbable (though fakery is almost never impossible when we are dealing with human ingenuity), tracks that have outward signs of reality and cannot be explained as cases of mistaken identity, and tracks found where a sighting also occurred and where a supporting photograph or film is also available. The one case that appears to fit this latter requirement has already been seriously questioned, of course. The others constitute a mystery that remains unsolved. It is this rather scanty evidence that will dimly haunt those of us who, like Thoreau, "need to witness our own limits transgressed, and some life pasturing freely where we never wander." But it will do little to convince skeptics or professional zoologists who must, after all, be doubtful about what is not proved. I suppose this same scanty evidence will also continue to persuade those who want to believe.

Sanderson included fecal matter in his "cognate" category of evidence. He claimed abundant evidence of droppings that are found in conjunction with footprints or sightings. Earlier it was shown how unreliable such evidence can be, but a specific case might illustrate the point. Not long after he found the strange pile of dung on the old railroad grade behind his property, Zane Gray was visited by Michigan's self-appointed Bigfoot expert, who whisked the noisome sample away to his Bigfoot Information Center, near Millington. Eventually the sample was sent to a resident biologist at Michigan's Department of Natural Resources, who tentatively suggested that the fecal matter contained horsehair, and possible deer hair. This expert avoided identification of the origin of the strange sample, which resembles a cow pie. This has been interpreted, however, as evidence that the dropping emanated from some unknown animal, probably Bigfoot, according to Wayne King. Such is the quality of most of the evidence from other samples of fecal matter.

It is true that a whole specialty, scatology, has emerged as a branch of biology. But nothing is ever cut-and-dried, so to speak. A field biologist will be aware of conditions of diet, health, season, activity, and even weather that directly affect the condition of the scat in question. But what can a Bigfoot expert do? Regarding the speculative and unclassified animal in question, he can make only educated guesses, since he cannot know details of the animal's habits, or even of its favored habitat. Pity the poor biologist who is expected to make some kind of clear identification regarding unsolicited samples of scat, often sent without pertinent details as to age, location, or other signs and conditions. If he refuses to analyze the sample, he risks the charge of deliberate suppression of "evidence." If he attempts an analysis and cannot make a positive identification of the source, he plays into the hands of those who will take his equivocal response as proof that the sample is "unknown" and must therefore come from an unknown animal—ergo, Sasquatch.

During my investigation into this somewhat distasteful subject it was perhaps inevitable that a bit of levity might creep in. For, in truth, it is difficult not to smile while picturing an intrepid hoaxer gathering and combining the various natural ingredients necessary to fake even the most minimally plausible Bigfoot feces, then to carry it reeking into the wilds and place it in the proximity of some recently discovered footprints. Yet an impartial look at the record seems to indicate that this has happened, at least on some occasions. It is one of those charges that are impossible to prove.

Since Sanderson's category of *corollary* evidence is the most ephemeral of all, it hardly seems necessary to press on. People who have had strange but unverifiable experiences may be confused, and there is usually only the "evidence" of their word. This category is therefore similar to eyewitness accounts. Reports of rocks or other objects being thrown against shelters, vehicles, or buildings, of oil drums being lifted and thrown about at construction or road-building sites, and reports of terrible odors are usually impossible to substantiate. Physical objects can easily be moved by humans, by animals, and by wind and water. (In traditional lore, rocks never fell from a mountainside without the impetus of physical being and deliberate intent, and trees never fell of their own accord, or even as a result of the wind.) Sounds can be recorded, but the recordings of alleged Bigfoot noises are akin to the samples of fecal matter, and to the photographs and films, in that they satisfy almost nobody except the most dedicated believers.

Much has been written about Sasquatch and whether or not it has the capacity to communicate. At least one theory of Bigfoot evolution strongly implies that oral communication of some kind ought to be expected. There is a weird story out of California, involving a man named Warren Johnson, his brother Lewis, and later his son and some friends, that makes the remarkable claim that a Bigfoot "rock-giant" living in the Sierra Nevada actually communicated with human beings on several occasions.

The story begins with an initial encounter in July of 1971 when a huge and terrifyingly noisy beast raided the Johnson camp in the night, apparently for food, making the place a shambles and leaving behind many footprints. Thereafter, the Johnson brothers returned often to the camp,* sometimes with other companions, and the experience was repeated several times. In the meantime the Johnson party reinforced the camp shelter—apparently a rough tripod of heavy logs—for their own protection, and were able eventually to coax the huge critter close enough to offer it food. They had by this time seen the creature several times through peepholes in the sides of the tepee-shaped shelter, and they described it rather vaguely as eight or ten feet tall, wide-shouldered, erect in posture, bull-necked, dark, and apparently very excitable. It is interesting that they stated that the beast was not black; at night, even in bright moonlight, the human eye lacks the capacity to discern color without the aid of an external light source, such as a lantern or flashlight, and therefore any dark color would be indistinguishable from black.

In time the monster returned with others of its kind, and for the first time sounds were recorded. Then, in the late summer

---

*The exact location of this camp seems to be unclear. In *Bigfoot,* by B. Ann Slate and Alan Berry, the area is described as the "mid-Sierra region." The site is described as a wooded ravine on a high volcanic plateau "once coveted by sheepherders." Other details are lacking.

of 1972, Alan Berry, a reporter for a small newspaper, joined the Johnson bunch at their Sierra camp, and in his presence they allegedly succeeded in talking to the creature and were answered in turn. They told Berry that the same thing had, in fact, happened before.

The sounds ranged from "drawn-out nasal" snarls and "barnyard" sounds to "the ring of monkeys' chatter" and various "rapid-fire chattering, a gibberish that came in spurts," mixed in with whistles, whines, and screams, all loud and raucous and (at the same time?) "clear and fluid." Berry described some of the sounds, along with a "voiceprint," as follows: "Gob-a-gob-a-gob, ugh, muy-tail."

Recordings of these and other sounds eventually found their way to experts, including a primatologist, a linguist, and a linguist with experience in primate vocalization, all of whom tentatively concluded that the sounds were either doubtful, phony, or reconstituted. This hardly satisfied the Johnsons, or the now-converted Berry. They had begun to believe—since the entire phenomenon was becoming increasingly linked with unidentified flashing lights, metallic clicking noises, strange disappearances, and an uncanny ability on the part of the creature to avoid being photographed—that the creature might not be a flesh-and-blood terrestrial animal after all. And, perhaps inevitably, the question of extrasensory perception was raised, and with it various theories of the paranormal, of psychic phenomena.

John Green has copies of certain tape recordings of these sounds, and of some recorded in a suburban area not far from Seattle. He played these back to me during my visit to his home in Victoria. To my ear these sounds seemed wholly unnatural; nothing I had ever heard in nature, or in any zoo, or on the soundtracks of scores of nature films remotely resembled this hodgepodge of incredible noises. I found it hard to believe that anyone could listen to such noises and still believe them to emanate from a single earthly beast of any kind. There were sounds slightly resembling those of a coyote, and others resembling a high-pitched human howl, or maybe that of a great ape, and others rather like a gibbon. (It happens that I had heard some excellent tapes of a gibbon's high-pitched hooting only a

few days before at the mammalogists' convention in Corvallis.)
Some of the noises seemed almost birdlike, and there were
screeches like those of a wildcat, and clicks like those of insects.
The main feature of these samples, particularly the California
ones, was that they combined many sounds of quite separate
quality, range, pitch, and frequency, and that there was no identifiable focus, as there is in all natural animal sound, whether it
be of a jackal, coyote, wolf, hyena, Colobus monkey, cuckoo,
touraco, woodpecker, vervet, chimpanzee, or elephant (all of
which I have heard in the wild). Even the best mimics in nature, the parrots and man himself (who is unsurpassed as a
mimic), cannot deviate beyond a certain quality and range of
sound. And this is identifiable in all species, except, perhaps,
man; a good human mimic might fool an expert with hundreds
of bird calls and scores of animal cries. But no human could
have made these noises unaided by electronic devices. The
range of human-produced sounds is limited. These recorded
sounds seemed to me so obviously concocted from several
sources that I could scarcely believe they have been produced
as evidence for Bigfoot.

I intend no scorn for the experiences of people that cannot,
perhaps, be explained by logic. Certainly, much of what I've
written here will be condemned by those who believe that critical objectivity about the Bigfoot phenomenon plays directly
into the hands of the "established" professional scientists who
have a vested interest—or so it is said—in pooh-poohing the
whole matter. It would certainly be naïve to assume that there
are no pressures within the scientific community to reject the
entire Bigfoot search out of hand. After all, any undue enthusiasm for the unproved and unknown only reinforces the rather
scornful attitude that the whole matter is a thorough waste of
time, a diversion from more important tasks. This is one reason
that the great museums, university departments, and other
scientific institutions won't throw their weight behind an organized search for Bigfoot.

This does not mean, however, that scientists have not in the
past been intrigued enough by the evidence for Bigfoot to
sponsor organized searches. The World Book Encyclopedia

sponsored a major expedition to the Himalayas in 1960–61—at the height of the abominable snowman craze—led by none other than Sir Edmund Hillary, conqueror of Everest. The joint objectives of this well-financed expedition were to establish or disprove the existence of the yeti and to carry out research into physiology of humans at high altitude. Marlin Perkins, of the Lincoln Park Zoo in Chicago and already a television personality, acted as the expedition zoologist. He was backed up by several other reputable scientists and respected Himalaya experts with first-hand knowledge of the region's animals and plants, and (of equal importance) of its peoples. One of these was Desmond Doig, whose primary task was to follow up any leads regarding the abominable snowman, including the many published reports about the yeti "scalps," mummified hands, and other relics in various lamaseries.

After an exhaustive search, Hillary and Doig, backed by Perkins and the other scientists, concluded that the yeti was mythological. In the book he coauthored with Doig, *High in the Thin Cold Air,* Hillary summed up their findings as follows:

> When faced with the universal collapse of the main evidence in support of this creature the members of my expedition—doctor, scientists, zoologists, and mountaineers alike—could not in all conscience view it as more than a fascinating fairy-tale, born of the rare and frightening view of strange animals, moulded by superstition, and enthusiastically nurtured by Western expeditions.

Doig was less willing than Hillary to accept the negative evidence of the expedition. He has retained hope, but he also ended his part of the book with these words:

> The hard fact is that one by one the supports to the Yeti theory have faded before the investigations:
>   Yeti tracks are readily moulded by the sun from the footprints of other animals;
>   The Khumjunk Yeti scalp is an interesting relic—but a fake for all of this;
>   The pangboche Yeti hand is largely human in origin;

The Yeti skins, so positively identified as such by any Sherpa,
are in truth the Tibetan blue bear;

And the myths and legends about the Yeti quickly move into
the sphere of fantasy when carefully investigated.

Most zoologists and anthropologists consider this much-
publicized expedition to have been quite enough. There have
been others, of less respectable nature, including the expeditions
sponsored by the late Texas millionaire Tom Slick. None of
these has come up with anything more convincing than the
original corpus of evidence that inspired the Hillary-Doig
effort.

More recently, in March 1977, a large Chinese expedition
led by Zhou Guoxing, an anthropologist with the Peking Museum of Natural History, searched in vain for a large bipedal
mammal with reddish hair that had been reported in southern
Hubei, and in the mountainous region called Shennongjia,
where the Hubei, Shanxi, and Sichuan provincial borders in-
tersect. The one-hundred-and-ten-member expedition included
biologists, zoologists, photographers, and infiltration teams of
soldiers equipped with rifles, tranquilizer guns, tape recorders,
cameras, and dogs. Footprints twelve to sixteen inches long
were reportedly found, as well as samples of feces. But nothing
conclusive enough was discovered to convince other scientists
at the Chinese Academy of Sciences in Peking that the expedition was not "running after shadows."

In North America the expeditions in search of Bigfoot have
not been of the kind to encourage faith in the competence of
the searchers. I've already noted the Pacific Northwest Expedition organized by Slick in 1959–60, which was a comedy of errors. In 1974 Peter Byrne, in company with Russ Kinne, a free-
lance photographer and filmmaker, went off on an expedition
into the wilds of British Columbia. They were awarded an Explorers Club flag to carry along on their search. Using Kinne's
private plane, and accompanied by a third man, they flew
around to various spots where Bigfoot reports had originated
in BC, landing at airstrips, fields, logging strips, and logging
roads. Altogether the three men flew some six thousand miles,

and they hiked, too—how far is not reported in Kinne's account, reported in the second issue, November 1974, of *Bigfoot News*. Nor is the duration of this aerial expedition mentioned.

Another expedition in that year was widely reported in the press to have been sponsored by the National Wildlife Federation. In the first issue of Byrne's *Bigfoot News,* dated October 1, 1974, an item appears on the second page: "WASHINGTON: National Wildlife Federation expedition concluded mid-September." This notice is followed by a report that says no finds were made during this four-month, fifty-thousand dollar search for Bigfoot. In the next issue there is a report stating that the expedition was "not a National Wildlife Federation project in the true sense in that no members of the NWF took part in it." The report goes on to say that the NWF only allowed its name to be used as a means to channel funds and that the Federation withdrew its name permanently in July of that year.

Then there is the embarrassing matter of the so-called Minnesota Iceman, which directly involved the prestigious Smithsonian Institution. This story is bizarre indeed. At the beginning it actually appeared to some people to be a genuine breakthrough in modern science, one of those unexpected discoveries in which the science of man and his relation to animals, indeed the whole evolutionary history of the higher primates, would be illuminated in exciting new ways. There are different versions of the specimen's actual beginnings, but the basic outlines are clear.

In late 1968 Ivan Sanderson and his associate in the science of the unknown, Bernard Heuvelmans, visited a remote farm near Winona, Minnesota, to investigate a weird creature frozen in a block of ice and housed in a mobile home equipped with an elaborate refrigeration unit. The animal, which measured about six feet tall and was completely covered with hair except on its face, had been exhibited around the country as part of a carnival during 1967 and 1968. People had paid thirty-five cents per person for a peek. Where the thing came from is uncertain. One story claimed it was found floating in the Sea of Okhotsk, off Siberia, in a block of ice. From there it somehow found its way to Hong Kong, where a mysterious West Coast millionaire "rediscovered" it and then rented it out to a carnival showman named Frank D. Hansen. Thus it was on tour until Sanderson got wind of it just before Christmas in 1968.

Another version claims that the creature was shot in Minnesota by Hansen hismelf—in 1970 he admitted to this in public, only to refuse further comment later—and there is a third and related tale reported in a sensationalist tabloid under the huge headline I WAS RAPED BY THE ABOMINABLE SNOWMAN by one Helen Westring, who said she was attacked while hunting alone near Bemidji, Minnesota.

In any case, when Sanderson heard news of the creature, probably through Hansen's instigation, Bernard Heuvelmans happened to be a houseguest, and the two at once made tracks for Winona. It took them three days of hard driving from New Jersey in the dead of winter to get to Hansen's ranch, where they were confronted with an incredible sight.

Lying on its back in a translucent block of ice, inside a metal coffin with a glass lid, was a humanoid creature that seemed in a macabre way to justify everything Sanderson and his Belgian colleague had hoped for for so many years. Despite patches of cloudiness in the ice and air bubbles that obscured the outline, the creature was plainly not human; nor was it any known species of ape.

Its hands and feet were huge in proportion to the rest of its body; the thumb was extraordinarily long, far longer than that of man or ape. The foot was broad, and the toes almost equal in length and breadth, with the big toe lined up with the others, as in man, rather than partially opposed, as in apes. There was no discernible waist, as in man, but the creature had a barrel chest similar to those of apes. The face was snub-nosed, with thin lips and very human-looking teeth, as far as could be seen through the layers of ice.

It is not hard to imagine the feelings that Sanderson and Heuvelmans must have shared. Surely this creature was the first genuine specimen that could account for the Bigfoot and abominable snowman tales. Both immediately set to work to write articles claiming the creature's authenticity—though neither had inspected the creature other than through its ice covering. Heuvelmans managed to publish an article in a respected Belgian scientific journal, complete with details on physiology, possible evolutionary origin, and classification. Sanderson followed with an article in *Argosy* magazine entitled "The Missing Link," with a lavish color drawing of the Iceman on the front cover of the issue.

Suddenly science had to take the phenomenon seriously. Despite their controversial inclinations, Sanderson and Heuvelmans were zoologists, and they had agreed that the creature was some form of humanoid previously unknown to science. Heuvelmans said the thing was a Neanderthaloid type, believed extinct for thirty thousand years—although Neanderthal fossil-skeleton remains differ only slightly from those of modern man. He also argued that it could not have been preserved in its present condition through the long ages—as mammoths have been preserved in certain types of frozen mud rather than in ice—and therefore it had to be one of a still-surviving species. Sanderson substantially agreed, though he was less willing to classify the creature without more study.

It was at this point that the Smithsonian entered the picture. Dr. Napier, who was then head of the primate-biology program at the Smithsonian's Natural History Museum, was invited by Sanderson to examine the specimen and to bring the weight of the Smithsonian behind a scientific investigation of the creature. A formal letter was thus despatched to Hansen in Minnesota to announce the Smithsonian's interest and to get his cooperation.

Then strange things began to happen. Confronted with the possibility that his carny exhibit would be melted from its icy sheath and examined by a team of scientists, Hansen responded with a letter so carefully worded with legal ambiguities it would put P. T. Barnum to shame. In essence what Hansen said was that although scientific authentication would be advantageous to his financial position, it might also prove to be the source of legal trouble. There were already stories circulating in the press that if the creature was humanoid, as it had been identified, and if it had actually been shot, then the question of a capital crime might be brought up. So the original specimen,

Hansen wrote, would have to disappear, and he would see to it that a good substitute was provided. Of course, this model of the original would be just different enough that observers who had already seen the original would know it was a substitute.

Soon various newspapers reported that the FBI had been informed of a possible homicide case, because of Heuvelmans's opinion, printed in his scholarly article, that the creature had apparently been killed by a high-caliber bullet through the eye.

Returning from a timely vacation in April of 1969, Hansen called a press conference and invited photographers and newsmen to view his new model of the original display, which he explained was an illusion, a "manmade fabrication." He was also careful to refer to the earlier display only as the "original," and not to use the word "real" in reference to it. In May Napier withdrew the Smithsonian's interest in the affair, especially after he and his associate George Berklacy, of the Smithsonian's public-relations office, had viewed a *Time-Life* film of the new model that clearly showed it to be slightly different from the Sanderson-Heuvelmans descriptions and drawings of the original.

By this time Napier was convinced that the whole case had been a hoax from the start—a clever and elaborate publicity stunt that almost misfired when Heuvelmans unexpectedly published his paper claiming the creature to be genuine and the Smithsonian decided to follow up. One can assume that Hansen had not expected his contrivance to attract the serious attention of the scientific world. Scientists characteristically ignore such specimens, as every carny huckster knows. When faced with exposure, Hansen presumably took the obvious course, but he acted in a clever way to keep the money flowing in from the suckers who viewed his model, now an admitted fabrication. Thereafter the model was displayed with a large placard on the trailer that read INVESTIGATED BY THE FBI. Hansen would know better than most that the public likes the idea that the authorities have been taken for a ride, and the fact that most of the displays in any carnival are fake has certainly never stopped people from paying money to see them.

Shortly after these events, Berklacy's office at the Smithsonian confirmed, by means of inquiries in the Los Angeles area, that a commercial organization on the West Coast had made the Iceman for Frank Hansen out of latex rubber and hair in April 1967.

In the meantime the Smithsonian had issued a press release disavowing any continued connection with the whole affair. Nevertheless, rumors have abounded ever since. The most common story is that the Smithsonian somehow got its hands on the original Iceman and for some reason decided to keep it secret. The fact that this rumor goes against the public record, and against Hansen's known actions and letters, is conveniently forgotten.

So there is really no justification for the widespread belief that the scientific community is engaged in a "conspiracy of silence" to obscure the truth about Bigfoot. The remarkable thing is not that established scientists and other authorities are skeptical and hence slow to act in support of ill-conceived private expeditions and the like but that so many respected biologists and others remain firmly open-minded about the possibility, if not the probability, that such an animal might exist.

In the final analysis, the paucity of evidence, despite contrary claims by nearly every Bigfoot investigator, is really striking. The continued failure to find physical evidence is far more compelling than the so-called evidence supporting the idea that the creature exists.

To support what remains of flagging curiosity and hope, we have a few uncertain footprints and perhaps a handful of fecal samples of even greater uncertainty. These are within that tiny proportion of the vast number reported in the last two decades that continue to defy alternative explanation. Then there are those few sightings, impossible to corroborate, that persist and nag at us, to tantalize our sense of mystery.

9. Beasts, Blood, and Things That Go Bump in the Night

From ghoulies and ghosties and long-leggety
   beasties
And things that go bump in the night,
   Good Lord, deliver us!

SCOTTISH PRAYER

Mankind evolved in a threatening world whose dangers were ever present and, for the most part, readily apparent. When our ancestors abandoned the relative safety of the rain forests and began themselves to stalk the game of the plains and woodlands, they entered a less sheltered landscape teeming with terrific and mortally dangerous creatures—charging, tusked tramplers; ungulates with razor hooves and impaling horns. Much less conspicuous but far more dangerous were the lurking predatory cats and other large meat-eaters that preferred to hunt in the darkness and whose teeth and claws came to symbolize both virile power and the threat of the silent attack in the night. When man moved into the mass of Eurasia, gigantic cave bears shared his collecting grounds and competed for shelter in caves, and no doubt occasionally hunted his helpless offspring. If the day was a time of visible dangers that had to be boldly confronted to get food, the night was a time of fear. And with the intelligence that was a component of communication, cooperation, and tool-making came that uniquely human capacity to project, to foresee, to imagine. Our ancestors' nights, even after fire was mastered, were filled with horrendous threats that were every bit as real as imaginary. Lions, leopards, hyenas, scimitar-toothed cats as big as any tiger, and huge wolves hunted nocturnally to glean their fare from the abundant Pleistocene. Just as the herbivores were more diverse than they are today, so were the carnivores. And, though by this time humans, too, were carnivorous by profession (if not by inheritance) they were most certainly prey as well.

This reality colored our earlier cultural patterns in subtle ways that continue, subconsciously and consciously, to influence our actions, especially when we feel threatened. Primeval fears of dangerous animals that intimately shared our waking and sleeping world were etched in our minds. And who knows how long ago it was that an old savant, sitting around a fire, first told gripping stories of strange beasts of humanoid aspect that came to take children away or appeared in remote places. Perhaps at that time there were a few such beings, early hominid relatives of man, or at least the dim memory of them. We *do* know that all folk have ancient stories of half-human beings. In legend these beings are never confronted during the hunt or caught in the deadfall, the snare, the net, the fire trap. They are not seen wandering among the other beasts at the trampled edge of the pond. In the tales these "manimals," these "were-beings," lurk at the edge of corporeality. They are often seen in dreams, and to distinguish between waking dream images is not so easy; even today our children cannot do so with ease. They are experienced in visions during the long rites of passage into adulthood that were once demanded of all youths, especially when fasting. They are glimpsed when questing for fast game, the hunter thirsty, hungry, tired, far from the security of camp. They are spotted fleetingly by lone hunters entering dark groves where imaginings create monsters out of unfamiliar shapes. Rarely does the witness see the legendary creature within the comforting company of the clan or among fellow hunters or gatherers; he sees it when he is alone, or at best among a group of two or three whose sharing makes them of one mind.

Who among us cannot remember the childhood terror of

walking alone in the dark past a cluster of trees—familiar by day, full of awful things at night—or quivering in some lonesome bed for the night sounds and shadows? Who can forget the certainty in a child's mind of the coming of the monster with hairy hands and glowing eyes, a being capable of penetrating even the barrier of the solid family doors, of father's protective presence, into one's own room? And how arrogant we are—in our awesome cities and our towns, amid our clutters of tools and engineered mountains of manufactures, encapsulated and cocooned against that ancient primitive world—to pretend that we are free of these night fears, echoes of our primeval origin.

The fact that we are not free from these fears is evident every day in our substitution of contrived evils for the real dangers of our world. We fantasize supernatural creatures, demons, vampires, ghosts, and extraterrestrial invaders in flying saucers instead of facing the awful threat that comes from ourselves; from our capacity for violence, destruction, and war.

Once upon a time we boldly confronted our fears. In our diurnal huntings and gatherings we went out into the land and took our meat and collected our roots, fruits, and nuts. When necessary we faced up to the cave bear, the lurking cat, and packrunning dogs (some of these we even domesticated), the trumpeting elephant, the charging bull. We took courage in numbers, and if we fell during the height of the hunt, we were honored, legendary within our own clan. Our death had meaning.

Primates that we are, we need not sleep the duration of the darkness. So we express imaginings, and we talk, and our stories reveal our hopes, our great fears, our failures and triumphs, our dreams and our desires. Even in ancient tales we continued to confront the world. We told our young how it was that the bear became the way it is, and how the elephant got its trunk and the leopard its spots. We familiarized the real animals of our world, and doing so we contained the genuine mystery of their behavior, and of our own. We fancifully and metaphorically explained how hare outsmarted fox, how tortoise in turn outwitted hare, and how spider outwitted them all. Each tale helped to make the world's creatures fit into the circle of being. Ignorance was muted. Sometimes in those tales we

lowered our voices, and in the hush of delightful fear (a titillating fear enhanced by the security of the band by the fire, strong
men holding their spears against the encircling darkness) we
told stories of man-monsters, of the *se'irim, pilosi, ulak, windigo,*
and *Hlo mung;* of Grendel and of the hero Beowulf; of cyclopes,
satyrs, and Fomorians; of *wudenwasa* and others of the race of
sylvan creatures; and of *sesqac, cyat-ko* or *soq'uiam, o-mah;* of the
alma and the yeti.

With few exceptions these creatures are not described as
werewolves or leopard-men. For the most part they are not supernatural creatures who can transform themselves to animal
and back to man, to do evil. Their behavior is, on the contrary,
all too human. In thousands of tales they lurk at the edge of humanity. Perhaps we need these man-monsters to be there,
whether or not they are or ever have been there.

There is undeniable tension between our contrived, yet often
comfortable, world of manmade things and the greater natural
world. We aspire to control even the weather. Our eternal
struggle for mastery over the natural environment is largely an
attempt to remove all threat and all uncertainty—in short, to
master even the winds and waters as we have mastered the
beasts of the field. So if a shark dares attack a human who en-
ters its boundless watery domain, we act as if the wolf of the sea
has personally insulted us, and we treat its kind like murderers
and set out to exterminate them. If a grizzly mauls a man running in fear—with their poor vision these big bears can easily
mistake a man for their more natural prey—or if a park bear turns
on a tourist who gets too close, we punish the culprit by killing
it, and sometimes we knock off all the others in the area. Often
we seem unsatisfied with the life of the particular "man-killer"
(which is certainly justified if the animal in question is in the
habit of killing people regularly), so we go beyond the bounds
of reason and demand more of its kind. Or we tame or even domesticate the beast, which in some cases is hardly better. For in
doing so we remove it from its evolutionary place in the world
and put it into ours, a shadow of its former self, emasculated,
caged, confused.

Paradoxically, many of us desire to enter the animals' world from time to time. Aside from watching from the safety of a zoo—which can be an exercise in futility for any animal admirer after perhaps two or three visits—we want to approximate the world we all once knew, where our elemental capacity to survive is at least moderately tested, a place where our shield of protective civilization is temporarily stripped away. Can we build that fire, catch fish, cache our food safe from bears? Most of us, if truly tested, want only to return at once to the safety of our cars and homes (an illusory safety, of course). To walk unprotected near a herd of elephants or buffalo, to encounter a bear in the woods, to see a poisonous snake in the grass, to camp within the laughter of hyenas and the roar of the lion beyond, to hike alone for any time through genuine wilderness, is to have an adventure. We have not entirely forgotten that this is the way we all lived not so long ago. In physical and evolutionary terms we are the same creatures we were twenty thousand years ago when we hunted amid the vast herds and when we in turn were stalked in the night. Our elemental wits are still intact—although we frequently appear not to know what to do with them outside our offices, cars, and TV rooms. And, puny though we are, our bodies are remarkably nimble and durable. So a few of us, very few, go partway back to that ancient mode and strike out for riverine wildernesses in Alaska, Siberia, Canada, South America, and trap and hunt for a living.

But many of us avoid such remnants of the wilderness altogether. We find zoos, TV specials, and books sufficient as stimuli, especially after the genuine fear of a long evening subway ride, or a walk through dirty streets where the most dangerous of all predators seeks its own kind. And yet a good number of us still live close by to vestigial segments of the natural world, in woodlots, near swamps, bogs, swales, and the ocean—where we do not yet rule beneath the waves—and near deserts and mountains. Many of us venture periodically into the preserved remnants of unspoiled wilderness, to hike, camp, fish, and hunt.

In many ways we who take part in the wilderness bear the brunt of that tension between what we were and what we remain in our deepest physical being—and what we have become in our social and psychological being. Those of us who at least visit the world of nature are minimally aware of its true force. We dimly comprehend that we, too, can pass, for we are subject to its rules, ultimately and finally. Those who try to ignore it (or through no fault of their own are ignorant of it) are reminded of reality only when a storm comes, or a flood. Then, bewailing the loss of a dwelling to a flood that only stays within its topographic limits, and demanding help from government, or crying "disaster" when a beach-built house is blown away, they draw attention to their folly. Meanwhile the animal part of that natural world grows ever more remote. Even the barnyard retreats.

Our fathers and grandfathers in their farmhouses—or in their close-knit European towns—knew cattle, sheep, horses, goats, domestic fowl, and the birds of the field. Our African ancestors knew these and many great wild beasts as well. On this continent they knew the taste of venison—beef did not become a staple of most of the Americas until barely a century ago— and of porcupine, of coon and quail, of catfish and trout. They also knew the rare but genuine threat of the wandering black bear in early spring, fresh from its den, and the wolfpack in February (a threat more imagined than real, with ten thousand years of folklore to back it up).

Indeed our forefathers soon killed off the predators and left a few coveted prey to hunt for sport in the places where farms or towns could not intrude. More recently we have acted to protect some of these prey species, especially deer and elk, and various fowl, and to hunt them seasonally. In recent decades those who hunt with guns usually know little or nothing about the animals they shoot; millions hunt for elemental reasons not yet fully understood, since meat seems to be a secondary motive. Those who hunt with cameras or binoculars or the naked eye, or go backpacking, snowshoeing, skiing, bird-watching, know considerably more on average. In scattered places the wilderness still presents a profusion of wild creatures, even to those oblivious of ecological principles, of the species of trees and flowering plants, and of insects. To enter that world on foot, especially where unspoiled nature dominates the landscape, is to become tuned to human limitations, to be made aware of one's weakness, of the weather and its promise or threat, and of the wild creatures that are potentially or really there.

Of course, as that wilderness shrinks, the tension grows apace. It appears that we cannot really be comfortable with it, and hence we willfully destroy the natural world. Yet we want it there for leisure and escape—within "manageable" bounds. It is as if we want to domesticate all of that remaining part of the biosphere as we long ago domesticated cattle and dogs; we desire it around us, but only in a state controlled by our agency. Thus it loses its savor, and we pine for untrammeled horizons, for places where our intrusive hand is not apparent, where roads do not or cannot go, where bears or lions are not airlifted out of designated campgrounds, where we know that we are but another animal under the same sun and breathing the same air as the hawk.

Should it be surprising, then, that contemporary folk resurrect ancient mythologies? Why should urban or semiurban people be less susceptible to the power of the old stories? Will a Sherpa have less need of faith in the yeti—which may exist, in any case, and which remains a more forceful symbol so long as it remains "legendary"—than a North American might have need for faith in Bigfoot? Probably the latter has the greater need, especially if he or she is abused by the constraints of our bureaucracies, by dehumanizing technologies, by impersonal forces beyond individual control. When we seek the great, hairy beast, a new quest is possible, something unknown still survives, and perhaps a tension is alleviated.

Thus, most Bigfoot stories, if studied within the framework of oral traditions and folklore, express symbolically—and often directly, through the fearfulness of the confrontation—certain unexpressed needs that are shared by urbanized man. History as we know it, or at least as it is presented to us in our popular culture, has sadly failed to unify our evolutionary past, our bionomic cycle of life and death, and our more recent "civilized" record. The links between mankind and the other life forms most intimately connected with humans—specifically those creatures we have always used for food and those we have long feared as efficient predators—are neglected or reduced to

Disney-like caricatures. We act as if the human story began only with agriculture, ignoring the fact that our hunting-gathering mode dominated for ninety-nine percent of our time on earth. We pretend that we moderns are somehow more human because of our most recent agricultural practices and that those still living within the more ancient patterns are mere primitives. Thus we alienate ourselves from our own earthly heritage and from the creatures, our evolutionary fellows, who have always been with us. Through our headlong subjugation of the biosphere we dimly sense our loss.

Classical mythology has often expressed this sense of alienation. The Bible tells of our Eden lost, and the prophets foresee a time when we shall be one with the beasts once more. The fact that the beasts of Eden are quite "unnatural" is beside the point. In many ways folklore, too, has sought explanation or at least some means of restoring our sense of place. Classic, unadulterated tales of our kinship with animals delight our little ones while they teach us a respectful sense of awe. But contemporary versions of these fables, cleaned up to exclude "violence," tend to make true and terrific beasts into infantile teddy bears, lap dogs, and pussycats. Our animals, we seem to be saying, must be placid, humanized creatures, the more like us the better, or else we will pay them only negative attention. Or else we will put them in zoos, behind bars, where they are safe—or, to put it more accurately, we are safe from them. Perhaps we must destroy them: We can henceforth make our wild lands into vast panoramas safe for the family photographer, empty of animal life.

Even those of us determined to protect what remains of our fellow creatures—not excluding domesticated animals—all too often tend to forget that we once lived with and in respect of the animals that we also killed for food and fiber. Thus, in a perverted new morality, the hunt becomes a moral negative where once it was a necessity. It has been truthfully said that the ecology of hunting has always involved a prudent policy of predation, in which man—who has never been *primarily* a predator—constrains his terrible killing potential and deliberately minimizes the kill. Apparently all of nature's predators, save man, act within biological restraints that more or less limit their kill to need, and because they are predators, their numbers are limited and their culling effect is an aid to the very species they prey upon. But humans, as we moved from tool to efficient tool, possessed the capacity to maximize the kill, and when agriculture was invented, to exterminate many of the very animals that we once needed for life itself. We cleverly domesticated various useful and adaptable animals such as swine, cattle, sheep, and goats, hence removing them from their ecological niches, substituting planned breeding for natural selection, until, in the words of the ecological philosopher Paul Shepard, "the animal ceases to be an adequate representation of a natural life form."

Meanwhile, the few remaining untamed beasts have been so widely studied, managed, and confined that they have lost much of their mystery. They have become almost akin to the predictable and boring animals of the barnyard, and the healthy awe we feel in the face of natural processes we cannot manage is thus reduced. In direct proportion to our capacity to control the wild beings of nature our deep-seated sense of unpredictability, of diversity, of danger, is reduced. We even confuse zoo-kept animals—with their progressive instinctual and physical degeneracy—with their still-free brothers, and we fool ourselves into believing that the sordid uniformity of the barnyard or the stinking routine of the cage is an improvement on the natural environment of risk, death, and regeneration. In doing so we seem to lose our capacity for surprise—to the point that we wish to eliminate it from our environment—and we substitute security for the stimuli of chance, the pleasure of risk.

We move forward amid scenes of collapsing ecosystems, replacing forests and savannas with empty manmade deserts, witnessing the accelerated disappearance of the earth's very soil. One scholar says that we moderns have only replaced the goat with the bulldozer in the last few decades, and that this process of ecodestruction is into its seventh millennium.

Meanwhile, we are horribly confused by our own behavior, alternately blaming "nature" and "society" for our malfunctions. We kill one another with even more ingenuity than we kill off the other life forms of this biosphere. Various thinkers recommend, in effect, that we turn our back's on our evolutionary past and act as if we share no heritage of predation (we once effectively distinguished between the needs of the hunt, interspecies killing for survival, and intraspecies murder); they suggest that our pathology is only socioeconomic. Others claim that we cannot adequately control ancient and innate aggressions, forgetting that animal aggression cannot be neatly separated from its counterpart: cooperative, violence-inhibiting, nurturing, and loving activity. We seem to be pulled hither and thither without compass. Few of us recognize that self-destructive violence—in humans as in animals—is but a perversion of natural behaviors that function quite well in an unspoiled and uncrowded biosphere. As we crowd ourselves and our fellow animals out, we deepen the pathology until we can no longer recognize what is good and what is bad.

In such a world our ancient myths and legends can have resurgent potency. The legendary giant *must* be out there; all the better if it is manlike. If so, it reminds us of the mysteries lost, of a time when we huddled in the night in the company of our familial band, our extended family, awaiting the dawn and the marvelous yet fearful chase that came with the sun; of a time when legend adorned even the most familiar creatures with an aura of unknowability, when even the slow-witted stallion could threaten death with flashing hooves even as it promised the feast; of a time when the young ventured alone into the hills to come to terms with the beasts and with the grasses, trees, and waters, accepting their mortal share of risk and death and thus confirming life; of a time when we learned, partly through the example of the animals we hunted, that life can be full only when lived in the full knowledge of death, of its appropriateness, its inevitability, and the cyclical pattern of which it is part.

Having lost this, or most of this, we seek pale and vicarious images of the unknowable. We make horror movies with the child-scaring bogeyman unleashed on a sleepy town at Halloween, to slaughter without meaning. We populate science-fiction dramas—mostly puerile and dull, propped up by pseudoscientific technology and gadgetry—with alien creatures that stalk us without cause (at least the saber-toothed tiger had cause). We desperately wish to find a lost Atlantis and to resurrect our dead gods through imagined and omnipotent visitors from outer space. We create inhuman cinematic monsters—with human traits only on the negative side—for diversion, having rid ourselves of the genuine threat of genuine beasts.

And we seek the shrinking wild woods for Bigfoot. For if he and his kind are there, in the fastness of inner Asia or in the rugged cordillera that ranges from California to Alaska, or even in the bottomlands of Michigan, Wisconsin, Minnesota, Iowa, Texas, Louisiana, and Florida, he is surely a mystery. He is beyond the contrivance of Hollywood, for only nature could have made him. In his presence we cannot assure ourselves of any outcome; we are at his mercy. Will he watch silently? Or flee? Or come after us? What are his needs, his patterns of action within the natural world? Does he breed as we do, affectionately and persistently rearing offspring through the many years that lead to physical maturity? Does he live alone, a wood-wanderer, mating only rarely and wary even of his own kind? Is he, like us, capable of towering rage (if he is an intelligent primate, he would have reason for anger)? Will he destroy willfully and yet meaninglessly, as we do? Is he a living reminder of our animal side, the wild man who exists outside the comforting yet stultifying grace of civilization, incapable of knowing God? Or is he a relic of our free and untrammeled past, going where he pleases when he pleases? If he does live out there, he is certainly a final symbol of the untamed.

Of course, thousands of people want him there. We may search for Bigfoot with passion, or believe in him the way many people believe in the healing power of the saints or in UFOs. Some may profess uncertainty tinged with sustaining hope, but they also search. For to refuse the *possibility* of Bigfoot would mean a kind of impending finality regarding man's control over nature, with the only remaining earthly mysteries being the inner structures, the biochemical, bioecological, and sociobiological roots of behavior. After all, what a disappointment it was— though no less fascinating—to discover that the wild gorilla is so gentle and acquiescent, almost asexual, that its terrible threats are ninety percent bluster and bluff; that despite its fearsome physiognomy and strength, it cannot protect its kind from the threat of extinction. What a shock it was to discover, many years into the labor of persistent observation, that the sociable and arboreal chimpanzee will kill and even eat its own kind; that it, too, might have a pathology.

Certainly there are many people, especially among scientists, who quite openly refuse the idea, or at least argue logically against the probability, that Bigfoot exists. Perhaps the pursuit of specialized research in more confined branches of zoology encourages acceptance of man's controlling influences and of the restrictions that go with control. It is interesting that among primatologists it seems to be the field ethologists who are most willing to accept, or at least hope, that a Sasquatch or yeti still wanders our world unknown. It is surely no accident that several field biologists recently argued, more from theory than experience, that although they think there probably is a yeti in the Himalayas, they fervently hope it is never discovered. Unfortunately, if it is there, it probably will be.

It is most probable our Bigfoot will never be found. But if there is such a strange monster out there, fulfilling a legendary role in our cybernetized, bureaucratized civilization, it would be a shame to reduce it to neat formulas, to type, to just another species.

I don't believe this will happen. And I will nod and even applaud when yet another René Dahinden packs into the woods and mountains in search of the monster, in a *quest,* like the heroes of old—like Nimrod, Hercules, Sir Gawain, St. George, Bilbo Baggins, Don Quixote.

Appendix A
The Patterson-Gimlin Film

One of the favorite charges of the Bigfoot fraternity is that the infamous film made at Bluff Creek in 1967 has been neglected by scientists, that it has not been seriously analyzed by experts. This is demonstrably untrue. In 1971 Dr. D. W. Grieve, an expert in biomechanics at the Royal Free Hospital School in London, carefully analyzed the film with the purpose of establishing the extent to which the alleged creature's gait resembled or differed from that of a human. As a basis for his analysis, Dr. Grieve compared measurements of stride length, time of leg swing, speed of walking, and the related movements of the lower limbs as these factors are known for humans walking at a particular pace.

Grieve at once pointed out that for purposes of quantitative analysis the film presents several problems. He noted the intermittent frame blurring in the film, caused by the unstable hand-held camera; the difficult lighting conditions and background foliage that together make it hard to establish accurate outlines of the creature's trunk and limbs even in the less blurred frames; and the fact that the figure is walking obliquely, at an angle, across the camera's field of view, especially in the part of the film that is most clear. Furthermore, no useful statements can be made about ankle movements, because the feet are not sufficiently visible. And the most important drawback is the fact that no information is available as to the frame speed used.

To measure body size and shape, Grieve used matching superimposition of images (comparing a human who walked over the same terrain to the figure in the film) to estimate the standing height of the alleged Sasquatch at not more than six feet five inches. This is approximately the height of the man used in the comparison. Hence the subject is well within human range. This estimate has been hotly disputed by many Sasquatch experts, but their contrary estimates of much greater height and weight are clearly biased by *a priori* assumptions. The fact is that the film is inconclusive in this respect. Grieve also adds that accurate measurements are impossible regarding "features that fall within the body outline."

Another important comment by Grieve that has been largely ignored is that his examination of several frames indicates that the height of the hip joint and the gluteal fold and the fingertips are similar to those of humans. The shoulder height—relative to standing height—appears "slightly greater" than in a human, and the hip width also seems somewhat greater. It should be noted that this effect could easily be produced by means of carefully placed pads.

On the basis of his careful analysis Grieve suggests that the body weight of the figure might be fifty to sixty percent greater than that of a normal man of the same height. He also states that earlier estimates that place the creature's height at around seven feet "seem rather extravagant." He calculates that the height of six foot five would suggest a weight of about 280 pounds.

The crucial part of Grieve's report, however, is his analysis of the timing of the gait. Since the frame speed was not known, Grieve was forced to estimate the timing of the different phases of the gait by an analysis of the number of frames relative to the motion. To attempt a comparison, he made five separate estimates in the sequence of right toe-off, left toe-off, right foot passing left, left foot passing right, and left heel-strike. These yielded a complete time cycle of 22.5 frames (within an estimated range of 21.5–23.5). Four independent estimates of the swing phase of the walk yielded 8.5 frames in each case.

Regarding stride length, Grieve points out correctly that the oblique view of the figure in the film makes it difficult to calculate any accurate measurement. He guesses the angle of the figure to be between 20 and 35 degrees relative to the image plane of the camera. This, he says, gives rise to an "apparent grouping of the left and right foot placements which could in reality have been symmetrical with respect to distance in the line of progression." Calculating the distances, on the film, between successive foot placements at 1.20 times the standing height, and assuming an obliquity of 27 degrees, Grieve estimates a stride length of 1.35 times the standing height. Corresponding values in man, for 20- and 35-degree obliquity, are 1.27 and 1.46.

Thus the stride length falls well within the human range. Anyone who has studied the film will surely agree, based on nothing more than visual observation, that there is nothing extraordinary about the figure's stride.

Grieve adds that the overall estimated measurements of knee flexion following toe-off and thigh angle behind the vertical, to total extension, are "very similar" to those of a human walking at high speed.

Grieve calculated from three possible frame speeds (16 fps, 18 fps, and 24 fps) and concluded that at 16 fps, the "cycle time and the time

of swing are in a typical human combination," though longer in duration than would be expected for the stride pattern. "It is as if a human
were executing a high-speed pattern in slow motion," Grieve adds.
He also pointed out that it is unlikely that such a combination of var-
iables could be produced by more massive limbs than humans have.
So he concluded that the film was probably not taken at 16 fps.

At 18 fps, almost the same conditions would be produced. However, if the film were taken at 24 fps, the subject in the film walked with
a gait pattern "very similar in most respects to a man walking at high
speed," though the cycle time is somewhat greater than expected and
the hip joint "appears to be more flexible in extension than one
would expect in man." The higher the frame speed, beyond 24 fps,
the more striking the similarity to the human gait.

Though Grieve admits to subjective impressions, when he studied
the film, that oscillated between acceptance of the Sasquatch because
such a film would be difficult to fake and "irrational rejection" based
on an emotional unwillingness to accept the possibility, he concludes
that the possibility of a "very clever fake cannot be ruled out on the
evidence of the film." Finally he suggests that a man of appropriate
height and weight proportions could mimic the longitudinal dimensions of Sasquatch and that a fake can only be ruled out if the film
speed is 16 or 18 fps.

A preliminary report on the Patterson-Gimlin film by two Russian
hominologists is interesting in its omissions and its emphases. Dmitri
Bayanov and Igor Bourtsev wrote this report after viewing a copy of
the film brought to them by René Dahinden in 1971. They began
their analysis by making a statement that the film shows a hairy creature walking erect, possessing "well-developed breasts and buttocks."
On this basis, assuming the figure's authenticity in advance, they proceed to an elaborate and tendentious series of speculations regarding
the morphology of the specimen in the film, including such elements
as its "simian" neck, the "flexibility" of its spine, the comparison of
its gait to that of Neanderthal man (this is based on an egregious hypothesis regarding Neanderthal's supposed gait put forth by the late
Boris Porshnev in 1963), the structure of its foot, and so on. It should
be noted that in the opinion of several scientists who have viewed the
film, virtually nothing conclusive can be inferred about the figure's
foot, and not much more can be inferred about the rest of the body.
Grieve's comment that the feet are not sufficiently visible to support
useful analysis is borne out by any careful viewing, even by an amateur. Some experts have suggested that the supposed "extension" that
seems to project slightly from the back or heel of the foot looks suspi-

ciously like a heavy sole attached to human footgear of some kind. Obviously, whether or not one is prepared to accept the hominologists' elaborate speculations regarding the meaning of this "protrusion" depends on one's degree of skepticism. (To many Bigfoot enthusiasts, an "open mind" means a willingness to suspend adherence to empirical arguments; in short, to accept the idea of the creature's existence in advance of the evidence, and hence to accept speculations such as the above.)

In another, somewhat more convincing report on the film footage, a Russian biomechanics expert named Dmitri D. Donskoy emphasized the "fully spontaneous and highly efficient pattern of locomotion" revealed by the figure in the film. He also noted the well-coordinated "cross-limb" interactions between the upper and lower limbs, the strong and energetic stride, the indication of massive and strongly muscled arms, the flexibility of the leg at each heel-strike, and so on. All of these, of course, fit any description of human locomotion.

Donskoy also makes repeated guesses based on his analysis of the film and presents these as if they are fact. A careful reading of his report in comparison with Grieve's judicious analysis is revealing. For example, much is made by Donskoy about the apparent knee bend at each heel-strike, and he suggests that in a normal human walk such knee flexion is not so noticeable, except perhaps in movements required by certain sports, like cross-country skiing. This, he implies, indicates that the alleged Sasquatch in the film is "very heavy with a powerful toe-off thrust."

Actually, even an amateur viewing the film might deduce that such a gait looks suspiciously like that of a human who is deliberately exaggerating his stride. Furthermore, people do walk with considerable knee flexion under certain circumstances. More than a century ago James Fenimore Cooper described such a ground-eating knee-flexed gait in *The Deerslayer* when explaining how his frontiersman hero emulated the long-distance hiking techniques of the Indians. It is also not unusual among certain overweight or heavyset people to walk with that peculiar bent-knee step that creates an impression of paradoxical athletic grace, the heavy torso seeming to float along above the legs.

Donskoy's comment that the "different parts of the limb lag behind the other." with the foot following the movement of the shank, and that, in turn, following the hip movement, is hardly surprising. He says that this kind of motion is peculiar to "massive limbs with well-relaxed muscles." Perhaps. But the emphasis here is certainly deceptive, though perhaps not deliberately so. All parts of a human leg, from the hip down to the toes, lag behind one another in a normal walk, otherwise how could the limb be moved forward prior to the heel-strike and then proceed to the toe-off, etc. The putative advantage of muscle resilience postulated by Donskoy is common to humans, whose gait, especially if well conditioned by activity, is also "fluid and smooth, with no breaking or erratic movement at the completion of each cycle." Likewise, assumptions about the absence of an arch on the foot of the alleged Sasquatch in the film, inferred from "study" of the bottom of the foot, are tendentious, simply not justified by any evidence in the film itself.

Interestingly Donskoy notes that because the figure in the film is manlike in appearance as well as bipedal, its gait resembles "in principle the gait of modern man." To this one might add a hearty amen, despite Donskoy's speculations about the figure's "expressiveness of movement."

Dr. John Napier's analysis of the film is pertinent and valuable. Basically Dr. Napier argues that the figure in the film is much too human. Napier is probably the best-qualified person to study the film, and since he believes in the probable existence of Sasquatch, his negative opinion of the film is highly significant. Napier says that the "cadence of the walk, the general fluidity of movements and the swing of the arms" are greatly exaggerated, and he adds that the walk seems "self-conscious." Also, the style of the walk, despite the visible pendulous breasts, is "essentially that of a human male." This has been noted by many observers. He points out that the cone-shaped crest on the top of the head is "definitely non-human" but adds that such a crest occurs in the adult-male gorilla and male orangutan and is a sex-linked characteristic, only minimally visible, if at all, in the females among the great apes. The presence of buttocks, a hallmark of human anatomy, "is at total variance" with the otherwise simian superstructure of the creature in the film. These buttocks are consistent, however, with the figure's walk and its inferred center of gravity. Such a combination—the upper half of the body seeming apelike, the lower half typically human—seems to Napier "almost impossible to conceive" as existing in nature.

It has been often pointed out that in his initial analysis Napier assumes things about the putative Sasquatch that are based entirely on the known anatomy of man and the great apes. This is true, but no one in this century has made more careful study of the various locomotion patterns of the primates. Napier's vital research on the locomotor functions of the hominids, along with his extensive publications on pongid locomotion, should not be lightly dismissed. Of course, Napier's initial criticism of the film does not prove it to be a fake.

Some time after his first viewing of it, Napier studied the film frame by frame dozens of times and deduced that the first impression he got of the film was only apparently paradoxical; that is, the impression of a "bad actor's interpretation of a classical human walking gait" was probably the consequence of the purported Sasquatch's attempt to assure that "every step, every footprint in the sandbar, told a tale." This is supported by the length of the step as measured, presumably on the spot, by Patterson and Gimlin—only forty-one inches. Such a step length is hardly consistent with the measured foot length of fourteen to fifteen inches. Grieve's conclusion that the figure in the film stands only about six feet five inches, Napier suggests, is especially pertinent to this analysis. He calculates that a creature with a foot length of between fourteen to fifteen inches ought to stand between seven feet eight inches and eight feet three inches tall. Anyone who has seen the film will observe the "exaggerated" stride. The figure is certainly not walking with a shortened, mincing step. If the creature actually did stand close to eight feet tall, as most Bigfoot enthusiasts argue, how can one reconcile the short stride as measured with the exaggerated stride that the eye sees? And how, if the creature stood only six foot five, can one accept the huge foot?

All this, along with Grieve's comments about the frame speed, would seem powerful reason to doubt the film, even without considering more recently discovered inconsistencies and outright discrepancies in the oral accounts. Napier's view that all of the scientific evidence points in the direction of some kind of hoax is impossible to disregard. Even Bigfoot hunter Peter Byrne has apparently decided no longer to include the Patterson-Gimlin film among his "convincing" pieces of evidence, even though he once devoted an entire chapter of a book to the infamous film, arguing for its veracity.*

---

*The texts of the reports by Grieve, Bayanov and Bourtsev, and Donskoy appear in Byrne's book *The Search for Bigfoot: Monster, Myth, or Man?* (pp. 152–166). Dr. Napier's analysis, summarized here, appears in his book *Bigfoot: The Yeti and Sasquatch in Myth and Reality* (pp. 90–95).

Appendix B
Bigfoot "Data" and Bionomic Factors

Some bionomic factors:
 A comparison between Bigfoot "data" and various relevant bionomic facts.

Bigfoot "data"	Pertinent bionomic factors
Morphological and other characteristics	
Height ranges in reports between 6 and 12 ft. Most often reported between 7 and 8 ft.	Within any species of mammal range of size is not great. Even in case of brown bears (a species including the grizzly and Kodiak bears) the normal range from smallest to largest is between 6 ft. and 8 ft. and between 600 to 1200 lbs. Great variation would require separate species.
Weight estimated between 250 and 1500 lbs., based entirely on footprint impressions and sightings.	
Footprint measurements vary between 12 and 24 in. long. Average about 16 in. Width averages about 7 in.	
Massive upper body, short neck, wide shoulders, deep chest.	Large size (according to Bergmann's rule) is a common northern adaptation. But it is associated with precise ecological niches—the high-fish diet, for ex., in the littoral zones where the brown bear grows largest. Likewise for polar bears. Even huge moose and elk, though widespread, exist only in specific

Bigfoot "data"	Pertinent bionomic factors
	environments. However vast their range, their habitat is limited. Hence the latter are easily hunted. Large omnivores and carnivores are similarly predictable.
	An interesting problem with Sasquatch (S.) data is the paucity of reported sightings of young in company with an adult. As with all mammals the young would possess immature morphological characteristics to distinguish them from mature adults (aside from size). One might reasonably expect frequent sightings of S. offspring in various stages of growth.
If described, stomach usually flat, as in humans.	Flat stomach in an omnivorous or carnivorous terrestrial primate of such bulk would be unprecedented.
Arms long, muscular, but not simian. Reaching only to knees or just above. Legs massive, muscular, but reported in considerable variation as to proportional length.	According to known biomechanical factors, huge stride length would require exceptionally long legs.
All or most of body hair-covered, except for face, or parts of face, palms, soles of feet.	Northern omnivorous mammals build up thick layers of fat, especially prior to winter.
Nothing specific reported about fat-layer beneath body hair.	
Coloration varies, from black, lt. brown to reddish brown, to	Among wild animals great variation in color is rare within

Bigfoot "data"	*Pertinent bionomic factors*
white. Sometimes described as "white-tipped" (an "agouti" pattern).	a species. Moderate seasonal changes are common. In some cases regional variations occur. "Agouti" patterns, with hair, are not a characteristic of higher primates.
Reports of powerful, lingering unpleasant odors.	Humans and the great apes have distinctive body odors. Not very strong compared to other mammals, however. Higher primates lack distinctive and powerful scent glands. Such glands among many mammals are also confined to a single sex, or vary from one sex to the other.
Reports of loud noises, howls, screams, screechings, hootings, whistlings, etc.	All mammals have identifiable core elements in their repertoire of sounds.
Feet similar to man's in structure but usually lacking visible arch. Toes often described as like "peas in a pod." Sometimes, however, reported with only 3 or 4 toes. Some are wedge- or swim-fin-shaped, others more like the yeti-type prints, very wide and "bestial."	Within the normal variation in size and shape among individuals within any species, a certain consistency is expected. Too much variation implies separate species.
Females reported with pendulous breasts, usually hair-covered (as in P-G film).	With exception of mankind, breasts of female primates are not noticeable, not especially pendulous, and almost hairless.
Males are sighted more often—if the lack of pronounced female characteristics is an indication. But there are almost no data	Male sexual organs are relatively prominent among all primates, including great apes, especially in man (probably for reasons of dominance and

Bigfoot "data"	Pertinent bionomic factors
on male sexual organs, which in man are obvious, partly because of erect posture.	threat display). Lack of data on such an obviously pertinent biological point re. the Sasquatch is significant.
Head large—small only in proportion to huge body—and usually cone-shaped. Ears small, if reported.	The sagittal ridge on certain great apes is to anchor strong jaw muscles; this goes with the massive paunch common to the great apes.
Face flat, lacking bestial snout. Described as humanlike or apelike. Eyes set full front, as in man, beneath massive brow ridge. Jaw massive, mouth wide. Lips variously described as thin and projecting.	Actually the human face is quite different from those of the apes, the human's decidedly infantile because of the huge brain case and the relatively small jaw.

Habitat, Range, Dispersal, Population, etc.	
Reports seem to include little useful data on any of these factors. Reports from the early to mid-'70s indicate rarity. Some "experts" made estimates between a few hundred to perhaps one or two thousand for all of N. America. Recent reports in great number, plus thousands of footprints, seem to indicate either many more or many pranks and hoaxes.	All wild mammals, particularly the higher primates, are limited in their dispersal (within their larger range) by physiography, and this is profoundly important in determining reproduction rates, success at rearing young, and overall population.

All animal populations must maintain a minimum food source (varies greatly from species to species) to sustain life in the wild. Many large omnivorous animals eating great quantities of food within a given zone is likely. |
| One popular theory postulates range *only* within the Pacific | If a given region lacks the requirements for the species, |

Bigfoot "data"	*Pertinent bionomic factors*
Northwest. Others include Montana, Idaho, Alberta, to the Rockies. Some suggest most of N. America, esp. the Midwest, Southeast, and Texas.	natural selection will weed it out.
Reports still most common in Pacific NW.	Ranges among mammals, except for man in recent millennia, vary seasonally, and somewhat during mating seasons. Primates characteristically remain within fairly well-defined "home ranges," patrolled by groups of varying size. Solitary existence is exceptional.
No consistent or conclusive data on overall dispersal within the Nearctic Region. No conclusive data on "home ranges" within any given region, even where sightings and footprints are frequent.	Among apes dispersal is limited by the tropical forest habitat. There's no evidence that any kind of ape ever evolved in, or migrated to, the Nearctic or the Neotropic Region (N. and S. America).
	Even relatively solitary browsers, like bears, rarely have home ranges larger than a few miles (ten or so for a grizzly) in diameter.
Most commonly reported in Pacific NW mountains and near ocean. In other regions of N. America most commonly reported in lowland forests and wooded swamps.	The great apes will range mostly in open-canopy forests (entirely tropical) up to 11,000 ft., down to near sea level in rain forests. Only chimps will browse in dry forests or forest savannas.
Increasing number of footprints found in both remote regions and close to dense human populations, with increased sightings in no discernible pattern.	Numerous footprints indicate abundance. Abundance means familiarity (as with rabbits, whitetail deer, even bears in certain favored regions).
	Normally, tracks of a given species, whether abundant,

Bigfoot "data"	Pertinent bionomic factors
	uncommon, or rare, are concentrated in favorable zones of habitation, clearly defined physiographically.
The contrast between this and earlier patterns of reports indicates unexplained paradox; completely inconsistent, esp. in face of human expansion in all zones.	Wild animal species (unless protected by conservation laws), decline in competition with growing and expanding human population.
No conclusive or consistent data on longevity, pattern of rearing young, growth rates to maturity, weaning, etc. No carcasses, bones, or other remains have been found.	Data of this nature on known animals come mostly from captive specimens. Nevertheless, expected mortality rates for a large wild species would be high, esp. for young.
No consistent data, hence no acceptable estimates on population density, even within a presumed favorable zone, such as Olympic Range in Washington and Coastal Range in Oregon.	Population density of the mountain gorilla, for example, averages about 1/sq. mile. Given roughly 150,000 sq. miles in NW area of purported sightings of Bigfoot, this ought to yield a population of 150,000, in order to approximate gorilla density.

Behavior	
"Sightings" indicate a shy, furtive, retiring creature, inoffensive, or at least nonaggressive. Sometimes said to be curious.	The most carefully studied mammals, both in captivity and the wild, are often unpredictable in their behavior, esp. in human company. Biology, reproduction, feeding, raising young, dictate certain predictable behaviors.
Only a few reports indicate violent or aggressive behavior; and a few reports of alleged kidnapping.	

Bigfoot "data"	*Pertinent bionomic factors*
Almost always seen alone. No mating behavior observed.	No large primates live entirely alone; even orangs are seen with young, and will associate during feeding, and esp. during mating.
No consistent data on feeding habits, food selection. No partly eaten vegetable or animal foods found and analyzed, etc.	Considering the impoverished understory of most of the woodlands of the Pacific NW, a large browsing primate would be expected to leave spoor. Even in the few favorable regions this would be the norm.
No data worth considering on regular use of trails, water, resting or sleeping places, dens, caves, nests, shelters, frequent feeding areas, etc.

Many droppings reported. Attempted analysis inconclusive or useless. | Animals leave discernible and usually predictable signs of their routine behaviors, even when rarely seen by man. Such things as trails, matted grass, broken branches, scratch marks, cropped branches, trampled areas, and above all droppings in home ranges. In such places droppings can be conveniently and effectively analyzed to determine health, diet, and other physiological factors. |
| No conclusive data indicating a discernible pattern of
1) territoriality,
2) hunting/gathering behavior,
3) favored foods during a given season,
4) cooperative or competitive behavior, or
5) exploitation of human- | All mammals behave within either discernible patterns of territoriality or other patterns of movement and association with others of the same species.

Extensive lists of diets of gorilla and chimp, for ex., are available. |

Bigfoot "data"	Pertinent bionomic factors
produced or human-managed foods.	All primates cooperate to a varying degree in seeking food, for ex.
	No matter how threatened by man, chimps, and on rare occasions even gorillas and orangs, will "raid" plantations, etc.
Apparently nocturnal.	All higher primates are diurnal.

Classification, Evolutionary Origins, etc.	
No data. Only conjecture and hypothesis. Unless or until a specimen is available, comparison with existing species and with fossils is impossible.	All existing species, including apes and humans, are classified according to order, family, genus, and species, on basis of comparisons of living (or dead) specimens and on fossil evidence.
These speculations include theories that Bigfoot originated from *Paranthropus, Gigantopithecus, Neanderthal* man, or perhaps some earlier dryopithecine type.	All evidence points to *Paranthropus*'s becoming extinct in the Middle Pleistocene, and it wasn't a giant form.
	Gigantopithecus, for which only parts of the jaw have been found in fossil form, was probably a large terrestrial ape, evolved from an earlier dryopithecine adapted to open savannas. Evidence points to extinction in the Middle Pleistocene.
	Neanderthal man has been classed as an early human for a long time. Besides, though adapted to the north, not a giant form. Completely diurnal, like all hominids,

Bigfoot "data"	Pertinent bionomic factors
	cooperative, living in extended family groups, etc.
(Regarding the alleged yeti, most theories postulate an origin from the line of a dryopithecine, or perhaps either *Gigantopithecus* or an ancestor of the modern orangutan. There is fossil evidence in Asia to support this hypothesis.)	The dryopithecines, *Gigantopithecus,* and the ancestral orangutans were found in Asia, many near the Himalaya, etc.

Locomotion	
Reports indicate exclusive or predominant bipedal gait. Footprint evidence supports this view. (Only evidence of a possible alternative mode is handprint data analyzed by Krantz.)	Man is the only tailless mammal consistently and exclusively bipedal. Gibbons can walk erect for some distance but their long arms are held erect or fully extended for balance. The great apes can walk erect, but they use all fours for normal movement, as do bears.
	The fossil record indicates that only the hominid line is truly bipedal, among all primates.

Bibliography

Bayanov, Dmitri, and Igor Bourtsev. "Bigfoot: Myth or Reality?" *Soviet Life,* vol. 3 (1979), pp. 54–58.

———. "On Neanderthal Versus Paranthropus." *Current Anthropology,* vol. 17 (1976), pp. 312–18.

———. "Reply." *Current Anthropology,* vol. 15 (1974), pp. 452–56.

Bourne, Geoffrey, and Maury Cohen. *The Gentle Giants.* New York: Putnam's, 1975.

Byrne, Peter, and Celia Killeen, eds. *Bigfoot News* (periodical) (1974–79), pp. 1–57.

Byrne, Peter. *The Search for Bigfoot: Monster, Myth, or Man?* Washington, D.C.: Acropolis Books Ltd., 1975.

———. "The Case for the Omah." *Explorers Journal,* vol. 50 (1972), pp. 83–92.

Campbell, Bernard G., ed. *Humankind Emerging.* Boston: Little, Brown, 1976.

Clark, Anne. *Beasts and Bawdy.* New York: Taplinger, 1975.

Cohen, Daniel. *Monsters: Giants and Little Men from Mars.* New York: Dell, 1975.

Coleman, Loren, and Jerome Clark. *Creatures of the Outer Edge.* New York: Warner Books, 1978.

Coon, Carleton S. *The Story of Man.* New York: Knopf, 1955.

———. Review of *Abominable Snowmen: Legend Come to Life,* by Ivan T. Sanderson. *Natural History,* vol. 71 (1962), pp. 4–5.

Critchfield, Richard. "Something's Out There: Nepal's Abominable Snowman Won't Go Away." *International Wildlife,* vol. 9 (1978), pp. 13–17.

Cronin, Edward W., Jr. "The Yeti." *Atlantic Monthly,* vol. 236 (1975), pp. 47–53.

Dahinden, René, and Don Hunter. *Sasquatch.* New York: New American Library, 1975.

Darlington, Philip J., Jr. *Zoogeography: The Geographical Distribution of Animals.* New York: Wiley, 1957.

De Gubernatis, Angelo. *Zoological Mythology.* London: Trubner and Co., 1872.

DeVore, B. I. *Primate Behavior: Field Studies of Monkeys and Apes.* New York: Holt, 1965.

Diolé, Philippe. *The Errant Ark: Man's Relationship with Animals.* Tr. by J. F. Bernard. New York: Putnam's, 1974.

Eisenberg, J. F., and W. Dillon, eds. *Man and Beast: Comparative Social Behavior.* Washington, D.C.: Smithsonian Institution Press, 1971.

Frazer, Sir James G. *The Golden Bough.* New York: St. Martin's, 1922.

Fossey, D., and A. H. Harcourt. "Feeding Ecology of Free-Ranging Mountain Gorilla." In *Primate Ecology: Studies of Feeding and Ranging Behavior in Lemurs, Monkeys and Apes,* ed. by T. H. Clutton-Brock. New York: Academic Press, 1977.

Fuller, Edmund, ed. *Bulfinch's Mythology.* New York: Dell, 1959.

Goodall, Jane. *In the Shadow of Man.* New York: Dell, 1971.

Graves, Robert. *The Greek Myths* (2 vols.). Harmondsworth, England: Penguin, 1948.

Green, John. *Bigfoot: On the Track of the Sasquatch.* New York: Ballantine, 1973.

———. *Sasquatch: The Apes Among Us.* Seattle: Hancock House, 1978.

———. *The Sasquatch File.* Agassiz, British Columbia: Cheam Publishers, Ltd., 1973.

Guenette, Robert and Frances. *Bigfoot, The Mysterious Monster.* Los Angeles: Sun Classic Publications, 1975.

Guerry, Vincent. *Life with the Baoulé.* Tr. by Nora Hodges. Washington, D.C.: Three Continents Press, 1975.

Hall, Mark A. "Contemporary Stories of 'Takutte' or 'Bigfoot' in South Dakota as Drawn from Newspaper Accounts." *The Minnesota Archaeologist,* vol. 37 (1978), pp. 63–78.

———. "Stories of 'Bigfoot' in Iowa During 1978 as Drawn from Newspaper Sources." *The Minnesota Archaeologist,* vol. 38 (1979), pp. 2–17.

Halpin, Marjorie. "Things That Go Bump in the Order." Review of *Sasquatch: The Apes Among Us,* by John Green. *British Columbia Studies,* vol. 39 (1978), pp. 61–66.

Harvey, Bill. "Cranks—and Others." *New Scientist,* March 16, 1978, pp. 739–41.

Heuvelmans, Bernard, and Boris Porshnev. *L'homme de néandérthal est toujours vivant.* Paris: Librarie Plon, 1974.

———. *On the Track of Unknown Animals.* New York: Hill and Wang, 1959.

Hill, W. C. O. "Abominable Snowman: The Present Position." *Oryx,* vol. 6 (1961), pp. 86–98.

Hillary, Sir Edmund, and Desmond Doig. *High in the Thin Cold Air.* Garden City, N.Y.: Doubleday, 1962.

Hulse, Frederick S. *The Human Species: An Introduction to Physical Anthropology.* New York: Random House, 1967.

Hunt, Sir John. "Triumph on Everest: Siege and Assault." *The National Geographic Magazine,* vol. 106 (1954), pp. 1–35.

Izzard, Ralph. *An Innocent on Everest.* New York: Dutton, 1954.

———. *The Abominable Snowman Adventure.* London: Hodder and Stoughton, 1955.

Jung, Carl G. *The Archetypes and the Collective Unconscious.* Tr. by R. F. C. Hull. New York: Pantheon, 1959.

_____. *Flying Saucers: A Modern Myth of Things Seen in the Skies.* New York: New American Library, 1969.

Kinne, Russ. "The Search Goes On for Bigfoot." *Smithsonian,* vol. 4 (1974), pp. 68–72.

Kirk, G. S. *Myth: Its Meaning and Functions in Ancient and Other Cultures.* London: Cambridge U. Press, 1970.

Kirtley, Bacil F. "Unknown Hominids and New World Legends." *Western Folklore,* vol. 23 (1964), pp. 77–90.

Königswald, G. H. von. *Meeting Prehistoric Man.* London: Thames and Hudson, 1956.

Krantz, Grover S. "Anatomy of the Sasquatch Foot." *Northwest Anthropological Research Notes,* vol. 6 (1972), pp. 91–104.

_____. "Sasquatch Handprints." *Northwest Anthropological Research Notes,* vol. 5 (1971), pp. 145–51.

Krantz, Grover S., and Roderick Sprague, eds. *The Scientist Looks at the Sasquatch* (vol. 2) Moscow, Idaho: University Press of Idaho, 1979.

Krutch, Joseph Wood. *The Most Wonderful Animals That Never Were.* Boston: Houghton Mifflin, 1969.

Landsburg, Alan. *In Search of Myths and Monsters.* New York: Bantam, 1977.

Leakey, Richard E., and Roger Lewin. *Origins.* New York: Dutton, 1977.

Lévi-Strauss, C. *Structural Anthropology.* New York: Basic Books, 1963.

MacDermott, W. C. *The Ape in Antiquity.* Baltimore: Johns Hopkins U. Press, 1938.

McNeely, J. A., E. W. Cronin, and H. B. Emery. "The Yeti—Not a Snowman." *Oryx,* vol. 44 (1973), pp. 65–73.

Marriot, Alice, and Carol Rachlin. *American Indian Mythology.* New York: Crowell, 1968.

Masters, John. "The Abominable Snowman." *Harper's,* vol. 218 (1959), pp. 30–34.

Matthiessen, Peter. "Stop the Go Road." *Audubon,* vol. 81 (1979), pp. 48–64.

_____. *The Snow Leopard.* New York: Viking, 1978.

Morris, Ramona and Desmond. *Men and Apes.* London: Hutchinson, 1966.

Muller, F. Max. *Contributions to the Science of Mythology* (2 vols.). London: Longmans, Green, 1897.

Napier, John R. and P. H. *A Handbook of Living Primates: Morphology and Behavior of Nonhuman Primates.* London: Academic Press, 1967.

Napier, John. *Bigfoot: The Yeti and Sasquatch in Myth and Reality.* London: Jonathan Cape., 1972.

_____. "The Locomotor Functions of Hominids." In *Classification and Human Evolution,* ed. by Sherwood L. Washburn. Viking Fund Publication in Anthropology, 1963.

New Larousse Encyclopedia of Mythology. Tr. by Richard Aldington and Delano Ames. London: Hamlyn Publishing Group, Ltd., 1968.

Parrinder, E. G. *African Mythology.* Feltham, England: Paul Hamlyn, 1968.

Patterson, Roger. *Do Abominable Snowmen of America Really Exist?* Yakima, Wash.: Franklin Press, 1966.

Peissel, Michel. "The Abominable Snow Job." *Argosy,* vol. 351 (1960), pp. 32–84.

Pilbeam, David. "Gigantopithecus and the Origins of Hominidae." *Nature,* vol. 225 (1970), pp. 516–18.

Pliny. *The Natural History of Pliny.* Tr. by John Bostock and H. T. Riley. London: Henry G. Bohn, 1855.

Porshnev, Boris F. "L'origine de l'homme et les hominides velus." *Revue Internationale de Sociologie,* vol. 2 (1966), pp. 76–83.

———. "The Troglodytidae and the Hominidae in the Taxonomy and Evolution of Higher Primates." *Current Anthropology,* vol. 15 (1974), pp. 448–50.

Pranavadanda, S. "The Abominable Snowman." *Indian Geog. Journal,* vol. 30 (1955), pp. 99–104.

Rawicz, Slawomir. *The Long Walk.* London: Constable, 1956.

Reynolds, Vernon. *The Apes: The Gorilla, Chimpanzee, Orangutan, and Gibbon— Their History and Their World.* New York: Dutton, 1967.

Robinson, Herbert Spencer, and Knox Wilson. *Myths and Legends of All Nations.* Totowa, N.J.: Littlefield, Adams, 1976.

Sagan, Carl. *The Dragons of Eden.* New York: Ballantine, 1977.

Sanderson, Ivan T. *Abominable Snowmen: Legend Come to Life.* New York: Chilton, 1961.

———. "First Photos of 'Bigfoot,' California's Legendary 'Abominable Snowman.' " *Argosy,* February 1968, pp. 23–31, 127–28.

———. "Preliminary description of the external morphology of what appears to be the fresh corpse of a hitherto unknown form of living hominid." *Genus,* vol. 25 (1969), pp. 249–78.

Schaller, George B. *The Mountain Gorilla.* Chicago: U. of Chicago Press, 1964.

Schlenker, C. V. *A Collection of Temne Traditions, Fables, and Proverbs.* London: Church Missionary Society, 1861.

Shepard, Paul. *The Tender Carnivore and the Sacred Game.* New York: Scribner's, 1973.

———. *Thinking Animals: Animals and the Development of Human Intelligence.* New York: Viking, 1978.

Simons, Elwyn L., and Peter Ettel. "Gigantopithecus." *Scientific American,* vol. 222 (1970), pp. 76–85.

Slate, B. Ann, and Alan Berry. *Bigfoot.* New York: Bantam, 1976.

Straus, William L., Jr. "Abominable Snowman." *Science,* vol. 123 (1956), pp. 1024–25.

Suttles, Wayne. "On the Cultural Track of the Sasquatch." *Northwest Anthropological Research Notes,* vol. 6 (1972), pp. 65–90.

Tchernine, Odette. *In Pursuit of the Abominable Snowman.* New York: Taplinger, 1971.

Thompson, Stith. 1955–58. *Motif-index of Folk-Literature* (6 vols.). Bloomington, Indiana: U. of Indiana Press, 1958.

Tschernezky, W. "A Reconstruction of the Foot of the 'Abominable Snowman.' " *Nature,* vol. 188 (1960).

Turnbull, Colin M. *The Forest People.* New York: Simon and Schuster, 1961.

Tylor, Edward Burnett. *The Origins of Culture.* (Originally published as chapters I–X of *Primitive Culture* in 1871.) New York: Harper & Bros., 1958.

Van Gelder, Richard G. *Biology of Mammals.* New York: Scribner's, 1969.

Vansina, Jan. *Oral Tradition: A Study in Historical Methodology.* Chicago: Aldine, 1965.

Vlček, Emanuel. "Old Literary Evidence for the Existence of the 'Snowman' in Tibet and Mongolia." *Man,* vol. 59 (1959), pp. 133–34.

Wade, Edwin L. "The Monkey from Alaska: The Curious Case of an Enigmatic Mask from Bigfoot Country." *Harvard* magazine, Nov.–Dec. 1978, pp. 48–51.

Wasson, Barbara. *Sasquatch Apparitions.* Bend, Oregon: privately printed, 1979.

Weidenreich, Franz. *Apes, Giants and Men.* Chicago: U. of Chicago Press, 1946.

Weinman, A. "Nittaewo." *Loris,* vol. 4 (1945), p. 337.

Werlhof, Jay von. "The Imperial County Footprint Site." *Pacific Coast Archaeological Society Quarterly,* vol. 14 (1978), pp. 1–9.

Wilson, Edward O. *Sociobiology.* Cambridge: Harvard U. Press, 1975.

Yeats, William Butler. *Mythologies.* London: Macmillan, 1959.

Yerkes, R. M. and A. W. *The Great Apes.* New Haven: Yale U. Press, 1929.

Index

abduction of women by wild men, 86
abominable snowman. *See* yeti.
ABSM. *See* yeti.
Academy of Applied Science, Boston, 176
Adam, Richard: *Shardik,* 48
Adams, Mt., Washington, 154, 155, 191
adaptation to climate, 45, 105–107
Africa
  Equatorial, inhabitants of, 75
  folklore, 74
  legend, 73
Ainu, 71–72
Akeley, Carl, 152
American Museum of Natural History, New York, 113, 144–45, 148, 176
American Society of Mammalogists, 173
  annual convention, 1979, Corvallis, Oregon, 188–89
Amerindians, 61, 79–82, 88, 137, 190
Andes: legend, 83
Anglo-Saxon literature, 65–66
animal behavior: misconceptions difficult to eradicate, 76–77
Ann, Lake, Michigan, 5, 126, 128, 131, 134, 138–40, 208
anthropologist and Sasquatch, 37–38
Anthropology of the Unknown Sasquatch and Similar Phenomena (conference, 1978, University of British Columbia), 176–79
  filming of, 178
ape, 67, 72–73, 76, 78, 90–91, 220.

  See also chimpanzee; gibbon; gorilla; orangutan; *Proconsul*; siamang.
adaptation, 105, 107, 110
Africa, 74
Asia, 35
brachiation, 102–103
evolution, 102
foot, 20–21
giant. *See Gigantopithecus.*
hand, 103
hibernation, 106
Himalayas, 117–18
Hindu lore, 71
-man, 71
migration, 107
Pacific Northwest, 82
skunk, 18, 50
tracking of, 210
unknown, 25–58
walking, 201
zoological classification of, 152–53
Arabian oryx, 85
archaeological evidence for Sasquatch, 81
archetype, 88–90
Argosy (magazine), 29, 50, 184, 221
Arthurian legend, 66
Asia, Southeast: folklore, 72–73
Australopithecus
  afarensis, 101, 110–11
  africanus, 99–100, 115
  robustus, 44, 88, 99–100, 115, 250
Auvergne, Captain d', 20

Baker, Mt., Washington, 165
Bare, John, 133

Bayanov, Dmitri, 25, 44, 79, 84, 92, 115, 239
bear, 93, 209–10
  behavior, 47–48
  Crawford County, Michigan, 141
  foot, 85
  grizzly, 189
  hibernation, 105–106
  photographing of, 209
  size, 243
  tracks, 198, 201
Bemidji, Minnesota, 220
Benzie County, Michigan, 5, 128, 136
Beowulf, 66, 89
Bergmann's rule, 45, 118, 243
Berklacy, George, 222
Bermuda Triangle, 95
Bernheimer, Richard, 168
  Wild Men in the Middle Ages, 67
Berry, Alan, 215
  Bigfoot, 28, 42, 214
Beulah, Michigan, 138
Bhutan, 34
Bible, 62, 231
  Genesis, 59
  giants in the earth, 59–91
Bigfoot. See Sasquatch; yeti.
Bigfoot News (monthly), 30–31, 219
bionomic factors compared with Sasquatch data, 243–51
biped, 35, 66, 70, 118, 199–200
bird, terrestrial, 199–200
Blue Creek Mountain, 80
Bluff Creek, California, 10, 12–14, 53, 56, 175, 182, 185–86, 206, 207, 210, 237
Blumenbach, Johann Friedrich, 153
bobcat, 194
Borneo
  legend, 73
  wildlife, 72
Bossburg tracks, 160, 206–207, 210–11
Boule, Marcellin, 112–13
Bourtsev, Igor, 25, 44, 79, 84, 92, 115, 239
brain size in evolution, 111
Brazil: legend, 83
British Columbia, 14-15, 192, 218
British Columbia Information Service Exchange, 122

British Columbia, Univeristy of, 177–78
Brittany, 66
Brocéliande (enchanted forest), 66
Browning, Mrs., 1–2, 7, 128, 132, 139
Buddhist medicine, 71
Burroughs, Edgar Rice: Tarzan, 48
Der Busant, 68
Byrne, Peter, 40, 43, 54, 127, 172–79, 211, 218, 242
  Bigfoot Information Center (Oregon-based), 29, 173–74
  Bigfoot News (monthly), 30–31, 219
  eyewitness rating, 53, 56
  The Search for Bigfoot, 29–30
Byron, Michigan, 123–24

California: Sasquatch research, 174, 207, 214
canine, 111
Cascade Range, Oregon, 9, 189
Castaneda, Carlos, 61
Caucasus Mountains, 77
Celtic legend, 65, 66
centaur, 61, 64
Cervantes Saavedra, Miguel de, 67
Ceylon, 73
Chandragupta (Indian king), 64
Charlevoix, Michigan, 1, 139
Chewbacca, 42
Chimera, 61
chimpanzee, 65, 72–76, 102–103, 118, 153, 210, 235
  cannibalism, 76
  pygmy, 152
China: "wild-man" legend, 71
Chinese Academy of Sciences, Peking, 218
Christianity: sylvan creature of pagan mythology transformed, 68
Clark, Jerome, 42
  Creatures of the Outer Edge, 28
Close Encounters of the Third Kind (movie), 89
Coleman, Loren, 42
  Creatures of the Outer Edge, 28
Columbia River, 9
Cooper, James Fenimore: The Deerslayer, 240

Crawford County, Michigan, 141
Crichton, Michael: *Eaters of the Dead*, 88
Ctesias: book about India, 64
Current Anthropology, 25, 28, 92
cyclopes, 58, 227

Dahinden, René, 31, 42, 56, 122, 144, 155–62, 164, 166, 173, 175, 177–78, 182–83, 185, 210–11, 235, 239
    evaluation by Barbara Wasson, 33, 156–57, 162
    Pacific Northwest Expedition, 1959–1960, 31, 207
    Sasquatch, 31–32
Daily Mail (newspaper), 21, 157
Däniken, Erich von: *Chariots of the Gods*, 26
Darwin, Charles, 102, 147
d'Auvergne, Captain, 20
deer, 107–108, 194
Defoe, Daniel: *Robinson Crusoe*, 197
dhole, 98
Doig, Desmond, 217–18
    High in the Thin Cold Air, 217–18
donkey, 77
Donskoy, Dmitri D., 240–41
dragon, 84–85
Dryopithecus indicus, 97, 99, 102, 117
Dyrrachium, 65

echo in the woods, 1–24
Eden, 231
eldritch beast, 81
    existence of, VII
    illness, etc. associated with encountering, 85–86
elephant
    symposium on the, 188
Enkidu, 63
Epic of Gilgamesh, 62–63
Eureka, California, 185
Everest, Mt., 20, 21, 202
evolution, 43, 198
    primate, 93-119
Explorers Club of New York, 192, 218

Fänke (or Fangge), 65
Fate (magazine), 29

faun, 63–65
Faunus (Roman god), 64
feces, 56–57
    bobcat, 194
    cow, 8, 212
    faking of, 213
    horse, 8
    Sasquatch. *See* Sasquatch: feces,
feral child, 48
Fife Lake State Forest, Michigan, 5
Fir Mountain, Oregon, 9
flying saucer. *See* unidentified flying object.
Flying Saucer Review, 28
flying squirrel, 194
folklore, 41, 59–91, 202, 224–35. *See also* legend; mythology..
    Africa, 74
    Amerindian, 39, 79–80
    geography and, 80–81
    Indonesia, 72–73
    Pacific Northwest, 39
    Southeast Asia, 72–73
Fomorians, 66
foot
    ape, 20–21
    human, 20, 200–201
    Sasquatch. *See* Sasquatch: foot.
    yeti. *See* yeti: foot.
footprint, 198–99, 204–205
    bear, 198, 201, 210
    frequency related to abundancy of a species, 209
    human, 201
    quadruped, 201
    Sasquatch. *See* Sasquatch: footprint.
    yeti. *See* yeti: footprint.
Fossey, Dian, 103
fossil evidence, 93, 198
    primate, 95–101, 104, 106, 113–17, 250–51
Fraser River, British Columbia, 158
Frazer, James G., 41
Freud, Sigmund, 41

Gardner, John, 66
Gates, Dennis, 177
Gawain and the Green Knight, 66, 89
geography and folklore, 80–81
George, St., 89
gibbon, 64, 72–73, 102–103, 152, 215

Gifford Pinchot National Forest, 164, 191
Gigantanthropus. See Gigantopithecus.
Gigantopithecus, 45–46, 49, 96–98, 100, 104, 115, 117, 125, 161, 250–51
Gilgamesh, 62–63
Gimlin, Bob, IX, 10–13, 177, 179–87. *See also* Patterson-Gimlin film.
Gobi Desert, 18
Goodall, Jane, 76, 103, 210
Gorgon, 61, 65
gorilla, 19, 65, 73–76, 86, 102–103, 109, 118, 147, 152–53, 170, 248, 250
Gray, Zane and family, IX, 3, 5–8, 128, 130–35, 138, 208, 212
Grayling, Michigan, 3
Green, John, IX, 26–28, 30–32, 39–43, 53, 55, 81, 84, 124, 125, 127, 144, 161, 163–71, 175, 177, 182, 185, 198, 207, 215
    British Columbia Information Service Exchange, 122
    Sasquatch: The Apes Among Us, 27, 186
Green Knight, 66
Grendel, 66, 227
Grieve, D. W.: analysis of Patterson-Gimlin film, 237–40, 242
grizzly bear, 189
Guatemala: legend, 83
Guinevere, 68
Guoxing, Zhou, 218

Halpin, Marjorie M., 172, 179
Hanno, 65
Hansen, Frank D., 220–23
Hanuman, 71
Harvey, Bill, 120
Hass, George, 177
hermit, human, 48–49
Herodotus, 64
Heuvelmans, Bernard, 84, 219–22
    On the Track of Unknown Animals, 37
hibernation, 105–106, 188–89
Hillary, Edmund, 21, 57, 217–18
    High in the Thin Cold Air, 217

Himalayas, 18–19, 34
    gorges unexplored, 47
    monkey, 115
    primate, 47
    wildlife, 19
    yeti. *See* yeti.
Hindu lore, 71
Hodson, Mr., 185
Hominidae, 44, 93–94, 101, 106, 206
Homo, 72, 115, 152
    erectus, 46, 100, 106–107, 110–11
    habilis, 100–101, 110
    sapiens, 111–14, 116–17
    sapiens neanderthalensis, 114
Hood, Mt., Oregon, 9
horse, 77
Howe, John, 3, 141–42
humanoid, 61, 70, 74, 87, 90, 93.
    See also ape; Sasquatch; yeti.
    abduction of women, 86
    adaptation, 110
    alcohol and, 86
    forest guardians, 86
    Greco-Roman literature, 63
    hairy, 62, 73, 86
    relic, 25–58, 61, 77–78, 110, 117
    South America, 83
    Southeast Asia, 72
Humboldt, Alexander von, 83
Hunter, Don: *Sasquatch,* 31–32

illness, etc. associated with encountering Sasquatch, 85–86
India, 175
    aboriginal inhabitants, 71
    book by Ctesias describing travel in, 64
Indians (Amerindians), 61, 79–82, 88, 137, 190
Indonesia: folklore, 72–73
Ireland: mythology, 66
Isaiah, 62

jaguar, 209
Japan: Ainu, 71–72
Jason, 89
Java: legend, 72
Java man, 46, 115
Jerome, St., 62, 68
Johanson, Donald, 101

Johnson, Warren, and family,
214–15
Juan de Fuca, Strait of, 165
Jung, Carl G., 41, 88–89

Khakhlov, V.A., 78
King, Wayne, 120–32, 134,
139–42, 212
Michigan Bigfoot Information
Center, 121–22
King Kong (movie), 79
Kingston, Michigan, 126
Kinne, Russ, 218–19
Kipling, Rudyard: Mowgli, 48
Kirtland's warbler, 2
Kirtley, Bacil, 71, 85–87, 168
Klamath, California, 22
Klamath River, California, 10
Klickitat River, Washington, 191
Komodo dragon, 84
Königswald, G. H. von, 98, 115
Meeting Prehistoric Man, 45
Krantz, Grover, 37–38, 251
editor: The Scientist Looks at the
Sasquatch, 38
Kwangsi cliffs, China, 97, 104
Kyle Lake, Michigan, 3

Lancelot: living in the woods like an
animal, 68
Landsburg, Alan, 40, 178
Myths and Monsters (documentary
film), 178
langur, 107
Lansing, Michigan, 126
Leakey, Louis B., 44, 100
Leakey, Mary, 99, 100
Leakey, Richard, 100
Leelanau County, Michigan, 5
Leelanau Peninsula, Michigan, 137
legend. See also folklore; mythology.
Africa, 73
Andes, 83
Borneo, 72–73
Brazil, 83
Ceylon, 73
Guatemala, 83
Java, 72
Mexico, 83
North America, 80–84
Sanskrit, 71

Sumatra, 72–73
Tibet. See yeti.
The Legend of Boggy Creek (movie),
42
lemur, 106
Lévi-Strauss, Claude, 41
Libya: humanoid described by He-
rodotus as living in, 64
Linnaeus, Carolus, 44, 72, 146
literature and Sasquatch, etc.,
25–39, 63. See also folklore; leg-
end.
Loch Ness Monster, 176
locomotion, 199–200
Lucretius, 61
On the Nature of Things, 59

macaque, 106–107
mammal, 145–46
mammoth in North America, 37
"manimal," 42
Marx, Ivan, 56, 207, 210
Masters, John, 51–52
Matthiessen, Peter, 118
The Snow Leopard, 51
Mead, Margaret, 147
media and Sasquatch, 22–23, 39–43
medicine, Buddhist, 71
Meganthropus, 115
Megasthenes, 64
Melville, Herman: Moby Dick, 82
Menlung Glacier, Nepal-Tibet, 20
Mica Mountain, British Columbia,
14
Mexico: legend, 83
Michigan, 125
description of flora and fauna,
134–37, 192
geology, 136
Indians, 137
Lake, 2, 5, 137
wildlife, 2–3, 5
Michigan Bigfoot Information Cen-
ter, 121–22
Michigan Department of Natural
Resources, 128, 212
Midnight Globe (newspaper), 123
The Minnesota Archaeologist, 55
"Minnesota Iceman," 37, 149–50,
219–23
Miocene Epoch, 96–97, 99, 102

Mongolia, 71
monkey
  Himalayas, 117
  Pacific Northwest, 82
"Monsters, Mysteries and Myths"
  (television program), 39
Mt. Hood National Forest, Oregon,
  9
Mowgli, 48
mulatto (word), 77
mule, 77
Murie, Olaus, J., 209
  Field Guide to Animal Tracks, 209
mythology, 41, 43, 85, 87–89, 231.
  See also folklore; legend.
  China, 71
  giants, 88
  Ireland, 66
  monster, 60–61
  wild man, 67
Myths and Monsters (documentary
  film), 178

Napier, John, 47, 50–51, 54–56,
  150, 160, 197, 200, 204–207,
  221–22, 241–42
  Bigfoot, 25, 33–36, 50
  study of footprint photographed
    by Eric Shipton, 203–204
The National Enquirer (newspaper),
  26, 123, 163
National Museum of Natural History, Smithsonian Institution, 150
National Wildlife Federation, 219
Neanderthal man, 43, 45, 46, 78,
  88, 111–14, 221, 239, 250
Nepal, 18, 34, 175
  lore, 69, 70
newspapers and Sasquatch coverage,
  22–23
Nittawo, 73
Norgay, Tenzing, 21, 85
North American Bigfoot. *See* Sasquatch.
nymph, 64

Odysseus, 89
ogre (word), 65
okapi, 147
Oligocene Epoch, 95, 102
Olson, Ron, 177

Olympic Mountains, Washington,
  165, 193
Olympic Peninsula, Washington,
  189
Olympus, Mt., Washington, 187
orang-pendek, 73
orangutan, 47, 72–73, 97, 102, 115,
  118, 147, 249, 251
  Linnaeus's knowledge of, 152
  word origin, 72
Orcus (god), 65
Oregon, 9
oryx, Arabian, 85
Ostman, Albert, 14–15, 20
  abduction and captivity by Sas-
    quatch, 14–15, 38

Pacific Northwest, 164, 174,
  187–88, 191–92, 206–207, 218
Paleolithic period, 114
Pamir Mountains, Asia, 77–78, 85
Pan paniscus, 152
panda, 94
*Paranthropus. See Australopithecus ro-
  bustus.*
parapsychology, 24
Partholón, 66
Patterson, Roger, 10–13, 56,
  180–82, 186. *See also* Patterson-
  Gimlin film.
Patterson-Gimlin film, 11–13, 32,
  36, 38, 40, 50, 53, 99, 148–49,
  161, 166, 179–85, 237–42
Peking man, 46, 115
Peking Museum of Natural History,
  China, 218
Perkins, Marlin, 217
Phidias, 64
Pickens, Ray, 211
Pithecanthropus, 46
Platte River, Michigan, 5
Pleistocene Epoch, 198, 225, 250
Pliny
  description of *silvestres* in India, 64
  Gorgon, 65
Pliocene Epoch, 97
Plutarch, 65
Pongidae, 72, 94, 102, 206
Ponginae, 72
Porshnev, Boris F., 43–44, 78, 84,
  115, 239

primatology, 25, 92–119, 210
  bionomic factors, 243–51
  comparative anatomy, 102
Proconsul, 101
psychology
  "ingroup," 88
  needs behind paranormal phe-
    nomena, 162
Pursuit (magazine), 29
pygmies
  Ceylon, 73
  Equatorial Africa, 75

quadruped, 98, 199
  footprint, 201
Quinault, 79

raccoon, 94
race
  "ingroup" psychology, 88
  tendency of one to mislabel an-
    other as completely different,
    77
Rainier, Mt., Washington, 154, 182
Ramapithecus, 99–101
Rawicz, Slavomir: The Long Walk,
    34–35
real (word), 168
Record Eagle (newspaper), 132
Redwood National Park, California,
    10
relic humanoid. See humanoid: relic.
rhinoceros, 85
Roethke, Theodore, 1
Romulus and Remus, 48
ruminant, 107–108
  stomach, 108
running, efficiency of, 111

Saanich inlet, British Columbia, 165
Saga (magazine), 29
Sagan, Carl, 152
  The Dragons of Eden, 88
St. Helens, Mount, Washington, 182
Sanderson, Ivan T., 69–71, 73–74,
    77, 83, 84, 87, 116, 118, 184,
    196–97, 206, 212–13, 219–22
  Abominable Snowmen, 36–37,
    49–50, 92, 196
  classification of Sasquatch evi-
    dence, 57, 146

The Dynasty of Abu, 50
  myths, legends, and folklore, 137
Sanskrit legend, 71
Sasquatch. See also yeti.
  alcohol and, 86
  anatomical detail, 17
  archaeological evidence, 81
  behavior, 248–50
  bionomic factors compared with
    data, 243–51
  buffs, 154–97
  California, 174, 207
  Cascade Range, Oregon, 189
  common sense about evidence,
    196–223
  conference, 1978, University of
    British Columbia, 176–79
  conundrums and controversies,
    120–43
  Crawford County, Michigan, po-
    lice report, 141
  description, 14–15, 17, 60, 79–80,
    129–30, 180–81, 220–21
  diesel fuel and, 141
  diet, 108–109
  doubtfulness of existence, 23–24,
    162, 190–91
  evidence, 52–58, 196–223
  evolutionary origins, 250–51
  existence, 25, 153, 168
  eyes, 17
  feces, 8, 56–57, 128–29, 131,
    150, 212, 223
  female, description of, 13
  filming of, 11–13
  foot, 85
  footprint, 6–8, 12–13, 17–18,
    20–22, 25, 35–36, 53–56, 128,
    131, 133, 175, 182, 184–86,
    202, 205–11, 223
  geographical extent of incidents
    concerning, 15, 17, 25–26, 30,
    125, 191
  habitat, range, dispersal, popula-
    tion, etc., 246–48
  hibernation, 188
  hoax, 137–40, 142–43, 149, 176,
    207, 210–12, 222
  hunter as con man, 160
  illness, etc. associated with en-
    countering, 85–86

Sasquatch *(cont.)*
  literature and, 25–39, 193
  locomotion, 38, 251. *See also* Sasquatch: footprint.
  lore, 18, 22, 59–91
  media and, 22–23, 39–43
  morphological and other characteristics, 243–46
  multiplicity, 190, 206
  mystery background, VII–IX
  mythology, 43
  newspaper use of caption "Bigfoot," 23
  odor, 7, 13, 18, 131, 139
  oral or folkloric tradition, 23
  Pacific Northwest, 164, 174, 191–92, 206
  phantasmagoria, 23
  photographing of, 11–13, 209
  police report, 141
  psychology of lore, 41
  questions about, 189
  recordings, 215
  scientific inquiry about, 24, 144–54
  searcher, psychology of, 33
  sighting, 2–3, 9–14, 19, 28, 126, 194–95, 214
  sound, 215–16
  specimen, 220–21
  speculation, 224–35
  steatopygia, 188
  stomach adaptation, 108–109
  story checking for detail, 187
  stride, 184
  theories, 43–52
  veracity, 181
  winter survival of, 188
  words for. *See* words for Sasquatch, yeti, etc.
  zoological classification, 220–21, 250–51
satyr, 58, 63–65, 227
  alcohol and, 86
scat. *See* feces.
Schaller, George, 51, 76, 103, 118, 147, 152
scientist as high priest, 159
sexual dimorphism, 82
Seymour Range, British Columbia, 165

shadow in the shade, 1–24
Shakespeare, William: *The Tempest,* 89
Shepard, Paul: *Thinking Animals,* 90
Sherpa
  lore, 18, 21, 69
  yeti identification, 20, 47
Shiawassee County, Michigan, 123–24
Shiawassee River, Michigan, 123
Shipton, Eric: photographing of large footprints, 20–21, 202–203, 206
siamang, 72, 102–103
Siberia, 34
Sierra Leone, 75–76
  wildlife, 65
Sierra Nevada Mountains, California, 214
Silenus (god), 64
Sinhalese Mountains, 73
Siskiyou Mountains, California, 10–11
The Six Million Dollar Man (television program), 42
Six Rivers National Forest, 10
skunk ape, 50
  odor, 18
Slate, B. Ann: *Bigfoot,* 28, 42, 214
Slick, Tom, 31–32, 218
  Pacific Northwest Expedition, 207, 218
Smithsonian Institution, 148, 153, 154, 158, 176, 219, 221–22
  "Monsters, Mysteries and Myths" (television program), 39
  National Museum of Natural History: Department of Vertebrate Zoology, 150
snowman, abominable. *See* yeti.
Society for the Investigation of the Unexplained: *Pursuit* (magazine), 29
Solomon Islands, 87
Southeast Asia: folklore, 72–73
Soviet Union, 77
Spenser, Edmund, 67
  The Faërie Queen, 68
squirrel, flying, 194
Stalo tribe, 86
Star Wars (movie), 42, 89
steatopygia, 188

stomach
  evolution, 109
  ruminant, 108
Strasenburgh, Gordon, 44–45
Stuht, John, 128
Sulla, 65
Sumatra
  legend, 73
  wildlife, 72
Suttles, Wayne, 79
  "On the Cultural Track of the
    Sasquatch," 38
sylvan, 63

Tarzan, 48
Tashtego, 82
Teutonic legend, 65
Thompson, Stith: *Motif Index of Folk
  Literature,* 85
Thorington, Richard W., Jr., IX,
  144, 150–54
Tibet, 34, 71
  lore, 70
Time-Life film of the "Minnesota
  Iceman" model, 222
Titan, 61
Titmus, Bob, 56, 186–87
Toba inlet, British Columbia, 14
Tolkien, J. R. R., 65
Tombazi, N. A., 19
Traverse City, Michigan, 130
  Record Eagle, 132
troglodytes, 28, 44, 115
Troglodytes recens, 115
Trout Lake, Washington, 191
True (magazine), 29
Tsimshian Indians, 81–82
Turnbull, Colin: *The Forest People,* 75
Tylor, Edward B., 41

UFO. *See* unidentified flying object.
UFO Report, 28
unicorn, 84–85
unidentified flying object, 28, 41,
  49, 159, 234
Union of Soviet Socialist Republics,
  77
United States Fish and Wildlife Service, 127
Ursidae. See bear.

Van Gelder, Richard G., 145–51,
  154, 188–89
Victoria, British Columbia, 164–65
Viking sagas, 88
vitamin B_{12}, 109
Vlček, Emanuel, 70, 84

Wade, Edwin L., 81–82
Walter, Steven, 3
warbler, Kirtland's, 2
Ward, Michael: photographing of
  large footprints, 20
Washington, Mt., New Hampshire,
  187
Wasson, Barbara, 162–63, 170,
  177
  Sasquatch Apparitions, 32–33, 156
Weidenreich, Franz, 98
  Apes, Giants and Men, 46
Westring, Helen, 220
wild child. *See* feral child.
wild man. *See* humanoid.
wildlife
  Borneo, 72
  Himalayas, 19
  Michigan, 2–3, 5
  misconceptions about, 201
  Sierra Leone, 65
  Southeast Asia, 72–73
  Sumatra, 72
Willow Creek, California, 13, 185
Winona, Minnesota, 219–20
wolf child. *See* feral child.
women, abduction of, by wild men,
  86
words for Sasquatch, yeti, etc.
  Africa, 74, 86
  Amerindian, 70, 79–84, 86
  Anglo–Saxon, 65
  Borneo, 73
  Chinese, 70
  Hebrew, 62
  Hindustani, 71
  Indonesia, 72–73
  Latin, 62
  Mongolian, 70
  Nepal, 69
  Sherpa, 22
  Soviet Union, 43, 77
  Spanish, 83
  Sumatra, 73

words for Sasquatch, yeti, etc. *(cont.)*
  Tibetan, 70, 104. *See also* yeti.
  United States, 77
World Book Encyclopedia, 216
Wylie, Kenneth, 191–95
  photographing of bear, 209
  research, VII-VIII, 168
  sighting of Sasquatch, 194–95

Yakima, Washington, 13, 14, 154,
    179, 185, 186
Yaqui Indians, 82
Yaqui sorcerer, 61
yeti, 10, 18, 20, 46–47, 50–51,
    69–70, 84, 118. *See also* Sas-
    quatch.
  Africa, 73–74
  alcohol and, 86
  buffs, 154–71
  description, 21, 35, 69
  evolution, 104

  expedition of Edmund Hillary,
    and, 57, 217
  foot, 85, 116
  footprint, 55, 118, 202–205
  geographical extent of incidents
    concerning, 22
  myth, conclusion of, 217
  reality of, 70
  scientific inquiry about, 144–54
  search for, 29, 218
  sublimation of snow, and foot-
    print, 202–205
  words for. *See* words for Sas-
    quatch, yeti, etc.

Zana, 79
Zemu Glacier, Himalayas, 19
Zhou Guoxing, 218
zoological classification, 72–73,
    92–119
zoology, 22, 147